Francis Wheen is an author and journalist who was named Columnist of the Year for his contributions to the *Guardian*. He is the author of *The Soul of Indiscretion: Tom Driberg, Who Was Dr Charlotte Bach?*, *Karl Marx*, which has been translated into over twenty languages, and *Hoo-Hahs and Passing Frenzies*, which won the George Orwell Prize in 2003.

'A wonderful, breakneck undressing of emperors . . . He is bullshit's enema number one.' Tim Adams, *Observer*

'If Wheen's book succeeds in starting to shift the balance between reason and sentimentality, between the lavish prompts of the heart and the colder ones of the brain, between rigorous analysis and twaddle cloaked in obscurity, then I think the ghost of [Thomas] Jefferson will have every right, and reason, to be proud of him.' David McKie, *Guardian*

'A brilliant, extended satiric essay . . . [Wheen's] book reads like a version of Frazer's *The Golden Bough*, with politicians, bankers and management consultants for shamans.'
Will Cohu, *Daily Telegraph*

'Francis Wheen is the intelligent sceptic's intelligent sceptic.'
Jeremy Paxman, *Mail on Sunday*

'Like Goya in *Los Caprichos*, Wheen depicts the sleep of reason bringing forth monsters. And like the weird, bat-like creatures in the etching, Wheen's demons are at the same time sinister and comic . . . Reaching the end of this short history of modern delusions, one wants it to go on and on.'
Dennis Sewell, *Literary Review*

'[Wheen] takes a bolt-gun to a herd of sacred cows: religious fundamentalism, New Age quackery, self-help hokum, think-tank Brent-spreak, economic voodoo, government-manufactured fear and hysterical celebrity worship. It's a bracing draught of common sense, and one gets the sense that Wheen found it difficult to know where to st▮

'In an earlier day this book ▮
public hangman. It is fun t▮
early-to-bed resolution. Fran▮

the last "tyrant of twaddle" is found drowned in the disused think tank.' E.S. Turner, *Times Literary Supplement*

'There are a lot of stupid people in the world, but Francis Wheen is not one of them. He admirably demonstrates this every time he puts pen to paper to debunk some nonsense or another. Fans of Wheen who have enjoyed his biography of Karl Marx as well as his journalism have a treat in store with *How Mumbo-Jumbo Conquered the World.*'

Suzanne Moore, *New Statesman*

'This amusing, intelligent and elegantly argued book is as good a demonstration of the values it defends as could be imagined.'

Philip Hensher, *Spectator*

'I expected a fun book about "mumbo-jumbo". This is, in fact, a manifesto for rescuing the greatest philosophical movement of the past millennium.' Johann Hari, *Independent on Sunday*

'Wheen slays sacred cows – homeopathy, astrology, Reaganomics, structuralism – with the gay abandon of a recalcitrant child with a big stick. Sensationally invigorating and very, very clever.'

Arena

'Wheen's assault on the pomposity and folly of the reason-free zone is important and timely.' Mark Henderson, *The Times*

'How welcome a book about Mumbo Jumbo! ... A well-informed polemic that most enjoyably challenges you to think.'

Peter Lewis, *Daily Mail*

'Francis Wheen is the small boy standing on the street-corner tugging at his father's sleeve. "Daddy," he is asking, "why is the emperor wearing no clothes?" The *Guardian* columnist has produced an at times hilarious, at others scary, compendium of collective madnesses. It is a joy, a tour-de-force polemic.'

Patrick Smyth, *Irish Times*

HOW MUMBO-JUMBO CONQUERED THE WORLD

A Short History of Modern Delusions

Francis Wheen

HARPER PERENNIAL

Harper Perennial
An imprint of HarperCollins*Publishers*
77–85 Fulham Palace Road
Hammersmith
London w6 8jb

www.harpercollins.co.uk/harperperennial

This edition published by Harper Perennial 2004

16

First published in Great Britain by Fourth Estate 2004

Copyright © Francis Wheen 2004
PS Section 'An Interview with Francis Wheen'
copyright © Simon Jones 2004

PS™ is a trademark of HarperCollins*Publishers* Ltd

Francis Wheen asserts the moral right to
be identified as the author of this work

A catalogue record for this book is
available from the British Library

ISBN 0-00-714097-5

Typeset in ITC New Baskerville by
Rowland Phototypesetting Limited
Bury St Edmunds, Suffolk

Printed and bound in Great Britain by
Clays Ltd, St Ives plc

Contents

For Bertie and Archie

Prologue

Two messiahs

Tehran, Wednesday 24 January 1979

Three army tanks block the entrance to Mehrabad International Airport, following an announcement by the Shi'ite Muslim leader Ayatollah Ruhollah Khomeini that he intends to return to Iran on 26 January after fourteen years of exile. 'Khomeini is not coming, not at all,' a major tells reporters.

It is eight days since Shah Mohammad Reza Pahlavi fled abroad, with mass demonstrations and strikes convulsing the country he has ruled for three decades. The tanks in the roadblock – British-made Chieftains – are themselves symptoms of the malaise which laid him low: both Muslims and Marxists were enraged by his dependence on Britain and the United States, his use of military force to crush dissent and his apparent contempt for Persian traditions.

Shahpour Bakhtiar, the prime minister, said after the Shah's departure that Khomeini was welcome to return home, but has adamantly refused to accept the Ayatollah's demand that he should yield power to an Islamic theocracy. As the tanks arrive at the airport, Khomeini's principal envoy in Tehran, Mehdi Bazargan, holds a news conference at which he describes his old friend Bakhtiar as a 'reasonable, logical and patriotic man' who must now accept the inevitable and give way to the Ayatollah. To mollify liberals, socialists and other secular opponents of the Shah, who have become increasingly fearful of Khomeini's ambitions, he adds that the proposed new government will be called an 'Islamic Democratic Republic' rather than merely an 'Islamic Republic'.

What will it mean in practice? In an interview with the newspaper *Ettelaiat* the Ayatollah denounces dancing and cinema as unIslamic, and limits his promises of free speech to exclude 'things not in the national interest'. At the Tehran news conference, Bazargan rejects models such as Libya and Saudi Arabia, explaining that he favours a government like that 'we had for ten years under the Prophet Mohammed and for five years under the Imam Ali'. In short, the intention is to restore a regime that last existed almost 1,300 years ago.

Monday 29 January

In Tehran, troops open fire on demonstrators who have burned two cinemas, two restaurants, a liquor shop, several bordellos and a nightclub. The protesters are seen 'chortling with delight' as they throw champagne bottles from the club's cellar on to a bonfire.

At the American embassy, Iranian soldiers guarding the grounds have to be replaced after one shoves an assault rifle into an American officer's belly and yells, 'Yankee go home!' As the original sixty-man contingent drive away in trucks, they all shout the same refrain.

Outside Tehran University, where at least thirty-five people were killed by army bullets yesterday, Major-General Taghi Latifi is dragged from his Mercedes 220 and badly beaten. A leaflet distributed on the campus says the time has come to establish a 'people's army' and attack the United States and Israel. 'We have to get guns,' it adds. Thousands of students take up the chant: 'Machine guns, machine guns, the answer to everything.' On sale inside the university are photographs of the Shah holding a glass of wine and Empress Farah wearing a one-piece swimming suit. Even girls whose blue jeans are visible beneath their ankle-length Muslim robes brandish the photos as proof of the royal couple's dissolute habits.

Alarmed by the crescendo of violence, Shahpour Bakhtiar announces that the country's airports will reopen tomorrow. Americans, Europeans and Iranian Jews make plans to leave as soon as possible. At his villa in the Parisian suburb of Neauphle-le-Château, Khomeini issues a statement confirming that he will return within the next forty-eight hours. 'If there is any blood to be shed, I want to be among my people.'

Thursday 1 February
Accompanied by a retinue of journalists and Iranian students, Khomeini boards a chartered Air France Boeing at Charles de Gaulle airport. Throughout the five-hour flight to Tehran, the black-robed, white-bearded seventy-eight-year-old reclines on a carpet in the first-class compartment. As they enter Iranian airspace, a French reporter asks: 'What are your emotions after so many years of exile?' The Ayatollah, who has ignored previous questions, murmurs 'Hichi' – the Farsi for 'nothing'.

Khomeini steps off the plane at 9.30 a.m. to a thunderous reception from at least a million supporters, many of whom have waited all night for a glimpse of their hero. In a brief statement at the airport, he says that 'final victory' will come only when 'all the foreigners are out of the country and uprooted ... I beg to God to cut off the hand of all evil foreigners and all their helpers in Iran.' He is then whisked into a limousine for a triumphal motorcade through the centre of Tehran to the cemetery of Behesht-e-Zahra, where he pays tribute to the hundreds who died in the months of demonstrations against the Shah. From there, he is flown by helicopter to his new revolutionary headquarters, a former girls' school near the Iranian parliament.

According to the BBC correspondent John Simpson, who travelled from Paris with Khomeini, 'a millennial frenzy took over the entire country. People wept and shouted and beat their chests in an ecstasy of hope and joy.' Newspapers publish ecstatic poems which reflect this chiliastic optimism:

> The day the Imam returns
> No one will tell lies any more
> No one will lock the doors of his house;
> People will become brothers
> Sharing the bread of their joys together
> In justice and sincerity.

London, Wednesday 10 January
James Callaghan, the British prime minister, looks tanned and relaxed on his return to England after six days at an international summit in Guadeloupe, where he was photographed swimming with young air-stewardesses during a break from discussing the Soviet nuclear threat. Britain, by contrast, is freezing and paralysed: thousands of lorry-drivers are on strike, most ports and many factories have shut down, all roads into the city of Hull are blockaded by secondary pickets, hundreds of schools have closed for lack of heating oil, supermarkets are running out of food and railway workers have announced that they will begin a national strike next week. And all because of Callaghan's insistence that no pay

rise in the private or public sector shall exceed 5 per cent, at a time when inflation is above 8 per cent.

Arriving at Heathrow airport, Callaghan is asked by a reporter about 'the mounting chaos in the country at the moment'. The avuncular smile that earned him the nickname Sunny Jim disappears at once. 'Please don't run your country down,' he admonishes. 'If you look at it from the outside, you can see you are taking a rather parochial view. I do not feel there is mounting chaos. I don't think that other people in the world would share the view that there is mounting chaos.'

A few hours later the political editor of the *Sun*, Walter Terry, files his report of the press conference: 'Sun-tanned premier Jim Callaghan breezed back into Britain yesterday and asked: Crisis? What crisis? . . . Not even the threat of up to two million people being laid off work next week worried jaunty Jim.' The *Sun*'s editor, Larry Lamb, adds the *coup de grâce* by repeating Terry's pejorative précis in a huge front-page headline: 'CRISIS, WHAT CRISIS?'

Wednesday 28 March
A day of high parliamentary drama. For the past couple of years Callaghan's minority Labour government has limped from one crisis to another, kept alive by wily parliamentary manoeuvring and makeshift alliances – first with the Liberals (during the 'Lib–Lab pact' of 1977–8) and then with the Scottish and Welsh nationalists, who were cajoled into acquiescence by the promise of a Devolution Bill. On 1 March, however, referendums in Scotland and Wales failed to deliver the support necessary for the home-rule proposals to become law, whereupon the nationalists abandoned Callaghan.

The Ulster Unionists have also backed the government in

recent months, but only in return for legislation increasing the number of parliamentary seats in Northern Ireland. When the Bill received the royal assent last week, they too decided there was no longer any advantage to be gained from propping up a wheezing and enfeebled administration. Seizing her opportunity, the Conservative leader Margaret Thatcher has tabled a motion of no-confidence in Her Majesty's government. If passed, it will precipitate a general election.

The debate is preceded by feverish and often farcical horse-trading. Having won round three Welsh Nationalists by promising a new scheme to compensate coal-miners suffering from lung disease, Callaghan still needs to find two more votes before tonight's division. The Labour minister Roy Hattersley gives Frank Maguire, the Independent member for Fermanagh and South Tyrone, three bottles of whiskey plus the promise of an inquiry into food prices in Northern Ireland. Some Ulster Unionists try unsuccessfully to trade their votes for a pledge to build an expensive natural-gas pipeline under the Irish Sea.

Opening the debate, Margaret Thatcher says that 'the government has failed the nation . . . Britain is now a nation on the sidelines. Rarely in the post-war period can our standing in the world have been lower or our defences weaker.' Labour has 'centralised too much power in the state', paying 'far too little attention to wealth creation and too much to its redistribution'.

The prime minister, who celebrated his sixty-seventh birthday yesterday, attacks the Conservatives and their 'lap dogs' in Fleet Street. He also sneers at the Liberals and Scottish Nationalists for allying themselves with the Tories: 'The minority parties have walked into a trap . . . It is the first time in recorded history that turkeys have been known to vote for an early Christmas.' He concludes with a surprise announcement that old-age pensions will be increased in November: 'Let need, not greed, be our motto.'

Ill and dying members are brought from their beds, some by ambulance, to be wheeled through the lobbies at 10 p.m. But the seventy-six-year-old Labour MP Sir Alfred Broughton, who suffered a heart attack a week ago, is too weak to leave hospital. If the vote is a tie, the Speaker would be obliged by precedent to exercise a casting vote on behalf of the government. Because of Sir Alfred's absence, however, the no-confidence motion is passed by 311 votes to 310.

Callaghan, the first British prime minister to have his government brought down by a censure motion since Ramsay MacDonald in 1924, announces that he will seek a dissolution of parliament and a general election as soon as essential business is cleared. 'Now that parliament has declared itself, we shall take our case to the country.'

Friday 4 May
The Conservatives have won an overall majority of forty-three seats in yesterday's general election – the biggest margin of victory by any party since 1966. Labour's share of the poll, at 36.9 per cent, is its lowest since 1931. While Audrey Callaghan moves the family's belongings out of the back door of 10 Downing Street, her husband leaves by the front door to ride to Buckingham Palace and hand in his resignation to the Queen. He then departs for his Sussex farm, pausing briefly *en route* to offer commiserations to staff at the Labour Party HQ in Smith Square.

Shortly afterwards Margaret Thatcher is summoned to the palace, where she formally accepts her appointment as prime minister by kissing the monarch's hands. She is then driven in a black Rover to Downing Street. Looking rather subdued and slight among the swirl of reporters and burly police officers, she quotes a favourite phrase of her former colleague Airey Neave, who was killed by a car-bomb at the beginning of the election campaign: 'There is now work to be done.' Before disappearing through the door of No. 10 to get on with it, she also recites 'some words of St Francis of Assisi, which I think really are just particularly apt at the moment':

> Where there is discord may we bring harmony,
> Where there is error may we bring truth,
> Where there is doubt may we bring faith,
> And where there is despair may we bring hope.

Introduction

Dare to know

The rapid progress true Science now makes, occasions my regretting sometimes that I was born too soon. It is impossible to imagine the height to which may be carried, in a thousand years, the power of man over matter. We may perhaps learn to deprive large masses of their gravity, and give them absolute levity, for the sake of easy transport. Agriculture may diminish its labour and double its produce; all diseases may by sure means be prevented or cured, not excepting even that of old age, and our lives lengthened at pleasure even beyond the antediluvian standard. O that moral science were in as fair a way of improvement, that men would cease to be wolves to one another, and that human beings would at length learn what they now improperly call humanity!

Letter from BENJAMIN FRANKLIN to Joseph Priestley
(8 February 1780)

In September 1784, a Berlin magazine invited several German intellectuals to answer the question 'What is Enlightenment?' They included the philosopher Immanuel Kant, who rose to the challenge with a vigour and clarity not always evident in his lengthier works:

Enlightenment is man's emergence from his self-incurred
immaturity. Immaturity is the inability to use one's own understanding without direction from another. This immaturity is
self-incurred if its cause is not lack of understanding, but lack
of resolve and courage to use it without another's guidance.
Sapere aude! Dare to know! That is the motto of Enlightenment.

The sprightly optimism of this venerable professor, then
already in his sixties, derived from his belief that a revolution
in human history was imminent. In the *Critique of Pure Reason*,
which had been published three years earlier and established
his reputation throughout Europe, Kant had sought to reconcile the two dominant schools of modernist philosophy –
the British empiricist approach of Bacon, Locke and Hume
(who held that knowledge was the product of experience and
experiment, and thus subject to amendment), and the continental rationalism exemplified by Descartes and Spinoza,
which maintained that certainty could be achieved by inferen-
tial reasoning from first principles. What these traditions had
in common was far more important than what divided them,
and by incorporating elements from both he was able to
demolish the pretensions of religion to superior knowledge
or understanding. 'The *critical* path alone is still open,' he
announced after almost seven hundred pages, having cleared
away the metaphysical obstacles.

If the reader has had the courtesy and patience to accompany
me along this path, he may now judge for himself whether,
if he cares to lend his aid in making this path into a high-road,
it may not be possible to achieve before the end of the present
century what many centuries have not been able to accomplish; namely, to secure for human reason complete satisfac-

tion in regard to that with which it has all along so eagerly occupied itself, though hitherto in vain.

From the vantage point of the twenty-first century, it is hard not to smile at the suggestion that the forces of reason might achieve 'complete satisfaction', and humanity grow out of its 'self-incurred immaturity', some time before 1800. 'I do not know whether we will ever reach mature adulthood,' Michel Foucault wrote in the 1980s, reflecting on the 200 years that had passed since Kant's famous essay for the *Berlinischer Monatsschrift*. 'Many things in our experience convince us that the historical event of the Enlightenment did not make us mature adults, and we have not reached that stage yet.' Foucault himself fiercely opposed the Enlightenment's universalism yet even he conceded its 'importance and effectiveness', arguing that it should 'be considered not, certainly, as a theory, a doctrine, nor even as a permanent body of knowledge that is accumulating; it has to be conceived as an attitude, an ethos, a philosophical life in which the critique of what we are is at one and the same time the historical analysis of the limits that are imposed on us and an experiment with the possibility of going beyond them.'

Just so: the Enlightenment was not so much an ideology as an attitude – a presumption that certain truths about mankind, society and the natural world could be perceived, whether through deduction or observation, and that the discovery of these truths would transform the quality of life. The foundations on which it built were those laid by the empirical philosophers and natural scientists of the seventeenth century – most notably Francis Bacon (1561–1626), John Locke (1632–1704) and Isaac Newton (1642–1727) – and the debt was fully acknowledged: Thomas Jefferson described them as the 'greatest men that have ever lived, without any exception', while d'Alembert and Diderot dedicated their *Encyclopédie*, that great monument of the French Enlightenment, to the trinity of English patron saints. (Rather less credit was given to Spinoza, the seventeenth-century Dutch philosopher who is only now beginning to receive his due. A recent study by Jonathan Israel presents him as the architect of the Radical Enlightenment – 'the chief challenger of the fundamentals of revealed religion, received ideas, tradition, morality and what was everywhere regarded, in absolutist and non-absolutist states alike, as divinely constituted political authority'.)

According to d'Alembert, 'once the foundation of a revolution has been laid down, it is almost always in the next generation that the revolution is accomplished'. The eighteenth century had no scientific advances comparable with those of Newton and Galileo, but the *philosophes* were standing on the shoulders of giants – and could therefore see further. 'By separating theology from natural philosophy, or by ingeniously arguing that natural philosophy *supported* theology, seventeenth-century scientists concealed from themselves, as much as from others, the revolutionary implications of their work,' the historian Peter Gay writes. 'Geniuses from Galileo to Newton lived comfortably with convictions that eighteenth-century *philosophes* would stigmatise as incompatible . . . For Newton, God was active in the universe, occasionally correcting the irregularities of the solar system. The Newtonian heavens proclaimed God's glory.' The achievement of the eighteenth century was to detach Newton's God from his physics, teasing out the implications of discoveries from the age of genius and pushing them to their logical conclusion: the professed aim of the Scottish philosopher David Hume was to be 'the Newton of the moral sciences'. As one modern commentator has said, the originality of the Enlightenment:

> lies not so much in what was preached as in the fervour of the preacher and the beneficial effects expected of the sermon. What distinguished the Enlightenment above all was its determination to subject all received opinions to the test of reason, to apply this test especially to views on human behaviour, to ethical and political theory, and to extract from the knowledge thus won whatever could be useful in improving the human lot.

Of course there were many different Enlightenments, each with its distinctive style, and scholars still argue about which was the real torch-bearer. Local particularities had a strong influence: in Germany and Scandinavia, characteristically, progressive thinkers sought to enlighten absolutist monarchs and create a modern, efficient polity; the French *philosophes* were more preoccupied with challenging aristocratic feudalism and the Roman Catholic church; in Britain, where a settlement of sorts had already been reached with both clerisy and monarchy, more attention was paid to the nature of liberal capitalism. Any movement which traced its ancestry to both Cartesian rationalism and Lockean empiricism could never be homogeneous. The Enlightenment encompassed optimists and pessimists, deists and atheists, democrats and elitists, Voltaire and Rousseau.

Despite their quarrelsome diversity, however, most Enlightenment thinkers shared certain intellectual traits – an insistence on intellectual autonomy, a rejection of tradition and authority as the infallible sources of truth, a loathing for bigotry and persecution, a commitment to free inquiry, a belief that (in Francis Bacon's words) knowledge is indeed power. That phrase is sometimes used by Machiavellian politicians to justify the restriction of valuable information, but for the *philosophes* it was a slogan of emancipation, a declaration of war against the impotence of ignorance. 'Enlightenment' had two meanings, both evident in the *Encyclopédie*: the discovery of truth and its subsequent diffusion. The purpose of the *Encyclopédie*, Diderot said, was to 'change the general way of thinking'; and it succeeded. The Enlightenment had many critics, but its illuminating influence and achievements were apparent in the history of the next two centuries – the waning of absolutism and superstition, the rise of secular democracy, the understanding of the natural world, the transformation of historical and scientific study, the new political resonance of notions such as 'progress', 'rights' and 'freedom'.

Does that light still shine today? If you type 'The Enlightenment' into a search engine at the online retailer Amazon, more than 1,500 books are listed. Look more closely, however, and you'll notice that many of them have nothing in common with what Kant, or indeed Foucault, meant by Enlightenment: *The Power of Now: A Guide to Spiritual Enlightenment*; *The Secrets of Kung Fu for Self Defence, Health and Enlightenment*; *Crystal Enlightenment: The Transforming Properties of Crystals and Healing Stones*; *The Rosicrucian Enlightenment*; *The Tibetan Art Colouring Book: A Joyful Path to Right Brain Enlightenment*; *Awakening the Buddha Within: Eight Steps to Enlightenment*; and *Golf for Enlightenment: Playing the Game in the Garden of Eden*, a recent title from the entrepreneurial mystic Deepak Chopra. 'The Enlightenment made explicit what had long been implicit in the intellectual life of Europe: the belief that rational inquiry leads to objective truth,' the British philosopher Roger Scruton wrote in

1999. 'Even those Enlightenment thinkers who distrusted reason, like Hume, and those who tried to circumscribe its powers, like Kant, never relinquished their confidence in rational argument ... For the ensuing 200 years, reason retained its position as the arbiter of truth and the foundation of objective knowledge. [But] reason is now on the retreat, both as an ideal and as a reality.'

For Scruton, this counter-revolution 'puts our entire tradition of learning in question'. Its leaders may seem an incongruous coalition – post-modernists and primitivists, New Age and Old Testament – but they have been remarkably effective over the past quarter-century. Nor are they merely dunderheads or fanatics who argue that 'ignorance is bliss' to assuage any prickings of guilt at their own imbecility: those who may know no better have been aided and abetted by a latter-day *trahison des clercs*. We have now reached the point at which a British prime minister who styles himself as a progressive moderniser (and recites the mantra 'education, education, education') can defend the teaching of creationism rather than evolution in school biology classes, with no apparent shame or embarrassment. Even intellectuals who respect Enlightenment values often seem reluctant to defend them publicly, fearful of being identified as 'liberal imperialists' or worse.

The sleep of reason brings forth monsters, and the past two decades have produced monsters galore. Some are manifestly sinister, others seem merely comical – harmless fun, as Nancy Reagan said of her husband's reliance on astrology. Cumulatively, however, the proliferation of obscurantist bunkum and the assault on reason are a menace to civilisation, especially as many of the new irrationalists hark back to some imagined pre-industrial or even pre-agrarian Golden Age. ('Where We

Stand. *The revolt against reason is the seed of insurgence*,' declares the manifesto of the Coalition Against Civilisation, a group of rural anarchists. 'We believe that through the invention and use of agriculture, certain people were able to force their lifestyles upon the rest of the world. What was being pushed is civilisation, the state of society that forces all to become domesticated and thus mediated from the natural world.') My purpose in this book is to show how the humane values of the Enlightenment have been abandoned or betrayed, and why it matters: those who rewrite or romanticise history, like those who rejoice in its demise or irrelevance, are condemned to repeat it. The story begins a quarter of a century ago, in 1979, when the Ayatollah Khomeini inaugurated an Islamist project to turn the clock back to medieval times, and Margaret Thatcher – who posed as a disciple of the Enlightenment giant Adam Smith – set out to re-establish 'Victorian values'. Neither could have dared imagine just how successful they would be.

1

The voodoo revolution

Why might not whole communities and public bodies be seized with fits of insanity, as well as individuals? Nothing but this principle, that they are liable to insanity, equally at least with private persons, can account for the major part of those transactions of which we read in history.

BISHOP JOSEPH BUTLER (1692–1752)

Although 1979 may not have the same historical resonance as 1789, 1848 or 1917, it too marks a moment when the world was jolted by a violent reaction to the complacency of the existing order. Two events from that year can both now be recognised as harbingers of a new era: the return of the Ayatollah Khomeini to Iran and the election of Margaret Thatcher's Tories in Britain. The Imam and the grocer's daughter represented two powerful messianic creeds whose 'conflict' – though often more apparent than real – found its most gruesome expression some twenty-two years later, when the twin towers of the World Trade Centre in New York were reduced to rubble by a small kamikaze squad of Islamist martyrs.

What seemed to be a straightforward battle between modernity and medievalism was in truth a more complex affair, ripe with ironies: the most ardent apostles of Thatcherite neo-liberalism were themselves engaged in a struggle against the world as it had evolved during the twentieth century (welfare states, regulated economies, interventionist governments, sexual permissiveness), while the pre-modern Islamic fundamentalists – commonly portrayed as bearded loons in an Old Testament landscape of caves and deserts – had a high-tech savvy that continually amazed and infuriated their enemies. Osama Bin Laden knew how to exploit the power of satellite TV and twenty-four-hour news channels; his lieutenants were Westernised enough to pass without notice in Europe and the United States. And it was a Boeing jet which carried the Ayatollah Khomeini back to Tehran on 1 February 1979.

'A nation trampled by despotism, degraded, forced into the role of an object, seeks shelter,' the Polish journalist Ryszard Kapuscinski wrote of the Iranian revolution. 'But a whole nation cannot emigrate, so it undertakes a migration in time rather than in space. In the face of circling afflictions and of reality, it goes back to a past that seems a lost paradise. The old acquires a new sense, a new and provocative meaning.' Although millions of Iranians celebrated the Ayatollah's arrival, by no means all were fundamentalist zealots yearning for jihad: Iran was a secular state by the standards of the region. What made his installation possible was that he was the only alternative on offer. Why? Because the increasingly corrupt and brutal Shah Mohammad Reza Pahlavi had suppressed the voices of democratic dissent. And who was responsible for this counter-productive folly? The United States, among others: the CIA had helped organise the coup which toppled Mohammed Mossadegh's left-liberal government and reinstalled the Shah on the Peacock Throne. Hence the seething resentment, felt even by some Westernised Iranians, against the 'great Satan' of America. It was President Carter's subsequent decision to let the Shah enter the US for medical treatment that provoked the storming of the American embassy and the 'hostage crisis'.

Ironically enough, Jimmy Carter was the only president who had dared to defy the conventional wisdom that guided American foreign policy for more than three decades after the Second World War: that in order to 'contain' the spread of Communism it was essential to support anti-Marxist dictators in Africa, Asia and South America, and to look the other way when they were torturing or murdering their luckless subjects. Although the founding fathers said in the declaration of independence that 'governments are instituted among men, deriving their just powers from the consent of the governed', and promulgated the American constitution to 'establish justice ... and secure the blessings of liberty', their successors in the second half of the twentieth century were reluctant to bestow these blessings beyond their own borders. Under Carter, however, even strategically important countries on America's doorstep – Nicaragua, El Salvador, Guatemala – were warned that further US aid was dependent on an improvement in their human-rights record. In an address at Notre Dame University on 22 March 1977, Carter deplored the 'inordinate fear of Communism which once led us to embrace any dictator who joined us in that fear', and called for a new foreign policy 'based on constant decency in its values and an optimism in its historical vision' – echoing Abraham Lincoln's description of liberty as 'the heritage of all men, in all lands everywhere'.

His conservative critics warned that by forcing right-wing despots to civilise themselves he was effectively hastening their downfall, to be followed by the installation of revolutionary dictatorships instead. The argument was summarised most bluntly by an obscure academic, Jeane Kirkpatrick, in her 1979 article 'Dictators and Double Standards', published in the neo-conservative magazine *Commentary*. 'Only intellectual fashion and the tyranny of Right/Left thinking', she wrote, 'prevent intelligent men of good will from perceiving the fact that traditional authoritarian governments are less repressive than revolutionary autocracies, that they are more susceptible of liberalisation, and that they are more compatible with US interests.'

Although Kirkpatrick was in fact a Democrat, her article found an admiring audience among gung-ho Republicans as they prepared for the 1980 presidential campaign. 'I'm going to borrow some of her elegant phraseology,' Reagan told a friend after reading *Commentary*. 'Who is she?' He found out soon enough: by 1981 he had appointed Jeane Kirkpatrick as his ambassador to the United Nations, and was using her distinction between jackbooted 'authoritarians' and Stalinist 'totalitarians' to justify sending arms to the bloodstained regime in El Salvador. Even when three American nuns and a lay worker were murdered by the Salvadorean junta, Kirkpatrick expressed no sympathy at all for the victims but continued to recite her glib theory of autocracy. 'It bothered no one in the administration that she had never been to El Salvador,' the *Washington Post* observed, 'and that one of the authorities she cited for her view of the strife there was Thomas Hobbes, an Englishman who had been dead for three centuries.'

Kirkpatrick shamelessly applied double standards of her own. Whereas right-wing tyrannies might take 'decades, if not centuries' to mature into democracies, she said, there was no example ever of a left-wing dictatorship making such a transformation. Hardly surprising, given that the world's first Marxist state was only sixty-three years old at the time; had she waited another decade or so, examples galore would have refuted the argument. Nor did the Iranian revolution bear out her thesis that it was better for the United States to prop up tottering autocrats than to back reformers. As Professor Stanley Hoffman pointed out in the *New York Times*, postponement of democratic reform 'prepares the excesses, sometimes the horrors, of the successor regimes'.

It has been said that opposition parties do not win elections: governments lose them. The rule applies in autocracies, too: hatred of the Shah, rather than universal Iranian longing for medieval theocracy, prompted the national rejoicing at the Ayatollah's coup. Three months later, in Britain, Margaret Thatcher won the votes of millions of electors who probably had little enthusiasm for (or indeed understanding of) monetarism and the other arcane creeds to which she subscribed. All they wanted was the removal of an etiolated, exhausted government which had no *raison d'être* beyond the retention of office. Jim Callaghan's administration had been limping heavily since 1976, when it was forced to beg for alms from the International Monetary Fund, and later that year he had formally repudiated the Keynesian theories of demand management that were accepted by all post-war governments, both Labour and Tory. In 1956 the Labour politician Anthony Crosland confidently declared that 'the voters, now convinced that full employment, generous welfare services and social stability can quite well be preserved, will certainly not relinquish them. Any government which tampered with the basic structure of the full-employment Welfare State would meet with a sharp reverse at the polls.' Twenty years later, following the onset of stagflation and the end of the long post-war boom, Callaghan informed the Labour Party conference that the game was up:

> What is the cause of high unemployment? Quite simply and unequivocally it is caused by paying ourselves more than the value of what we produce. There are no scapegoats. That is as true in a mixed economy under a Labour government as it is under capitalism or communism. It is an absolute fact of life which no government, be it left or right, can alter . . . We used to think that you could spend your way out of a recession and increase employment by cutting taxes and boosting government spending. But I tell you in all candour that that option no longer exists, and that insofar as it ever did exist, it only worked on each occasion since the war by injecting a bigger dose of inflation into the economy, followed by a higher level of unemployment as the next step. Higher inflation followed by higher unemployment. We have just escaped from the highest rate of inflation this country has known; we have not yet escaped from the consequences: high unemployment. That is the history of the last twenty years.

Callaghan's regretful message soon became Thatcher's triumphant catchphrase, and was later adopted as the mantra of American evangelists for untrammelled global capitalism: there is no alternative.

At first, the new Tory prime minister proceeded with caution. There were plenty of old-style Tory gents in her Cabinet, and few people guessed what she would do to sabotage the post-war consensus – not least Thatcher herself. It was often remarked that, even when she had taken up residence in 10 Downing Street, the new prime minister continued to sound like a politician from the opposition benches, or even an impotent street-corner orator. When she censured her own employment secretary on the BBC's *Panorama* programme, the *Economist* complained that 'it is doing no good to the cause of party morale for the Cabinet's most strident critic to seem to be the prime minister, especially on the highly public platform of a television interview'. Help was at hand, however, as neo-liberal soulmates cheered her on from across the Atlantic: in the same editorial, the *Economist* reported 'the arrival of the ideological cavalry' from the United States to rally the troops and stiffen the sinews.

'The importance of Margaret Thatcher stems not from the fact that she is a woman and one who is both an attorney and the first-ever British Prime Minister with a science degree,' Kenneth Watkins wrote in *Policy Review*, journal of the right-wing Heritage Foundation.

> Her importance stems from the fact that she has a profound conviction, based on her birth, family upbringing and experience, that a successful free enterprise economy is the only secure basis for individual freedom for even the humblest citizen ... If Margaret Thatcher fails, the door in Britain will be open for the headlong plunge to disaster in the form of the irreversible socialist state. If she wins, and win she can, she will have made a major contribution to the restoration of Britain's fortunes and, in so doing, will inscribe her name in the history books as one who will have led the way not only for her own country but for the entire Western world.

Another conservative Washington think-tank, the American Enterprise Institute, despatched Professor Herbert Stein, who had chaired the Council of Economic Advisers under

Presidents Nixon and Ford, to spend three weeks in Britain during the summer of 1979. He returned in high spirits. 'The regime is dedicated to restoring the work ethic, initiative, personal responsibility, and freedom,' he wrote in *Fortune* magazine.

> It stresses these values not only as spurs to GNP growth but also as ends in themselves – quite simply the right way to live ... The government wants to correct what it regards as the intellectual errors that have dominated British thinking for the past forty years. It finds the Socialist and Keynesian doctrines by which Britain has been governed since World War II to be intellectually uncongenial and economically self-defeating. To replace these obnoxious doctrines, it is resolved to preach what it holds to be economic truth and sense.

Even more gratifyingly, she won the approval of the two economists she most revered, both of them Nobel laureates. Milton Friedman, founder of the 'Chicago school' of monetarism and free-market theory, wrote an ecstatic column for *Newsweek* ('Hooray for Margaret Thatcher') urging American politicians to heed the British example. 'What happens in Britain is of great importance to us. Ever since the founding of the colonies in the New World, Britain has been a major source of our economic and political thought. In the past few decades, we have been moving in the same direction as Britain and many other countries, though at a slower pace. If Britain's change of direction succeeds, it will surely reinforce the pressures in the United States to cut our own government down to size.' Three months after Friedman's rousing hurrah, *Forbes* magazine sought a verdict from the other Thatcherite icon, Friedrich von Hayek, whose influential anti-Keynesian polemic *The Road to Serfdom* had been written in the final months of the Second World War. 'I admire her greatly,' Hayek confirmed. 'Her policies are the right ones, but whether she'll be able to get done what she knows must be done is another question.' Quoting John Stuart Mill's description of the Tories as 'the stupid party', he expressed his suspicion that Thatcher, like himself, was more of a nineteenth-century liberal than a conservative – an opponent, in other words, of any interference with the marketplace, whether from social democrats bent on social engineering or captains of industry who wished to keep out cheap imports.

Milton Friedman returned to Britain in February 1980 to launch an ideological *Blitzkrieg* – meeting Thatcher at Downing Street, promoting his new book *Free to Choose* and presenting a series of televised lectures in which he advocated 'the elimination of all government interference in free enterprise, from minimum wage to social welfare programmes'. He cited the economies of Japan, South Korea and Malaysia to prove that prosperity depended on allowing the 'invisible guiding hand' of the free market to hold the tiller. 'What happens here in Britain will have a very important influence in the US,' he told the *Washington Post*'s London correspondent. 'If Thatcher succeeds, it will be very encouraging. It is a fascinating experiment, and a good deal depends on it . . . Britain, and much of the world, is at a turning point after a fifty to sixty-year run of Fabian socialism.' Thatcher's election, he believed, 'could mark the turning away from the welfare state back to the free-market economies of the nineteenth century'.

By then, Thatcher's application of Friedmanite principles – restricting the money supply, cutting public spending – was indeed producing results. During her first year inflation surged from 9 per cent to more than 20 per cent; interest rates and unemployment both rose sharply; and Britain's manufacturing industry, the legacy of that energetic nineteenth-century entrepreneurialism which Friedman and Thatcher so admired, was battered by recession.

This news escaped the attention of her transatlantic disciples, perhaps because they were distracted by the emergence of a hero on their own side of the pond – the old Hollywood actor Ronald Reagan, who entered the presidential primaries of 1980 reciting the incredible but irresistible promise that he would cut taxes, increase defence spending and still balance the budget by 1983. The wondrous alchemical formula had been devised by Arthur Laffer, a colleague of Milton Friedman at the University of Chicago, whose 'Laffer Curve' seemed to demonstrate that a government could actually increase its revenue by *reducing* tax rates. The rich would no longer feel impelled to seek out ingenious tax-dodging ruses, and the lower rate would stimulate economic growth, thus expanding the national revenue anyway.

Although the 'supply-side economics' espoused by the Reaganites had a veneer of scientific method, not least in the elegant parabola of Laffer's curve, it was indistinguishable from the old, discredited superstition known as 'trickle-down theory': the notion that if the rich were encouraged and enabled to make themselves as wealthy as possible – through low taxes, huge salaries, stock options, bonuses and perks – the benefits of this bonanza would somehow, magically, reach the pockets of the humblest hop-picker or crossing-sweeper. In his *Political Dictionary*, William Safire attributes the theory (though not the title) to the presidential candidate William Jennings Bryan, who in 1896 referred to the belief 'that if you will only legislate to make the well-to-do prosperous, their prosperity will leak through to those below'. The actual phrase 'trickle-down theory' first appeared in the 1932 presidential campaign, when Democrats mocked Herbert Hoover's plan to engineer an economic recovery by making the rich richer. 'It's kind of hard to sell "trickle down",' Reagan's budget director, David Stockman, admitted in an incautious interview with the *Atlantic Monthly* soon after the 1980 election. 'So the supply-side formula was the only way to get a tax policy that was really "trickle down". Supply-side is "trickle-down theory".'

Even on the right, Reaganomics was not universally popular. One of Britain's most fervent monetarists, Professor Patrick Minford, advised Margaret Thatcher that the Laffer Curve was nonsense; Reagan's Republican rival George Bush mocked supply-side theories as 'voodoo economics'. Only a few months later, however, Bush accepted the role of candidate Reagan's running mate, and by 1981 the new president and vice-president were working their voodoo magic. Reagan's first budget included a modest reduction in the basic tax rate, but his indiscreet colleague David Stockman revealed that this was merely a 'Trojan horse' for the far more drastic slashing of the top rate from 70 to 50 per cent – and, later, to 28 per cent. Tax-cuts for the rich were central to the supply-side superstition.

According to the Laffer Curve, the public coffers should then have swelled with extra revenue, so much so that the budget could be balanced within a year or two. The reality could hardly be further from the theory: during Reagan's eight years in the White House the total federal deficit swelled from about $900 billion to more than $3 trillion. While his tax policies certainly precipitated an orgy of speculation in stocks and real estate, they did nothing to induce genuine economic progress: as Americans stopped saving and started spending, throughout the 1980s there was a continuous decline in the long-term capital investment on which growth and jobs depended. At the start of 1981 the new administration was assuring the nation that there would be no recession, but by the autumn it had already arrived, as the Federal Reserve raised interest rates to dampen the inflationary effects of the tax cuts. A year later unemployment in the US rose above 10 per cent for the first time since the 1930s.

Ronald Reagan was an incorrigible fantasist. (He once told the Israeli prime minister that he had been present at the liberation of Nazi death camps in Europe; in fact, his wartime duties in the army film unit never took him further afield than California.) Like many sentimental old hams, he could not always distinguish between his own life and the roles he acted. More surprisingly, others believed his fantasies: even today, tough conservative journalists come over all lyrical and moist-eyed when writing about the years of Reaganomics, recalled as a Gilded Age of prosperity and contentment.

It was indeed reminiscent of that previous Gilded Age a century earlier, notably in the widening gulf between a wealthy elite and the rest. As the political analyst Kevin Phillips recorded in his influential book *The Politics of Rich and Poor* (1990), 'no parallel upsurge of riches had been seen since the late nineteenth century, the era of the Vanderbilts, Morgans and Rockefellers'. Income tax was abolished in the United States in 1872, not to be reimposed again until the First World War, and it was during this period that the great dynasties built their fortunes – and flaunted them. An ostentatious 1980s mogul such as Donald Trump, who erected the Trump Tower as a vainglorious monument, was merely following the example of those earlier *nouveaux riches* who built outrageously gaudy palazzos and châteaux on Fifth Avenue. The conspicuous extravagance of late-Victorian millionaires – exemplified by Mrs Stuyvesant Fish's famous dinner in honour of her dog, which arrived wearing a $15,000 diamond-studded collar – was more than matched by the glitzy parties chronicled and celebrated every month in *Vanity Fair*, relaunched under the editorship of Tina Brown in 1983 as a parish magazine for the new plutocracy.

As in the first Gilded Age, scarcely any of the new abundance trickled down to the middle or working classes. Under Ronald Reagan, it was not until 1987 that the average family's real income returned to the levels enjoyed in the 1970s, and even this was a misleading comparison since they were now working far harder for it: whereas in 1973 average Americans had 26.2 hours of 'leisure time' every week, by 1987 the figure had fallen to 16.6 hours. They were less secure, too, as short-term or temporary contracts demolished the tradition of full-time, well-paid and often unionised employment. The earnings of male blue-collar workers in manufacturing industry fell throughout the 1980s as their employers threatened to close the factory or move production overseas if American labour 'priced itself out of a job'. There was also a revival of Herbert Spencer's social Darwinism, which had last been in vogue at the turn of the previous century, as right-wing triumphalists argued that government should not interfere with the 'natural selection' of commercial markets.

Curiously, however, they seemed quite willing to let the government clear up any ensuing mess. In 1982 members of Congress were bribed to 'liberalise' the Savings & Loan industry, effectively promising that the public purse would cover any losses from bad investments made with savers' money but also undertaking not to oversee or regulate these investments.

The consequences, predictably enough, were rampant fraud, the collapse of more than 650 S&L companies – and a bill of $1.4 trillion, to be met by the taxpayer. In 1988 a report from the General Accounting Office, *Sweatshops in the US*, noted that another feature of the Gilded Age had returned, partly because of the official mania for deregulation: reasons cited for the reappearance of sweatshops included 'enforcement-related factors, such as insufficient inspection staff, inadequate penalties for violations [and] weak labour laws'. But since the victims were penniless and often voteless workers, rather than middle-class mortgage-owners, the Reaganites blithely left them to the market's tender mercies. Nor did they complain when the deregulatory zeal of Reagan's Federal Communications Commission enabled a tiny and ever-shrinking group of large corporations to control most of the nation's media enterprises – even though this concentration of power thwarted their professed desire for greater competition and choice.

The trouble with the Conservatives, Evelyn Waugh once said, was that they never put the clock back, even by five minutes. He could not have made the same complaint about Ronald Reagan or Margaret Thatcher, both of whom had a single-minded mission to free the capitalist beast from the harnesses and bridles imposed upon it during the previous half-century. In January 1983, when the television interviewer Brian Walden suggested that Thatcher seemed to yearn for 'what I would call Victorian values', she replied: 'Oh exactly. Very much so. Those were the values when our country became great.' Delighted by the cries of horror her remarks elicited from the liberal intelligentsia, she returned to the theme in subsequent speeches and interviews. As she explained:

I was brought up by a Victorian grandmother. We were taught to work jolly hard. We were taught to prove yourself; we were taught self-reliance; we were taught to live within our income. You were taught that cleanliness is next to Godliness. You were taught self-respect. You were taught always to give a hand to your neighbour. You were taught tremendous pride in your country. All of these things are Victorian values. They are also perennial values. You don't hear so much about these things these days, but they were good values and they led to tremendous improvements in the standard of living.

Margaret Thatcher had a hostility to organised labour that would have won the respect of any grim-visaged Victorian mill-owner or coalmaster – as did Ronald Reagan, even though (or perhaps because) he himself was a former president of the Screen Actors' Guild. 'I pledge to you that my administration will work very closely with you to bring about a spirit of cooperation between the President and the air-traffic controllers,' Reagan promised PATCO, the air-traffic controllers' union, shortly before polling day in the autumn of 1980. But there was little evidence of this spirit when its members went on strike the following August: the new president announced that they would all be sacked unless they returned to work within forty-eight hours. More than 11,000 duly received their pink slips, their leaders went to jail and fines of $1 million a day were levied on the union.

Margaret Thatcher waited slightly longer for her own showdown. A thirteen-week strike by steel-workers in 1980, which ended with no obvious victor, convinced her that she must remove unions' legal immunities and outlaw secondary picketing before turning the full armoury of state power against militant labour. Besides, other preparations had to be made.

The union she most dearly wished to destroy was that of the mineworkers, who had brought down the previous Tory government in 1974 and were now led by the Marxist Arthur Scargill, but a lengthy pit strike could be resisted only if coal stockpiles were high enough to keep the home fires burning for the duration. So, as her biographer Hugo Young reported, from 1981 onwards the National Coal Board was 'given every financial and other encouragement to produce more coal than anyone could consume, and the Central Electricity Generating Board given similar inducements to pile up the stocks at power stations'. At the same time the police were equipped with new vehicles, communications equipment, weaponry and body armour. When the National Union of Mineworkers went on strike in 1984, a year after Thatcher's re-election, the government was ready for a long and bloody war.

With a belligerence that unnerved even some of her Cabinet colleagues, she described the miners as 'a scar across the face of the country' and likened them to the Argentine forces whom she had routed in the Falkland Islands two years earlier. 'We had to fight an enemy without in the Falklands,' she declared, in her best Churchillian style. 'We always have to be aware of the enemy within, which is more difficult to fight and more dangerous to liberty . . . There is no week, nor day, nor hour when tyranny may not enter upon this country, if the people lose their supreme confidence in themselves, and lose their roughness and spirit of defiance.' That autumn, when the IRA bombed a Brighton hotel where she was staying, she used the atrocity as further rhetorical ammunition: murderous terrorists and striking coal-miners were both conspiring 'to break, defy and subvert the laws'. For Margaret Thatcher, the miners' eventual and inevitable defeat represented nothing less than a victory of good over evil.

The prime minister could not claim the credit which she undoubtedly felt was her due, however, since throughout the dispute she had insisted that the war against 'the enemy within' was being prosecuted by the National Coal Board rather than Downing Street. The pretence fooled nobody – least of all the chairman of the NCB, who after one meeting at No. 10 complained to a reporter that 'I have weals all over my back, which I would be happy to show you' – but she felt obliged to maintain it, having often expressed her vehement dislike for government intervention in industry, or indeed in anything else. Even those branches of the state that enjoyed almost universal acceptance, such as public education and the National Health Service, appeared to Thatcher as quasi-Soviet abominations. 'As people prospered themselves so they gave great voluntary things,' she said in one of her many nostalgic eulogies to Victorian England. 'So many of the schools we replace now were voluntary schools, so many of the hospitals we replace were hospitals given by this great benefaction feeling that we have in Britain, even some of the prisons, the Town Halls. As our people prospered, so they used their independence and initiative to prosper others, not compulsion by the State.'

This was Margaret Thatcher's own version of trickle-down economics. Despite her notorious comment that 'there is no such thing as society; there are individual men and women, and there are families', she had limitless faith in the social conscience of the rich and might even have endorsed the mystical credo issued by an American coal-owner, George Baer, during the 1902 miners' strike: 'The rights and interests of the labouring man will be protected and cared for – not by the labour agitators, but by the Christian men to whom God in his infinite wisdom has given the control of the property interests in this country.' Since God, in his infinite wisdom, presumably had similar influence over those who control the White House, he must have changed his mind during the middle decades of the twentieth century: from Franklin Roosevelt's New Deal of 1933, which laid the foundations of a rudimentary welfare state, through Harry Truman's 'Fair Deal' to Lyndon Johnson's 'Great Society', the consensus was that even a prosperous capitalist nation should protect its weaker citizens – and its natural resources – against the depredations of the rich. To Thatcher this may have seemed tantamount to Communism, but it was also accepted by many conservatives. As the American author William Greider points out:

> The ideas and programmes that formed the modern welfare state originated from the values of the right as well as the left, from the conservative religious impulse to defend the domain of family, community and church against the raw, atomising effects of market economics as well as from the egalitarianism of anti-capitalist socialism. The welfare state was, in fact, an attempt to devise a fundamental compromise between society and free-market capitalism.

It was a Republican president, Richard Nixon, who created the Occupational Safety and Health Administration, the Food and Drug Administration and the Environmental Protection Agency. 'We are all Keynesians now,' he explained.

By the 1980s, however, God had apparently become a champion of *laissez-faire* again. Whereas Margaret Thatcher's twentieth-century predecessors mostly kept their Christianity to themselves, her own 'crusade' – as she often called it – was thoroughly religious in both content and style. Her father had been a Methodist lay preacher, and in her memoirs she proudly acknowledged the influence of a stern Christian upbringing: 'I believe in "Judaeo-Christian" values: indeed my whole political philosophy is based on them.' In 1951, as the prospective parliamentary candidate Miss Margaret Roberts, she told the Dartford Free Church Council that 'the future of the world depended on the few men and women who were Christians and who were willing to practise and propagate that faith abroad'.

From the moment when 'Thatcherism' was first articulated as a distinctive brand of Conservatism, soon after she and her intellectual mentor Sir Keith Joseph established the Centre for Policy Studies in 1974, its disciples emphasised that this was not mere materialism but an entrepreneurial theology. Sir Keith's famous Edgbaston speech of October 1974 caused a furore by proposing that low-income women should be discouraged from breeding, but its peroration (scarcely noticed at the time) was no less astonishing, and probably more significant. 'Are we to move towards moral decline reflected and intensified by economic decline, by the corrosive effects of inflation?' he asked, his face characteristically furrowed in anguish. 'Or can we remoralise our national life, of which the economy is an integral part?'

Modern British politicians hadn't previously used such language, but over the following two decades the evangelical message was heard again and again. 'I am in politics because of the conflict between good and evil,' Thatcher said, 'and I believe that in the end good will triumph.' Speaking to the Zurich Economic Society in 1977, she warned that:

we must not focus our attention exclusively on the material, because, though important, it is not the main issue. The main

issues are moral ... The economic success of the Western
world is a product of its moral philosophy and practice. The
economic results are better because the moral philosophy is
superior. It is superior because it starts with the individual,
with his uniqueness, his responsibility, and his capacity to
choose ... Choice is the essence of ethics: if there were no
choice, there would be no ethics, no good, no evil; good and
evil have meaning only insofar as man is free to choose.

She explicitly associated her belief in economic freedom of
choice with the Christian doctrine of the same name, as a
means of salvation. Self-reliance and property ownership were
'part of the spiritual ballast which maintains responsible citi-
zenship'. (Many Christians, of course, remained unpersuaded
that the prime minister was doing God's work. Anglican
bishops such as David Jenkins and David Sheppard protested
against the mass unemployment which she had created, and
the 1985 report *Faith in the City*, commissioned by the Archbishop of Canterbury, blamed the Tories' social Darwinism
for the squalor, decay and alienation found in Britain's inner
cities. Thatcher reacted furiously to the criticisms, arguing
that men of the cloth had no business commenting on her
industrial and economic policies – apparently oblivious to the
fact that her own metaphysical and religious justifications for
the new 'enterprise culture' had legitimised these clerical
ripostes.)

As the daughter of a man who had been both a preacher
and a local councillor, Thatcher knew how usefully scriptural
texts could be deployed to suggest divine sanction for political
prejudice. Speaking to the general assembly of the Church
of Scotland in 1988, she justified her blitz on benefit-
claimants by quoting St Paul's epistle to the Thessalonians:

'If a man will not work he shall not eat.' In another startling biblical exegesis, she said that 'no one would remember the Good Samaritan if he'd only had good intentions. He had money as well.' Like Reagan, Thatcher often implied that most public welfare provision was unnecessary: if the nation had enough millionaires, their natural benevolence and wealth-spreading talents would suffice. (Alas for the theory, charitable giving by Americans with annual salaries above $500,000 actually fell by 65 per cent between 1980 and 1988; the real Good Samaritans, who raised their donations by 62 per cent, turned out to be humbler souls earning between $25,000 and $30,000. Even more remarkably, the poorest in the land – those on $10,000 a year or less – gave 5.5 per cent of their income to charity, a higher share than anyone else.)

While affecting to admire Victorian philanthropy, Thatcher displayed a visceral contempt for the *noblesse oblige* of the wealthy paternalists in her own ranks – 'the wets', as she called them, who 'drivel and drool that they care'. Her real heroes were buccaneering entrepreneurs, and it sometimes seemed that no other way of life, including her own, was truly virtuous. (The political writer Hugo Young recalled one social encounter with Thatcher which 'consisted of a harrying inquiry as to why I didn't abandon journalism and start doing something really useful, like setting up a small business'.) 'These people are wonderful,' she raved. 'We all rely upon them to create the industries of tomorrow, so you have to have incentives.' Every obstacle to money-making – corporation taxes, anti-monopoly rules, trade unions' bargaining rights, laws protecting workers' health and safety – had to be minimised or swept away altogether. No wonder the stock market on both sides of the Atlantic went wild in the 1980s. For all Thatcher's pious injunctions about living within one's income, this was a decade of borrowing and spending. Between 1895 and 1980 the United States had shown a trade surplus every year, but during the presidency of Ronald Reagan it was transformed from the world's biggest creditor nation into the biggest debtor – and tripled its national debt for good measure.

Most people would regard it as suicidally irrational to embark on a credit-card splurge without giving a thought to how the bills can ever be paid. Yet when the denizens of Wall Street did just that in the 1980s, they were lionised. Gossip columnists and business reporters alike goggled in awe at the new financial titans – men such as Ivan Boesky, 'the great white shark of Wall Street', who was said to be worth $200 million by 1985, and Michael Milken, 'the junk-bond king', who earned $296 million in 1986 and $550 million in 1987. Boesky liked to describe himself as an 'arbitrageur' but the title of his 1985 book, *Merger Mania*, summarised the source of his wealth in plainer language. He had an enviable talent for buying stock in companies which, by happy coincidence, were targeted for takeover shortly afterwards, thus enabling him to sell at a profit. As it transpired, this owed less to the mysterious arts of 'arbitrage' than to old-fashioned insider-trading: Dennis Levine, a broker at the Wall Street firm Drexel Burnham Lambert, was tipping him off about imminent mergers or acquisitions in return for a percentage of Boesky's spoils. Meanwhile Levine's colleague Michael Milken was pioneering the use of high-risk, high-yield 'junk bonds' – essentially a means of converting equity into debt – to finance the merger mania. In May 1986 Boesky gave the commencement address at Milken's alma mater, the Berkeley business school at the University of California, and won loud applause when he said: 'Greed is all right, by the way. I want you to know that. I think greed is healthy. You can be greedy and still feel good about yourself.' Six months later he was indicted for illegal stock manipulation and insider dealing, charges that eventually landed him in Southern California's Lompoc federal prison. By 1991 Milken was also in a Californian jail, having incurred a ten-year sentence and a $600 million fine for fraud and racketeering.

As with 'junk bonds', almost all the macho financial neologisms of the 1980s were euphemisms for debt in one form or another. A 'leveraged buyout', for instance, involved purchasing a company with borrowed funds. More often than not, the security for these loans would be the target company itself, which would thus have to repay the debt from its own profits – or from the sale of assets – once the deal had gone through. Then there was 'greenmail', a technique pioneered by corporate raiders such as T. Boone Pickens and Sir James Goldsmith who would acquire a menacingly large stake in a company and then terrify the firm's owners into buying it back at a premium in order to avoid a hostile takeover. This reaped huge rewards for the predators but left their victims fatally indebted or dismembered: when the Goodyear Tire and Rubber Company fell prey to Goldsmith and his associates, it had to spend $2.6 billion paying off the greenmailers.

Where once businesses made products, now they made deals. As more and more money was borrowed from abroad to cover the difference between what Americans produced and what they consumed, a few voices began to question how and when the IOUs for this bogus prosperity would be honoured. 'This debt is essentially the cost of living beyond our means,' the economist Lester C. Thurow warned in the late summer of 1987, when the US trade-account deficit reached $340 billion. 'If the money we were borrowing from abroad all went into factories and robots, we wouldn't have to worry because the debt would be self-liquidating. It's the fact that we are using it entirely for consumption that makes it a serious problem.'

As any three-card-trick hustler knows, legerdemain depends for its success on fooling all the audience all the time: any members of the crowd who point out that the entire operation is a con must be silenced at once, or else punters will be markedly more reluctant to hand over their ten-dollar bills. So it was with the stock market in 1987, after five continuous years of giddy ascent. John Kenneth Galbraith, the grand old man of American Keynesianism, can probably claim the credit for being the first observer to state what should have been obvious: that Wall Street prices no longer had any relation to actual economic conditions. Writing in the January 1987 issue of the *Atlantic Monthly*, he argued that the market was now driven solely by 'a speculative dynamic – of people and institutions drawn by the market rise to the thought that it would go up more, that they could rise up and get out in time'. It had happened before, in the months preceding the Great Crash of 1929, and as the historian of that disaster Galbraith was struck by several other parallels – most notably the faith in seemingly imaginative, currently lucrative but ultimately disastrous innovations in financial structures. 'In the months and years prior to the 1929 crash there was a wondrous proliferation of holding companies and investment trusts. The common feature of both the holding companies and the trusts was that they conducted no practical operations; they existed to hold stock in other companies, and these companies frequently existed to hold stock in yet other companies.' The beauty of this exaggerated leverage was that any increase in the earnings of the ultimate company would flow back with geometric force to the originating company, because along the way the debt and preferred stock in the intermediate companies held by the public extracted only their fixed contractual share. The problem, however, was that any fall in earnings and values would work just as powerfully in reverse, as it duly did in October 1929. Nearly sixty years on, Galbraith wrote, leverage had been rediscovered and was again working its magic in a wave of corporate mergers and acquisitions, and in the bank loans and bond issues arranged to finance these operations.

The *Atlantic* magazine was the perfect pulpit from which to deliver such a sermon. Three years after the 1929 débâcle it had published the following *mea culpa*, written by an anonymous denizen of Wall Street, which now reads like a pretty accurate history of the 1980s as well:

In these latter days, since the downfall, I know that there will be much talk of corruption and dishonesty. But I can testify that our trouble was not that. Rather, we were undone by our own extravagant folly, and our delusions of grandeur. The gods were waiting to destroy us, and first they infected us with a peculiar and virulent sort of madness.

Already, as I try to recall those times, I cannot quite shake off the feel that they were pages torn from the Arabian Nights. But they were not. The tinseled scenes through which I moved were real. The madcap events actually happened – not once, but every day. And at the moment nobody thought them in the least extraordinary. For that was the New Era. In it we felt ourselves the gods and the demigods. The old laws of economics were for mortals, but not for us. With us, anything was possible. The sky was the limit.

It is a familiar delusion, the conviction that one has repealed the laws of financial gravity. (Even Isaac Newton, the man who discovered physical gravity, succumbed. 'I can calculate the motions of the heavenly bodies, but not the madness of people,' he said, selling his South Sea Company stock for a handsome profit in April 1720 before the bubble burst; but a few months later he re-entered the market at the top and lost £20,000.) Writing of a Wall Street boom at the very beginning of the twentieth century, Alexander Dana Noyes recalled that the market 'based its ideas and conduct on the assumption that we were living in a New Era; that old rules and principles and precedents of finance were obsolete; that things could safely be done today which had been dangerous or impossible in the past'. Days before the crash of October 1929, the Yale economist Irving Fisher (himself an active share-buyer) pronounced that 'stock prices have reached what looks like a permanently high plateau'.

All the familiar portents of disaster – swaggering hubris, speculative dementia, insupportable debt – were evident by 1987. 'At some point something – no one can ever know when or quite what – will trigger a decision by some to get out,' Galbraith predicted. 'The initial fall will persuade others that the time has come, and then yet others, and then the greater fall will come. Once the purely speculative element has been built into the structure, the eventual result is, to repeat, inevitable.' He added, however, that there was a compelling vested interest in prolonging financial insanity, and anyone who questioned its rationale could expect rough treatment from the spivs organising the three-card trick, just as the eminent banker Paul Warburg had been accused of 'sandbagging American prosperity' when he suggested in March 1929 that the orgy of 'unrestrained speculation' would soon end in tears. Galbraith's own article in the *Atlantic* had originally been commissioned by the *New York Times* but was spiked because the editors found it 'too alarming'.

Its eventual publication did nothing to puncture Wall Street's exuberance, at least for a while. ('Galbraith doesn't like to see people making money' was a typical reaction.) On 8 January 1987, a few days after the professor's gloomy New Year message, traders on the floor of the stock exchange were cheering and hurling confetti in the air as the Dow Jones industrial average broke through the 2,000 level for the first time. 'Why is the market so high when the economy continues to be so lacklustre?' *Time* magazine wondered. 'Considering such questions mere quibbles, many optimistic analysts are convinced that the crashing of the 2000 barrier is the start of another major market upsurge that might last anywhere from two to five years.' By the end of August the Dow had climbed to 2,722.42, the fifty-fifth record high achieved that year. Employing a system known as Elliott Wave Theory, the Wall Street guru Robert Prechter calculated that it would gain another thousand points in the next twelve months. Others put their trust in the so-called Super Bowl Theory, which held that the stock market always rose when a team from the original National Football League won the championship. And why not? The theory had been vindicated in eighteen of the previous twenty years, a more impressive success rate than conventional forecasting methods.

Against the madness of crowds, Friedrich von Schiller once wrote, the very gods themselves contend in vain. What hope was there for mere mortals wishing to understand the logic of a bull market that seemed unaffected by sluggish economic growth and a decline in business earnings? To quote Galbraith again:

Ever since the Compagnie d'Occident of John Law (which was formed to search for the highly exiguous gold deposits of Louisiana); since the wonderful exfoliation of enterprises of the South Sea Bubble; since the outbreak of investment enthusiasm in Britain in the 1820s (a company 'to drain the Red Sea with a view to recovering the treasure abandoned by the Egyptians after the crossing of the Jews'); and on down to the 1929 investment trusts, the offshore funds and Bernard Cornfeld, and yet on to Penn Square and the Latin American loans – nothing has been more remarkable than the susceptibility of the investing public to financial illusion and the like-mindedness of the most reputable of bankers, investment bankers, brokers, and free-lance financial geniuses. Nor is the reason far to seek. Nothing so gives the illusion of intelligence as personal association with large sums of money.

It is, alas, an illusion.

During the South Sea Bubble of 1720 investors hurled their money into any new venture, however weird its prospectus: 'For extracting of Silver from Lead'; 'For trading in Human Hair'; 'For a Wheel of Perpetual Motion'; and, most gloriously, 'a Company for carrying on an Undertaking of Great Advantage, but Nobody to know what it is'. Similarly, some of Wall Street's best-performing stocks in 1987 were enterprises that had neither profits nor products – obscure drug firms which were rumoured to have a cure for AIDS, or AT&E Corp, which claimed to be developing a wristwatch-based paging system. 'The thing could trade anywhere – up to 30 times earnings,' a leading analyst, Evelyn Geller, said of AT&E. 'So you're talking about $1,000 a share. You can't put a price on this – you can't. You don't know where it is going to go. You are buying a dream, a dream that is being realised.'

AT&E soon went out of business, its dream still unrealised, but Geller's rapturous illusion shows how the market was kept afloat at a time when any rational passenger should have been racing for the lifeboats.

By the second week in October, a few dents were appearing in the hitherto impregnable dreadnought. Some blamed a spate of investigations by the Securities and Exchange Commission into Wall Street's biggest names – Drexel Burnham Lambert, Goldman Sachs, Kidder Peabody – following the arrest of Ivan Boesky. Others complained that the fall in the dollar (caused by a widening foreign trade deficit) was weighing on the market. An additional factor was 'portfolio insurance', the high-tech innovation which set off waves of computerised selling as soon as the market fell below a certain level, prompting a downward stampede and foiling any attempts to recover equilibrium. Meanwhile, the risk-free yield on thirty-year government bonds had risen to an unprecedented 10.22 per cent, only slightly below the risk-heavy 10.6 per cent return from the stock market. Some investors wondered why they bothered to buy shares at all.

The economic tsunami of 19 October 1987 – 'Black Monday' – began with panic selling on the Tokyo stock exchange and then surged through Asia and Europe, following the sun, before engulfing Wall Street. The Dow Jones plummeted by 508.32 points, losing 22.6 per cent of its total value – almost twice the 12.9 per cent plunge during the crash of October 1929 which precipitated the Great Depression. 'Of all the mysteries of the Stock Exchange,' J. K. Galbraith had written in his history of the 1929 disaster, 'there is none so impenetrable as why there should be a buyer for everyone who wants to sell. 24 October 1929 showed that what is mysterious is not inevitable. Often there were no buyers.' Sure enough, on the morning of 20 October 1987 ('Terrible Tuesday'), with no one willing to purchase stocks at any price, there was a full hour in which trading ceased altogether: it appeared that the world's dominant financial system had simply curled up and died. What saved it from extinction was not the 'invisible hand' but the new chairman of the Federal Reserve Board, Alan Greenspan, who flooded the market with cheap credit shortly after midday and strong-armed the big banks to do the same, thus preventing Wall Street from dragging the whole US economy into recession. Meanwhile, the regulators of the New York stock exchange also intervened to 'preserve the integrity of the system'.

Did chastened right-wing triumphalists notice that capitalism had been rescued only by swift action from the federal government and the regulators, precisely the kind of 'interference' they would usually deplore? Apparently not. Ronald Reagan signalled a return to business as usual by dismissing Black Monday as 'some kind of correction', and magazines such as *Success* continued to glamorise the casino culture. Neo-liberals applauded the 'creative destruction' of manufacturing industry, old work practices, public institutions and anything else that stood in their path. In Washington and London, right-wing institutes and foundations proliferated like bindweed, fertilised by the enthusiasm with which Thatcher and Reagan greeted their crackpot schemes. The bow-tied young men in these think-tanks prided themselves on 'thinking the unthinkable', coming up with ideas such as privatisation – which would later become an unchallengeable gospel, spread everywhere from Russia to Mexico. 'We propose things which people regard as on the edge of lunacy,' Dr Madsen Pirie of the Adam Smith Insitute boasted in 1987. 'The next thing you know, they're on the edge of policy.' By a blissful irony, it was one such 'unthinkable' scheme – the poll-tax, dreamed up by the Adam Smith Institute and recklessly adopted by Thatcher against the advice of her colleagues – which helped to bring her down in November 1990.

By then, however, her task was effectively accomplished anyway. The demise of the Marxist states in Eastern Europe seemed to vindicate all that she and Ronald Reagan had done: both socialism and Keynesianism had been pronounced dead, and unrestrained turbo-capitalism installed as the new orthodoxy. 'What I want to see above all,' Reagan said, 'is that this remains a country where someone can always get rich.' And there was no shortage of hucksters willing to explain, for a fee, just how this could be achieved.

2

Old snake-oil, new bottles

There is an universal tendency among mankind to conceive all beings like themselves, and to transfer to every object those qualities with which they are familiarly acquainted, and of which they are intimately conscious. We find human faces in the moon, armies in the clouds . . . In proportion as any man's course of life is governed by accident, we always find that he increases in superstition, as may particularly be observed of gamesters and sailors, who, though of all mankind the least capable of serious reflection, abound most in frivolous and superstitious apprehensions . . . All human life, especially before the institution of order and good government, being subject to fortuitous accidents, it is natural that superstition should prevail everywhere in barbarous ages, and put men on the most earnest inquiry concerning those invisible powers who dispose of their happiness or misery.

DAVID HUME, *A Natural History of Religion* (1757)

Money is power, and power is the ultimate aphrodisiac. The logic is inescapable: rich people are sexy.

Logic has seldom been applicable to the mysteries of desire, and five minutes in the company of a typical tycoon should be enough to deflate this particular syllogism. The sheen of narcissism, the indiscriminate smile, the fawning gaggle of sycophants – what could be less alluring? One of the most resonantly repulsive images from the 1980s is of Michael Douglas, in shirtsleeves and braces, playing the snake-eyed corporate raider Gordon Gekko in *Wall Street*. Yet the fact that Oliver Stone's film was a moral fable with a message as old as the Bible (love of money is the root of all evil) eluded many moviegoers, mesmerised as they were by the seductive energy of sheer wickedness, and Gekko's 'greed is good' mantra soon became the catchphrase of every Big Swinging Dick in New York and London – Masters of the Universe, as Tom Wolfe called them in *The Bonfire of the Vanities*. For ambitious young things who had yet to join the club, there was one urgent question: I've got the red braces, I've got the attitude, I've got greed in abundance, so how can I grab some of the loot?

Help was at hand. In 1982 a young management consultant from McKinsey & Co., Thomas J. Peters, co-wrote *In Search of Excellence*, a relentlessly optimistic primer which celebrated America's best companies and sought to identify the secrets of their success. As the *Economist* noted, Peters had 'a knack of saying the right thing at the right time': *In Search of Excellence* was published in the very week when unemployment in the US reached its highest level since the 1930s, and it found a ready audience in a nation worried about declining competitiveness but sick of hearing about the Japanese miracle. (Perhaps Peters had learned from the precedent of Dale Carnegie, whose equally cheerful and vastly popular *How to Win Friends and Influence People* had appeared in 1936, in the depths of the Depression.) *In Search of Excellence* sold five million copies, and Peters used the proceeds to buy a 1,300 acre farm in Vermont, complete with cattle and llamas.

After that, the deluge: *The Seven Habits of Highly Effective*

People by Stephen R. Covey, *The Fifth Discipline* by Peter Senge, *The One-Minute Manager* by Kenneth Blanchard and Spencer Johnson, *Awaken the Giant Within* by Anthony Robbins . . . The *New York Times* list of non-fiction bestsellers soon became so clogged with inspirational tracts that the paper established a separate category for 'Advice, How-to and Miscellaneous'. Even men who had already made their fortune hastened to cash in: the Chrysler boss Lee Iacocca, the gloriously vulgar property developer Donald Trump and the rebarbative media mogul Al Neuharth all dashed off inspirational, ghost-written blockbusters that sold by the ton. (Neuharth's title, *Confessions of an S.O.B.*, perfectly evokes its rancid flavour.) Victor Kiam – the tiresome self-publicist who liked Remington razors so much that he bought the company – passed on the ideas which had propelled him to plutocracy in *Go for It* and *Keep Going for It*. 'Turn those negatives into positives!' 'A little bit of courtesy and caring. It goes such a long way.' 'Business is a game. Play it to win.' 'When you're an entrepreneur, you don't look a gift horse in the mouth.' 'When opportunity knocks, the entrepreneur is always home.' 'Any job worth doing is worth doing well.'

The authors of the American declaration of independence had prefaced their statement of human rights by announcing 'we hold these truths to be self-evident'. If Thomas Jefferson and his colleagues didn't flinch from stating the obvious, why should Victor Kiam or his rivals? Had the founding fathers only thought of copyrighting the text, they too could have enjoyed huge royalty cheques. One man who certainly understood how to profit from ideas that had hitherto been regarded as common property was Benjamin Franklin, whose *Poor Richard's Almanack* (1733) is a pot-pourri of similarly banal yet uplifting mottos – 'early to bed, early to rise, makes a man healthy, wealthy and wise', 'little strokes fell great oaks', and so forth. Pleasantly surprised by its reception, Franklin reworked the aphorisms into bestselling pamphlets such as *The Way to Wealth* and *Advice to a Young Tradesman*.

Two and a half centuries later, the market for platitudes became so crowded that ever more exotic angles were required to catch the eye of airport browsers. In the words of Mike Fuller, author of *Above the Bottom Line*, 'you have to have a shtick of some kind'. One promising approach, as the emphasis shifted from 'management' to 'leadership', was to seek out historical analogies, though the history usually turned out to be a mere promotional gimmick rather than a serious examination of past experience. The pioneer here was Wess Roberts (or Wess Roberts PhD as he styled himself, forgetting that non-medical 'doctors' who insist on drawing attention to their postgraduate qualification – Henry Kissinger in the US, Ian Paisley in Northern Ireland – always bring disaster in their wake: it's tantamount to having the warning 'This Man is Dangerous' tattooed on one's forehead). Roberts's book *The Leadership Secrets of Attila the Hun* appeared in 1991 and soon found its way on to the bookshelves of every middle manager in the United States. Described as a 'fantastic' guide which 'will help you make the most of your leadership potential', it vouchsafed these truly fantastic discoveries: 'You must have resilience to overcome personal misfortunes, discouragement, rejection and disappointment'; 'When the consequences of your actions are too grim to bear, look for another option.' Could anything be sillier? You bet: other authors have since come up with *Gandhi: The Heart of an Executive, Confucius in the Boardroom, If Aristotle Ran General Motors, Make It So: Management Lessons from 'Star Trek the Next Generation', Elizabeth I CEO: Strategic*

Lessons in Leadership from the Woman Who Built an Empire and *Moses: CEO*. The ten commandments, we now learn, were the world's first mission statement.

Recognising that not everyone wanted to be Donald Trump, or even Queen Elizabeth I, publishers extended their self-help lists to include more emollient titles on 'personal growth' – *Chicken Soup for the Soul, The Road Less Travelled* and *Men Are from Mars, Women Are from Venus* – or even out-and-out fiction such as James Redfield's novel *The Celestine Prophecy,* allegedly based on a manuscript revealing the secrets of the ancient Mayans, which sold five million copies in the United States alone. These might seem more New Age than New Economy, but it is instructive to note how often the two overlapped, as in Barrie Dolnick's *The Executive Mystic: Psychic Power Tools for Success* or Paul Zane Pilzer's bestseller, *God Wants You to be Rich*. When Anthony Robbins performed for a 14,000-strong crowd at a stadium in Dallas, the supporting speakers included John Gray, the man who inflicted *Men Are from Mars, Women Are from Venus* on the world. (Also on stage were country-music singer Trisha Yearwood, Dallas Cowboys quarterback Troy Aikman and General Norman Schwarzkopf: one is irresistibly reminded of early Beatles concerts featuring guest appearances by Freddie and the Dreamers, the Yardbirds and Rolf Harris.)

The juxtaposition of Robbins and Gray was all too congruous: there had long been a powerful spiritual impetus in American can-do literature. The popular nineteenth-century author Horatio Alger, who in novels such as *Do and Dare* and *Strive and Succeed* strove to persuade the nation that perseverance will always be rewarded, was a former Unitarian minister, defrocked for 'unnatural familiarity with boys'. Norman Vincent Peale, a Methodist minister, became the most successful self-help guru since Dale Carnegie with *The Power of Positive Thinking* (1952), which argued that Christians had a head-start in business: a typical anecdote concerned a saleswoman who told herself, 'If God be for me, then I know that with God's help I can sell vacuum cleaners.' One of Peale's modern counterparts, Stephen Covey, is a devout Mormon from Salt Lake City.

The marriage of mysticism and money-making reached its consummation in Deepak Chopra (or rather, Deepak Chopra MD), a Harvard-trained endocrinologist who turned to tran-scendental meditation (TM) and ayurvedic medicine in the early 1980s. He began marketing TM herbal cures – and indeed praised them in the *Journal of the American Medical Association* without mentioning that he was the sole share-holder in the distribution company. Chopra's transformation from an obscure salesman of alternative potions to a national guru can be dated precisely to Monday 12 July 1993, when he appeared on the Oprah Winfrey show to promote his book *Ageless Body, Timeless Mind.* His revelation that 'love is the ultimate truth' was perfectly pitched for Oprah and her millions of fretful yet hopeful viewers. Within twenty-four hours of the broadcast 137,000 copies of *Ageless Body, Timeless Mind* had been ordered, and Chopra's publishers – the deliciously named Harmony Books – were reprinting round the clock. By the end of the week there were 400,000 copies in circulation.

Since then he has published twenty-five books and issued at least 100 different audiotapes, videos and CD-ROMs, in which Eastern philosophy, Christian parables and even Arthurian legends are distilled into a bubble-bath for the soul. (One video offers 'Lessons from the Teaching of Merlin'.) Like Covey and Robbins, he understands the magic allure of numbered bullet-points: hence titles such as *The Seven Laws of Spiritual Success* and *Way of the Wizard: 20 Spiritual Lessons for Creating the Life You Want*. In public performances, the soothing effect of his Hallmark-card ruminations – 'Everything I do is a divine moment of the eternal', 'You and I are nothing but saints in the making' – is intensified by his mellifluous Anglo-Indian cadences and the mellow sitar riffs that often accompany them. Those who want the full-immersion experience can book in to the Chopra Centre for Well-Being in La Jolla, California – dubbed 'Shangri-La Jolla' by the irreverent – where their 'profound personal transformation can be customised for stays of 1–7 days'. The Centre grosses about $8 million a year, though Dr Chopra himself no longer attends to customers personally. 'It wouldn't be in the best interest of patients,' a spokeswoman said, 'because of his writing and speaking engagements.' Perhaps wisely, Deepak Chopra MD ceased renewing his California medical licence after the *annus mirabilis* of 1993 and therefore cannot be held professionally accountable for the consequences of his advice. 'I don't consider myself a religious or spiritual leader,' he has said. 'I consider myself a writer who explains some of the ancient wisdom traditions in contemporary language.' And for contemporary rewards, one might add: his speaking fee is about $25,000 per lecture. One corporate client, Atlantic Richfield Co., employed Chopra for almost a decade to teach employees how to find their inner space. 'We were going through a lot of changes at the time,' a company spokesman explained. 'We needed to impress on people the need to look at the world differently.'

Harold Bloom argued in his 1992 book *The American Religion* that many Americans are essentially Gnostics, pre-Christian believers for whom salvation 'cannot come through the community or the congregation, but is a one-on-one act of confrontation'. Clearly this does not apply to the more traditional churchgoing masses, but it suits solipsistic New Agers seeking the 'inner self' – and high-achieving materialists who like to think that fame and riches are no more than their due, reflecting the nobility of their souls. Chopra is happy to oblige: 'People who have achieved an enormous amount of success are inherently very spiritual . . . Affluence is simply our natural state.' Vain tycoons and holistic hippies alike can take comfort from Chopra's flattery ('You are inherently perfect'), and from his belief that the highest human condition is 'the state of "I am"': since we reap what we sow, both health and wealth are largely self-generated. Following this logic *ad absurdum*, he argues that 'people grow old and die because they have seen other people grow old and die. Ageing is simply learned behaviour.' Demi Moore was so impressed by this *aperçu* that she named him as her personal guru, announcing that 'through his teachings I hope to live to a great age, even 130 years isn't impossible'. Chopra himself, rather more cautiously, says that 'I expect to live way beyond 100.' Why the longevity formula failed to work for Princess Diana, with whom he lunched shortly before her death, remains a mystery.

Other famous admirers have included the former junk-bond king Michael Milken, Michael Jackson, Elizabeth Taylor, Winona Ryder, Debra Winger, Madonna, Mikhail Gorbachev, Hillary Clinton and Donna Karan, who expressed her gratitude by supplying the dapper doctor with free designer suits. Alas, as Karan looked to the east her business went west: she was replaced as chief executive of her own company in the summer of 1997, under pressure from investors who feared that a growing obsession with herbs, healing crystals and reincarnation was blinding her to the financial imperatives of running a publicly traded corporation.

For celebrities – and many others – Chopra offers a meta-physical justification for smug self-absorption, and requires no effort or sacrifice. Gita Mehta summarised the trade-off as long ago as 1979, in her excellent book *Karma Cola*:

> The westerner is finding the dialectics of history less fascinat-ing than the endless opportunities for narcissism provided by the Wisdom of the East ... Coming at the problem from separate directions, both parties have chanced upon the same conclusion, namely, that the most effective weapon against irony is to reduce everything to the banal. You have the Karma, we'll take the Coca-Cola, a metaphysical soft drink for a physical one.

The comic writers Christopher Buckley and John Tierney attempted to satirise the phenomenon in their book *God is My Broker: A Monk Tycoon Reveals the 7½ Laws of Spiritual and Financial Growth* (1998) – supposedly written by one 'Brother Ty', a failed, alcoholic Wall Street trader who saves his soul and earns a fortune after joining a monastic order devoted to the great Chopra. Brother Ty's 'laws', though amusing enough ('If God phones, take the call'; 'As long as God knows the truth, it doesn't matter what you tell your customers'; 'Money is God's way of saying "Thanks!"'), serve only to confirm that the genre is beyond parody, and probably immune to mockery anyway. Is Brother Ty's second law – 'God loves the poor, but that doesn't mean He wants you to fly coach' – any more hilariously absurd than Chopra's advice in *Creating Affluence*: 'B stands for better and best ... People with wealth consciousness settle only for the best. This is also called the principle of highest first. Go first-class all the way and the universe will respond by giving you the best'? And Brother Ty's seventh law – 'The only way to get rich from a get-rich book is to write one' – does not seem to apply to piss-takes. Although the publishers of *God is My Broker* claimed that it was 'destined to be a cult bestseller', it remained all cult and no bestseller. Chopra himself continued to flourish, heedless of the sniggering sophisticates. Named by *Time* magazine as one of the hundred top Icons and Heroes of the twentieth century, he is reported to earn more than $20 million a year from his spiritual business empire. No coach class for him.

In style, as in content, the sub-genres of self-help literature had much in common. Jonathan Lazear's *Meditations for Men Who Do Too Much,* aimed at workaholics who burned themselves out by reading *Keep Going for It* and *The Leadership Secrets of Attila the Hun,* had clearly bought its wisdom off the peg from the same retail chain patronised by the management gurus, Statements of the Obvious Inc. 'Our families, our partners, our extended families, our children will always be there for us if we can make the decision to be there for them'; 'We need to learn to pace ourselves'; 'Wealth doesn't really translate to happiness'; 'Trusting no one can be as dangerous as trusting everyone'; 'We can learn from our failures'; 'No one is happy all of the time.'

The gurus who were chortling and whooping all the way to the bank might have questioned that last assertion. Kenneth Blanchard parlayed the success of *The One-Minute Manager* into an income of $6 million a year from videotapes and lectures promoting his message that 'people who produce good results feel good about themselves'. In the late 1990s Stephen Covey's Utah-based consultancy had annual revenues of more than $400 million, and employed 3,000 people in forty countries to spread his gospel of 'Principle-Centered Leadership'. Anthony Robbins, who once worked as a school janitor, had earned about $80 million – some of it from books such as *Awaken the Giant Within* and *Unlimited Power*, but mostly from his talent for persuading sober-suited executives to shout 'Yes! I can do it! I will lead not follow!' while Tina Turner's 'Simply the Best' blasted out of the PA system. John Gray had an 'income-stream' of $10 million in 1999, partly from 350 Mars and Venus 'facilitators' who paid him for the privilege of distributing his books at monthly workshops. By the end of the century, self-help publications were worth $560 million a year, and according to the research firm Marketdata Enterprises the total income of the 'self-improvement industry' in the US – from seminars, personal coaching, CDs and videos – was $2.48 billion. As *Newsweek* reported, 'With slick marketing and growing acceptance by mainstream Americans, authors like Covey, Anthony Robbins and John Gray are amassing fortunes that rival those of Hollywood moguls.'

Why would mainstream Americans pay to be told what they knew already? One of Blanchard's satisfied customers tried to explain. 'What he's saying is a lot of common sense and not really new,' the executive manager of B. H. Emporiums, a Canadian retail chain, conceded. 'But if I pay him $15,000 to say it, my general managers and my people listen. If I'm paid to say it, my people don't listen in the same way.' The mega-stars in this branch of showbiz may have had nothing original to impart, but they knew how to put on a performance. Anthony Robbins, a six-foot-seven Superman lookalike, would ask his audience to take off their shoes and socks and walk across hot coals while he repeated the soothing mantra 'cool moss, cool moss'. The frenetic stage persona of Tom

Peters, former McKinsey man, was a cross between Mick Jagger and Pete Townshend – arms flailing, sweat drenching his shirt.

So what are the seven habits of highly effective people? How do we awaken the giant within? The short answer is: never overestimate the intelligence of your audience. 'Did you ever consider', Stephen Covey asks in *The Seven Habits of Highly Effective People* (1989), 'how ridiculous it would be to try to cram on a farm – to forget to plant in the spring, play all summer and then cram in the fall to bring in the harvest? The farm is a natural system. The price must be paid and the process followed. You always reap what you sow.' The echo of Chauncey Gardener, the idiot savant who dispensed horti- cultural wisdom in Jerzy Kosinski's satire *Being There*, is presumably accidental.

Anthony Robbins prefers to take his imagery from the kitchen rather than the farmyard. 'A nice metaphor for the components and use of strategies is that of baking,' he observes in *Unlimited Power* (1986). 'If someone makes the greatest choc- olate cake in the world, can you produce the same quality results? Of course you can, if you have that person's recipe . . . if you follow the recipe to the letter, you will produce the same results, even though you may never have baked such a cake before in your life.' This weary analogy clearly had a profound effect on at least one reader. 'There is no better metaphor for the products of the knowledge economy than the recipe,' the British guru Charles Leadbeater writes in *Living on Thin Air: The New Economy* (1999). 'Think of the world as divided up into chocolate cakes and chocolate-cake recipes . . . We can all use the same chocolate-cake recipe, at the same time, without anyone being worse off. It is quite unlike a piece of cake.' Tony Blair, in turn, was deeply impressed, hailing Leadbeater as 'an extraordinarily interesting thinker' whose book 'raises critical questions for Britain's future'. Another Labour minister, Peter Mandelson, described *Living on Thin Air* as 'a blueprint for what a radical modernising project will entail in years to come'.

The man ultimately responsible for all this lucrative twaddle is Dale Carnegie, and most of his successors stick pretty closely to the formula (oh, all right, recipe) devised by the pioneer. It was certainly Carnegie who cottoned on to the selling power of animal analogies, peppering his prose with such eternal verities as 'no one ever kicks a dead dog' and 'if you want to gather honey, don't kick over the beehive'. Studying the titles on display in the management section of Borders' bookshop, you might assume that you'd stumbled into the natural history department by mistake: *Lions Don't Need To Roar: Stand Out, Fit In and Move Ahead in Business,* by Debra Benton, *Swim with the Sharks Without Being Eaten Alive* by Harvey Mackay and *Teaching the Elephants to Dance: Empowering Change in Your Organisation* by James A. Belasco. Charles Handy's *The Age of Unreason* has a picture of a leaping frog on its front cover. Why? 'If you put a frog in water and slowly heat it, the frog will eventually let itself be boiled to death,' he explains. 'We, too, will not survive if we don't respond to the radical way in which the world is changing.' Not to be outdone, Stephen Covey includes a section on fish in his *Principle-Centred Leadership*. 'I've long been impressed', he reveals, 'with the many parallels between fishing and managing. In reality, senior-level executives are really fishing the stream. That is, they're looking at the business in the context of the total environment and devising ways to "reel in" desired results . . .' And what does it get them? A pile of dead trout.

Apart from dancing elephants and boiling frogs, the other

essential ingredient of these books is lists. Following the distinguished example of God, who condensed the laws of
righteousness into ten easy-to-understand instructions, the
authors seek to persuade their readers that the secrets of
success are finite and can be briefly enumerated. Again
Carnegie was the pioneer, offering 'seven ways to peace and
happiness' and 'four good working habits that will help prevent fatigue and worry'. Having hit the jackpot with *The Seven
Habits of Highly Effective People*, Covey went even further in his
sequel, whose chapter headings include 'Three Resolutions',
'Six Days of Creation', 'Six Conditions of Empowerment',
'Seven Deadly Sins' (didn't someone else think of that first?),
'Seven Chronic Problems', 'Eight Ways to Enrich Marriage
and Family Relationships' and, generously enough, 'Thirty
Methods of Influence'. Meanwhile, Anthony Robbins has discovered the 'Five Keys to Wealth and Happiness' and 'Seven
Lies of Success'. More ambitiously still, his book *Giant Steps*
provides no fewer than '365 lessons in self-mastery' – though
some of them are pretty skimpy. Here is Lesson 364, in
its entirety: 'Remember to expect miracles ... because you
are one.'

If the gurus offered nothing but cracker-mottoes, their
appeal might have been limited to a few simpletons; but the
faux naivety was cunningly seasoned with an equally *faux*
sophistication. They made liberal use of neologistic jargon –
're-engineering', 'demassing', 'downsizing', 'benchmarking'
– to give their twee clichés an appearance of scientific method
and intellectual rigour. And it worked: even grizzled New York
police chiefs and four-star generals began babbling about 'the
mobility pool' and 'proactive outplacement'. ('Of course this
benchmarking is only a rough guide,' one Pentagon official
told a reporter. 'The ultimate benchmarking exercise is war.')

Stephen Covey's client-list in the US included the departments of energy, defence, interior and transportation, the postal service – and Bill Clinton, who invited both Covey and Anthony Robbins to spend the weekend with him in December 1994.

Reeling from his party's defeat by Newt Gingrich's Republicans in the previous month's congressional elections, the president summoned no fewer than five feelgood authors to help him 'search for a way back'. The other three were Marianne Williamson, a glamorous Hollywood mystic (and, one need hardly add, bestselling author) who had performed the marriage rites at Elizabeth Taylor's 1991 wedding to Larry Fortemsky; Jean Houston, a self-styled 'sacred psychologist' whose fourteen books included *Life Force: The Psycho-Historical Recovery of the Self*; and her friend Mary Catherine Bateson, an anthropology professor whose study of 'non-traditional life paths' had been praised by Hillary Clinton.

This quintet of sages asked the president to describe his best qualities. 'I have a good heart,' he said. 'I really do. And I hope I have a decent mind.' (If so, one might ask, why seek solace from snake-oil vendors?) As they talked long into the night, and all the following day, the conversation was increasingly dominated by Hillary's problems – the constant personal attacks she endured, and the failure of her plan to reform health-care. Jean Houston, who felt that 'being Hillary Clinton was like being Mozart with his hands cut off', informed the First Lady that she was 'carrying the burden of 5,000 years of history when women were subservient . . . She was reversing thousands of years of expectation and was there up front, probably more than virtually any woman in human history – apart from Joan of Arc.'

The latter-day Joan was understandably flattered. Over the

next six months Houston and Bateson often visited Hillary Clinton in Washington, urging her to talk to the spirits of historical figures who would understand her travails and thus help her 'achieve self-healing'. Sitting with her two psychic counsellors at a circular table in the White House solarium, she held conversations with Eleanor Roosevelt (her 'spiritual archetype') and Mahatma Gandhi ('a powerful symbol of stoic self-denial'). It was only when Houston proposed speaking to Jesus Christ – 'the epitome of the wounded, betrayed and isolated' – that Hillary called a halt. 'That', she explained, 'would be too personal.' The reticence seems rather puzzling: don't millions of Christians speak to Jesus, both publicly and privately, through their prayers?

There was little the Republicans could do to exploit 'Wacky-gate', as it became known: too many people remembered Ronald Reagan's dependence on Nancy's astrologer. Those with longer memories might even have recalled that Norman Vincent Peale, the man who brought God into the selling of vacuum-cleaners, was a regular visitor to the White House during Eisenhower's presidency and presided at the wedding of Richard Nixon's daughter Julie. Indeed, a few months before Clinton's chinwag with the gurus, three former presidents – Ford, Reagan and Bush – had joined Peale's widow, the Rev. Robert Schuller and Zig Ziglar ('America's No. 1 motivational speaker') in a forty-one-gig travelling show titled Success '94. Ten days after the Camp David self-help session, the Republican congressman John Kasich, chairman of the House Budget Committee, invited his staff to a seminar with Doug Hall, author of *Jump Start Your Brain*. 'Hall blasted the old Sam the Sham song "Woolly Bully" in the committee room,' the *Washington Post* reported, 'while the staffers shot at one another with Nerf guns.'

No wonder President Clinton remained so stubbornly popular, however many scandals buffeted his reputation: his dabblings in alternative psychology and New Age management techniques must have been a great reassurance to many fellow-citizens who had previously felt slightly shamefaced about their own dalliance with Deepak Chopra or Anthony Robbins. As *Newsweek* pointed out when the story of Hillary's chats with ghosts eventually leaked, 'From Atlantic Richfield to Xerox, corporate America has spent millions every year putting managers through the same kind of exercises in personal transformation the Clintons have been sampling for free. Houston herself has run seminars for the Department of Commerce and other federal agencies. At Stanford Business School, Prof. Michael Ray has prepared future captains of industry with Tarot cards and chants to release their deeper selves.'

Everyone was at it. In Britain, allegedly the home of the stiff upper lip, the loopier manifestations of soul-baring may have been mocked but managerial mumbo-jumbo found an eager market. By 1995 the British government was spending well over £100 million a year on management consultants, as branches of officialdom were forcibly transformed into 'agencies'. What had once been straightforward public services, such as the health system or the BBC, acquired their own internal markets – which in turn created new blizzards of paperwork and extra layers of bureaucracy, all in the name of efficiency. The ensuing chaos was best described by an official inquiry into the semi-privatised British prison service, commissioned after two murderers and an arsonist escaped from Parkhurst jail in January 1995: 'Any organisation which boasts one Statement of Purpose, one Vision, five Values, six Goals, seven Strategic Priorities and eight Key Performance

Indicators without any clear correlation between them is producing a recipe for total confusion and exasperation.' The home secretary promptly sacked the director-general of the prison service, Derek Lewis, a businessman who knew nothing about jails or indeed public administration. Lewis was understandably puzzled: the same government which recruited him three years earlier to give the penal system a dose of management theory had now punished him for doing just that.

This fiasco did nothing to dampen the Tories' enthusiasm for merchants of gimmickry and gobbledegook; and the only difference made by the election of New Labour in 1997 was that that the Blairites seemed even more susceptible. Government spending on private consultants rose by 25 per cent in both 1998–9 and 1999–2000, and by more than 50 per cent the following year – from £360 million to £550 million. The recipients of this largesse could hardly believe their luck. 'Go back two or three years,' the trade journal *Management Consultancy* commented in August 2001, 'and it would have been difficult, if not impossible, to find anyone anticipating an increase in spending of that magnitude from the state.' Not so: Tony Blair had never concealed his reverence for management gurus. In the summer of 1996 he despatched 100 Labour frontbenchers to a weekend seminar at Templeton College, Oxford, where a posse of partners from Andersen Consulting lectured the wannabe ministers on 'total quality service' and 'the management of change'. (The veteran Labour politician Lord Healey, who also spoke at the event, was unimpressed: 'These management consultants are just making money out of suckers.') When Blair entered Downing Street, several executives from Andersen – and McKinseys, the other leading management consultancy – were seconded to Whitehall with a brief to practise 'blue skies thinking'. Soon afterwards, in perhaps the most remarkable manifestation of New Labour's guru-worship, they were joined by Dr Edward de Bono, whose task was 'to develop bright ideas on schools and jobs'.

In the autumn of 1998 more than 200 officials from the Department of Education were treated to a lecture from de Bono on his 'Six Thinking Hats system' of decision-making. The idea, he explained, was that civil servants should put on a red hat when they wanted to talk about hunches and instincts, a yellow hat if they were listing the advantages of a project, a black hat while playing devil's advocate, and so on. 'Without wishing to boast,' he added, 'this is the first new way of thinking to be developed for 2,400 years since the days of Plato, Socrates and Aristotle.' In similarly unboastful fashion, de Bono often says that he invented 'lateral thinking' – which is like claiming to have invented poetry, or humour, or grief – and takes pride in having devised a system of 'water logic'. Here is an example of water logic in action: 'How often does someone who is using a traditional wet razor stop to consider whether instead of moving the razor it might be easier to keep the razor still and to move the head instead? In fact it is rather better. But no one does try it because there is "no problem to fix".' If his pupils in Whitehall tried this shaving technique they would soon discover why it hasn't caught on: the result looks like an out-take from *The Texas Chainsaw Massacre*. So far as can be discovered, the education department has yet to order those coloured hats, but no doubt it benefited from his other creative insights: 'You can't dig a hole in a different place by digging the same hole deeper'; 'With a problem, you look for a solution'; 'A bird is different from an aeroplane, although both fly through the air.'

Who could disagree? Gurus are safe enough while peddling ancient clichés disguised as revolutionary new strategies. It is when they seek out instances of this wisdom in action that they come a cropper: the entrepreneur-as-hero often turns out to be merely human after all. In his 1985 book *Tactics: The Art and Science of Success*, Edward de Bono offered the lessons that might be learned from a number of people who 'would generally be regarded as "successful"'. After studying these inspiring examples, 'the reader should say, "Why not me?"' The millionaires he extolled included US hotelier Harry Helmsley, later convicted of massive tax evasion, and Robert Maxwell, subsequently exposed as one of the most outrageous fraudsters in British history.

One of the Thatcherites' most frequently repeated injunctions in the 1980s was that until Britain learned to love wealth-creators it was doomed to economic decline. As the Tory minister Lord Young said in 1987 while presenting the *Guardian*'s Young Businessman of the Year Award, there is a 'strong anti-business, anti-entrepreneurial streak' in British society. (Not that it deterred his lordship: soon afterwards he left the Cabinet for the lusher pastures of the chairman's office at Cable & Wireless.) Jonathan Aitken, another wealthy Conservative, made the same point twenty years earlier in his book *The Young Meteors*. 'One reason why we are so ill-equipped on any level to compete in manufacturing fields', he argued, 'is that as a nation we are only just beginning to regard profit-making through manufacturing as respectable.' To conquer this lingering prejudice, he drew attention to some thoroughly respectable entrepreneurs – such as Gerald Ronson, aged twenty-seven, 'one of Britain's youngest self-made property millionaires', and Jim Slater, the 'brilliantly successful' founder of Slater-Walker. Slater-Walker later

performed so brilliantly that it had to be bailed out by the
Bank of England, and Jim Slater was found guilty of fifteen
offences under the Companies Act. Gerald Ronson, not to
be outdone, served a term in Ford open prison for his partici-
pation in an illegal share-ramping operation. The catalogue
of woe was completed in June 1999 when Jonathan Aitken
himself, who had served as a Cabinet minister until 1995,
was jailed for perjury and attempting to pervert the course
of justice.

Hence the traditional British resistance to the allegedly
aphrodisiac qualities of tycoons: we can't help suspecting that
they wear their socks in bed and snore all night. Even those
politicians and pundits who approve in principle of capitalist
self-enrichment will often join the chorus of insults directed
against 'fat cats' who put the theory into practice, and the
few attempts to idolise business chieftains have invariably
ended in embarrassment. Consider the fate of the London-
based American author Jeffrey Robinson, who has tried for
years to persuade his adopted country that cigar-chomping
magnates are sexy. In 1985, the high noon of Thatcherism,
he published *The Risk Takers*, a collection of conversations
with British businessmen who 'turn me on'. Gerald Ronson
once again paraded himself for our titillation ('a man with a
proven knack for making money'), as did Robert Maxwell.
'He is', Robinson announced, 'a survivor.' Yet another pin-
striped pin-up was Asil Nadir, whose fruit-packing company
Polly Peck had long been a favourite of awestruck stock-
brokers. Nadir complained to his sympathetic interviewer that
'in this country there are people who believe it's a sin to be
successful'.

In 1990, with his promiscuous ardour apparently undimin-
ished, Robinson produced *The Risk Takers Five Years On*, in

which he boasted that some of his original interviewees, including Robert Maxwell and Asil Nadir, had 'gone from strength to strength'. Maxwell, he predicted, would eventually retire, covered in glory, leaving his sons Kevin and Ian with the exciting challenge of 'keeping dad's ship afloat'. Well, at least the buoyancy metaphor was accurate: Maxwell's corpse was found floating off the coast of Spain on 5 November 1991, after a fall from his yacht.

For his revised edition, Robinson added several chapters on 'big players' he had missed the first time around – among them Gerald Ratner, 'the world's largest jeweller', and Michael Smurfit, an 'indisputable success'. Once more, alas, the demon lovers turned out to be all mouth and no trousers. With the subsequent admission that one of his products was 'crap', Ratner managed to transform his firm's annual profit of £112 million into a loss of £122 million and was forced to quit. Smurfit resigned as chairman of Irish Telecom only a few weeks after Robinson's book appeared, when it was revealed that he had bought a new corporate HQ without informing his fellow-directors, and that he was a shareholder in a company which had previously owned the property. At the same time, he invested heavily in the Brent Walker group – which duly went belly-up, taking £10 million of his money with it.

What of the *Guardian*'s own small endeavour to burnish the image of go-getters, the Young Businessman of the Year competition? At the 1987 ceremony, where Lord Young advised that 'people should look up to successful businessmen in the same way that they look up to successful sportsmen and successful pop stars', the winner was John Ashcroft of Coloroll, who repeated the leitmotif in his acceptance speech. 'We live in an age which applauds the millionaire McCartneys and Simon Le Bons and is now beginning to accept the large salaried superstar creations of the manufacturing sector. Long may it continue.' Within three years, Coloroll had collapsed, crushed by £400 million of debts. The dashing Mr Ashcroft then started up a chain of shops; by 1993, it too was in the hands of the receivers.

The *Guardian*'s annual mating ritual with 'business success' only served to confirm the old proverb: *post coitum omne animal triste est*. The 1988 prize went to John Gunn of British & Commonwealth Holdings; two years later B&C crashed with £1 billion in liabilities. Richard Brewster, chief executive of the packaging group David S. Smith (Holdings), took the palm in 1990, praised by the judges for his 'management skills in rebuilding an important British industry'. By 1991, he had gone – 'hounded', as one City commentator cruelly observed, 'by the curse of having been nominated *Guardian* Young Businessman of the Year'. The award itself, like so many of its winners, conked out soon afterwards.

Typical British defeatism, some might say: a true professional would heed Victor Kiam's wise words and 'turn those negatives into positives!' In 1987, five years after Tom Peters initiated the craze for management blockbusters with *In Search of Excellence*, most of the US firms he had marked as 'excellent' were in steep decline. The cover of *Business Week* magazine, which first noticed his remarkable inability to pick winners, carried the single word 'Oops!' Worse still, a comparative study in the *Financial Analysts' Journal* found that whereas stocks in two-thirds of Peters's model corporations had underperformed Standard & Poor's 500 index, those in thirty-nine companies which were reckoned abysmal by Peters's six 'measures of excellence' had actually outperformed the market over the same five-year period.

Was Peters abashed? Of course not: when opportunity knocks, the entrepreneur is always home! With admirable chutzpah, he capitalised on the blunder by writing another bestseller, which advocated entirely different solutions to the problems of American business. 'Excellence isn't,' he announced in the opening sentences of *Thriving on Chaos* (1987). 'There are no excellent companies.' With his customary impeccable timing the book was published on Black Monday, when the Dow Jones plummeted by 20 per cent – thus apparently confirming his new discovery that the world had spun out of control and 'no company is safe'.

Or, to quote the unimprovable headline on a despatch from the Agence France Presse news agency in the closing months of the year 2000: 'Order, Chaos Vie to Shape 21st Century'.

3

It's the end of the world
as we know it

'*Before I draw nearer to that stone to which you point,*' said Scrooge,
'*answer me one question. Are these the shadows of the things that
Will be, or are they the shadows of the things that May be only?*'
　Still the Ghost pointed downward to the grave by which it stood.
　'*Men's courses will foreshadow certain ends, to which, if persevered
in, they must lead,*' said Scrooge. '*But if the courses be departed from,
the ends will change. Say it is thus with what you show me!*'

CHARLES DICKENS, *A Christmas Carol*

For public intellectuals in the early 1980s, one little prefix
was obligatory. Post-modernism, post-feminism, post-Fordism
and 'post-culture' (a term coined by Professor George
Steiner) all joined the lexicon of modish discourse. Within a
few years, however, even these concepts had been superseded.
When the economist Lester C. Thurow said that 'the sun
is about to set on the post-industrial era', James Atlas of
the *New York Times* posed the obvious question: 'What
follows post?'

In *The Sense of an Ending*, the British literary critic Sir Frank
Kermode argued that humans require an illusion of order

and narrative: 'To make sense of their span they need fictive concords with origins and ends, such as give meaning to lives and to poems.' With the *fin de siècle* and indeed the end of the millennium looming, there was a palpable sense of imminent closure and conclusion: the critic Arthur Danto announced 'the end of art'; the *New Yorker* writer Bill McKibben was paid a $1 million advance for his book *The End of Nature*; an editor at the *Scientific American,* John Horgan, published *The End of Science: Facing the Limits of Knowledge in the Twilight of the Scientific Age.* As Atlas commented, 'clearly, it's late in the day'. President Reagan had celebrated the arrival of 'morning in America'; before most people had even managed to finish their breakfast, however, the shadows of evening were already lengthening, and citizens who had been enchanted by the Gipper's sunny optimism now seemed to have an almost masochistic yearning for gloomy jeremiads.

One unlikely beneficiary of this new appetite was Paul Kennedy, a bearded, soft-spoken Englishman from the history faculty at Yale University, whose 677-page tome *The Rise and Fall of the Great Powers: Economic Change and Military Conflict from 1500 to 2000* was published by Random House in January 1988, with an initial print-run of 9,000. By mid-February it had sold more than 100,000 copies. Few of these readers, one must assume, were particularly curious about the old imperial powers of China, Spain, Holland or Britain, whose histories comprised most of the book. Nor, one guesses, would Kennedy have been inundated with requests from TV talk shows or invitations to address congressional committees had he stuck to his original plan and ended the narrative in about 1945. Deciding that this would be 'a cop-out', he added a speculative final chapter predicting that American hegemony was waning. Simply put, the Kennedy thesis asserted that great empires establish themselves through economic might, but are then obliged to spend an ever larger proportion of their wealth on military prowess with which to protect themselves from upstart rivals. The consequent 'imperial overstretch' seals their fate. It happened to the Bourbons and the Habsburgs, and would just as surely happen to the apparently omnipotent United States within a few years.

'When a serious work of history with more than a thousand footnotes starts selling in Stephen King-like quantities,' the *New Republic* commented, 'you can be sure it has touched something in the popular mood.' And, sure enough, a great power overburdened with defence commitments duly succumbed to imperial overstretch soon afterwards. Alas for Kennedy, it was not the United States but the Soviet Union, whose speedy and spectacular demise he had quite failed to foresee. Undaunted, he interpreted this unexpected plot-twist as confirmation of his prophecy of American decline, since the end of the Cold War reduced 'the significance of the one measure of national power in which the United States had a clear advantage over other countries', that is military strength. (The other measures of American dominance – economic, cultural, technological – were apparently invisible from Professor Kennedy's study at Yale.) Besides, didn't the collapse of Soviet Communism, which even many American Cold Warriors had thought impossible, re-emphasise his central point: that nothing lasts for ever? With that, at least, few could take issue – or so it seemed until the summer of 1989, when the *National Interest* magazine carried a fifteen-page article entitled 'The End of History?' Its author was an obscure young official from the policy planning staff of the US State Department, Francis Fukuyama.

Once again, a shy, tweed-jacketed historian woke up to find

himself famous. Even those who disagreed with Fukuyama paid tribute to his intellectual audacity, which was further rewarded with book contracts, lecture invitations and a professorship at the Johns Hopkins School of Advanced International Studies. 'How is it that some people become famous while others do not?' a jealous rival asked. 'Of course, it smacks of sour grapes for one of the latter to ask this about one of the former, but Francis Fukuyama's career begs for the question. How exactly do you get ahead by boldly making one of the worst predictions in social science?' The question answers itself: if you are going to be wrong, be wrong as ostentatiously and extravagantly as possible. Had Fukuyama confined himself to saying that the end of the Cold War marked a victory for economic and political liberalism, scarcely anyone would have paid attention, since identical observations could be found in newspaper editorials any day of the week. But he understood what was required to titillate the jaded palate of the chattering classes: simplify, then exaggerate. 'What we are witnessing', he proclaimed, 'is not just the end of the Cold War, or a passing of a particular period of postwar history, but the end of history as such: that is, the end point of mankind's ideological evolution and the universalisation of Western liberal democracy as the final form of human government.' By the time he had expanded his essay into a book, two years later, even the question-mark in the title had disappeared.

The obvious flaws in this terminalist teleology were magicked away with similar nonchalance. The German philosopher G. W. F. Hegel, who was cited by Fukuyama as his chief inspiration, also believed that we had reached 'the last stage of history, our world, our own time' – but dated it to Napoleon's victory at the Battle of Jena in 1806. Some political soothsayers might interpret this precedent as a cautionary tale of reckless complacency, but not Fukuyama. With nimble dialectic – or, if you prefer, shameless chutzpah – he argued that Hegel was right after all, since 'the present world seems to confirm that the fundamental principles of socio-political organisation have not advanced terribly far since 1806'. Ergo, we had reached the zenith and terminus of political evolution: Nazism and Communism were mere 'bypaths of history'. ('How far shall we trust a "Universal History" that relegates the conflagrations of two world wars and the unspeakable tyranny of Hitler and Stalin as "bypaths"?' the American commentator Roger Kimball asked in a review of Fukuyama's book. 'I submit that any theory which regards World War II as a momentary wrinkle on the path of freedom is in need of serious rethinking.')

History is itself an ambiguous term, of course. It can mean no more than what occurs in the world, or the techniques for finding this out, but it is also the discipline that orders events and experiences into an evolutionary narrative – summarised by the Enlightenment historian Lord Bolingbroke as 'philosophy teaching by examples', and later defined by R. G. Collingwood (in *The Idea of History*) as the reality of the present tempered by the necessity of the past and the possibilities of the future. This too was declared obsolete by the Terminalists. Fukuyama did not merely foreclose all possibilities other than the universal and perpetual reign of liberal American capitalism, the predominant present reality; he was also implicitly slamming the door on the past, muffling the cries and whispers of previous generations. Since 'all of the really big questions had been settled', he argued, 'in the post-historical period there will be neither art nor philosophy, just the perpetual caretaking of the museum of human history'.

Imagination, heroism and idealism would be supplanted by economic calculation.

Not the most appealing manifesto for a brave new world, you might think. And Fukuyama would agree – sometimes. When celebrating the ultimate triumph of liberal capitalism he chides those tiresome nations which are still somehow 'stuck in history', and means it as an insult; yet in his more wistful moments he admits that 'the end of history will be a sad time'. Sad, and deeply dull: he fears that sheer boredom, married to 'a powerful nostalgia for the time when history existed', may yet 'serve to *get history started again*'. The incredulous italics are mine: having asserted that modern American-style capitalist democracy is so manifestly unimprovable that it has seen off every conceivable challenger, Fukuyama casually concedes that this invincible titan could yet be overthrown by nothing stronger than the sleepy ennui of its beneficiaries. One is reminded of Karl Marx's private confession to Frederick Engels after writing a newspaper article on the likely outcome of the Indian mutiny in the 1850s: 'It is possible that I shall make an ass of myself. But in that case one can always get out of it with a little dialectic. I have, of course, so worded my proposition as to be right either way.'

Fukuyama's dialectic is similarly artful. He parades Hegel's philosophy of history as supporting evidence for his own blithe certainty; yet he acknowledges (if only in a footnote) that the Hegelian historical terminus, the supreme desideratum, was not American capitalism but the absolute monarchy of nineteenth-century Prussia, described by Hegel as 'the achievement of the modern world, a world in which the substantial Idea has won the infinite form'. No doubt Stone Age men and women, if they ever gave it a moment's thought, assumed that their own way of life was just as immutable: few people have ever been able to imagine any kind of society other than the one that they inhabit. If Hegel was wrong about the eternal reign of Prussian absolutism, why should we believe that the present system has any more staying power? Fukuyama has an answer to that, too: 'We cannot picture to ourselves a world that is *essentially* different from the present one, and at the same time better. Other, less reflective ages also thought of themselves as the best, but we arrive at this conclusion exhausted, as it were, from the pursuit of alternatives we felt *had* to be better than liberal democracy.'

The contempt for 'less reflective ages' is deliciously ironic. Fukuyama's beloved Hegel had a fatal penchant for concepts such as the Substantial Idea and the World Spirit – the *Geist* – but, thanks to the Enlightenment's legacy, he did work in an era which enjoyed an *embarras de richesse* of truly imaginative reinterpretations of the world. After the collapse of Communism there was an eruption of grand universal theories whose reflectiveness was in inverse proportion to their *réclame*. Cretinous oversimplification seemed to be what policy-makers and political analysts required. Where Fukuyama led, his old tutor from Harvard, Samuel Huntington, soon followed. His pitch for the Big Idea market – global chaos theory – mimicked Fukuyama's own product-launch so closely, indeed, that one wondered if both men had taken the same correspondence course on How to Be a Modern Political Guru in Three Easy Lessons.

First, summarise your tentative thesis in an American policy journal: Huntington's essay 'The Clash of Civilizations?' (note the query) was published by *Foreign Affairs* in the summer of 1993.

Secondly, devise a concept so arrestingly simple that it can be understood and discussed even by half-witted politicians or TV chat-show hosts. Again, Huntington was happy to oblige. 'It is my hypothesis that the fundamental source of conflict in this new world will not be primarily ideological or primarily economic,' he wrote. 'The great divisions among humankind and the dominating source of conflict will be cultural. Nation states will remain the most powerful actors in world affairs, but the principal conflicts of global politics will occur between nations and groups of different civilisations. The clash of civilisations will dominate global politics. The fault lines between civilisations will be the battle lines of the future.'

Finally, having got everyone talking about your provocative new idea (Huntington's article was translated into twenty-six languages), reap the rewards by expanding it into a bestselling book. *The Clash of Civilizations and the Remaking of World Order* was duly published in 1996.

There, however, any resemblance to Fukuyama ceased – or so it appeared. Huntington's paradigm was generally taken as a rebuttal of Fukuyama's Panglossian optimism. As well it might be, for Huntington was a perfect specimen of the gloomy realist, committed to maintaining the balance of power and profoundly mistrustful of utopian dreamers – or indeed anyone who thought or hoped that the human condition was susceptible to improvement. As he told an interviewer, 'I am a child of Niehbur' – Ronald Niehbur, a Protestant theologian who believed that order could be preserved only by severe restrictions designed to bridle humanity's inherent wickedness.

Huntington's fellow-postgraduates at Harvard in 1950 included a chubby, precocious *émigré* called Henry Kissinger; a few years later, as a young don at the university's School of Government, his closest colleague was Zbigniew Brzezinski, later a hawkish National Security Adviser to President Carter. Unlike his friends Kissinger and Brzezinski, Huntington remained in academe, seeking inspiration from tutorials and seminars rather than crisis meetings in the Oval Office (though he did advise Lyndon Johnson's administration in 1967, and wrote a few speeches for Jimmy Carter a decade later). His modus operandi was set out in his first book, *The Soldier and the State*, in 1957. While admitting that 'actual personalities, institutions and beliefs do not fit into neat logical categories', he nevertheless insisted that 'neat logical categories are necessary if a man is to think profitably about the real world in which he lives and to derive from it lessons for broader application and use'. Without abstraction, generalisation and simplification there could be no understanding. One reviewer complained that the text was 'noisy with the sounds of sawing and stretching as the facts are forced into the bed that has been prepared for them'.

This was the technique he exercised thirty-five years later (and rather profitably, to purloin his own adverb) when formulating the Clash of Civilisations theory. He divided the world into 'seven or eight' distinct civilisations – Western, Islamic, Hindu, Latin American, Slavic–Orthodox, Confucian, Japanese and 'possibly' African. The artificiality of this taxonomy became most apparent with his startling declaration that Greece 'is not part of Western civilisation'; because it happened to have the wrong sort of Christianity, the birthplace of European culture was filed alongside Russia under 'Orthodox'. Guessing that this might raise eyebrows, Huntington cited an extra reason for excluding Greeks from the Western bloc: for a few years in the 1960s and 1970s they were ruled by a military dictatorship. Yet Spain, which endured the dictatorship of General Franco at the same time, was welcomed into his club without any awkward questions from the membership secretary.

The categorisation unmistakably reflected his own values and prejudices, as when he rebuked politicians in Australia for betraying the country's Western heritage by seeking to 'cultivate close ties with its [Asian] neighbours'. Mixed marriages between countries representing different cultures can never succeed, Huntington said, because 'successful economic association needs a commonality of civilisation'. With characteristic perversity, however, he decided that incongruous alliances outside the Western world were entirely natural: hence, for example, his warning that an Islamic–Confucian coalition 'has emerged to challenge Western interests, values and power', as proved by the sale of Chinese weapons to Iran and Pakistan in the 1980s. The supply of Western arms to Saudi Arabia in that period, exemplified most conspicuously by the multi-billion-dollar Al-Yamamah contract, did not lead him to conclude that there is an equally 'natural' Christian–Islamic connection.

As the argument proceeds, it becomes increasingly clear that pedantic distinctions between, say, Japan and Thailand or Italy and Greece are a flimsy camouflage intended to disguise his even cruder overstatement: that the modern world can be defined as 'the West vs the Rest'. Not that any camouflage was necessary. In a further article published by *Foreign Affairs* later in 1993, Huntington replied to those who had accused him of oversimplification with a defiant plea of guilty as charged: 'When people think seriously, they think abstractly; they conjure up simplified pictures of reality called concepts, theories, models, paradigms. Without such intellectual constructs, there is, William James said, only "a bloomin' buzzin' confusion".'

True enough, up to a point: free thinkers should always keep Occam's Razor within reach, to cut through needless complexities and obfuscation. But Huntington's arbitrary bladework served only to obliterate the reality that most conflict is not between civilisations but *within* them, as the inhabitants of Rwanda, Northern Ireland and countless other tribal cockpits know to their cost. As Edward Said pointed out, the theory made no allowance for 'the internal dynamics and plurality of every civilisation; or for considering that the major contest in most modern cultures concerns the definition or interpretation of each culture; or for the unattractive possibility that a great deal of demagogy and downright ignorance is involved in presuming to speak for a whole religion or civilisation'.

Each of Huntington's supposedly monolithic 'civilisations', even that of the West, includes different currents – fundamentalism, traditionalism, modernism, liberalism and so on. Timothy McVeigh's bombing of the Murrah Building in Oklahoma, like the sarin gas attack on Tokyo subway passengers by the Aum Shinrikyo cult, was a spectacular (though mercifully rare) manifestation of the tensions to be found within even modern and democratic cultures. These destructive assaults differ only in scale, not in kind, from the more frequent atrocities perpetrated by groups such as the Muslim Brotherhood in Egypt, the Taliban in Afghanistan or the Islamic Salvation Front in Algeria against fellow-members of their own 'civilisation'.

For all its apparent novelty, Huntington's eye-catching model was largely a reworking of the classical 'realist' theories that have long dominated the study of foreign relations, in which international politics is essentially an unending struggle for power between coherent but isolated units, each striving to advance its own interests in an anarchic world. The only difference, as critics pointed out, was that Huntington 'has replaced the nation-state, the primary playing piece in the old game of realist politics, with a larger counter: the civilisation. But in crucial respects, the game itself goes on as always.'

Curiously, Samuel Huntington's conservative pessimism – with its emphasis on cultural predestination, its narrow religio-cultural definition of what constitutes a 'civilisation', its reluctance to accept the possibility of cross-pollination between cultures – echoed many of the tenets promoted by those self-styled radicals in the West who had marched down the dead-end of 'identity politics'. Both effectively denied people the freedom to choose their own affiliations and associations, imposing lifelong allegiance to a club which they never applied to join. The Nobel laureate Amartya Sen described the Clash of Civilisations theory as nothing less than 'a violation of human rights', which may sound like hyperbole until one recalls that the Ayatollah Khomeini ordered the murder of Salman Rushdie because the London-based 'blasphemer' had Muslim forebears; had *The Satanic Verses* been written by a white Anglo-Saxon, no fatwa could have been promulgated. Professor Sen cited the bloodshed in Rwanda, Congo, Bosnia and Kosovo – and the rise of violent Hindu chauvinism in his own birthplace, India – as further evidence that the amplification of one distinctive identity 'can convert one of many co-existing dividing lines into an explosive and confrontational division'.

The Clash of Civilisations and the End of History were invariably regarded as opposites – often, indeed, the only two alternatives available. 'These are the two touchstones of any debate about the future direction of the world,' the

Washington Post reported. 'They're the theoretical elephants in the room. The old debate about capitalism vs. communism has been replaced by Fukuyama vs. Huntington.' Because of the yearning for binary simplicity, and the obvious tonal contrast between the respective optimism and pessimism of these two academic jumbos, few noticed just how much they had in common. Both were rigidly determinist in their insistence that humanity's fate had been preordained, whether ideologically or culturally, and grotesquely reductionist in their refusal to acknowledge the complex pluralities that constitute those vague abstractions 'history' and 'civilisation'. Just as Fukuyama effectively erased Nazism and Stalinism from his account of the past 200 years because they didn't fit, so Huntington ignored the fact that neither the number nor the causes of conflicts had changed much over the years. People still took up arms for the traditional reasons – territorial hunger, economic desperation, religious zeal, lust for power, defence against external threats or internal rivals. Nevertheless, the polished sheen of his neat Manichean theorising dazzled many Western policy-makers – not least because the phrase 'global chaos theory' gave an extra veneer of scientific method to his coarse generalisations. Although he would be horrified by the comparison, Huntington aped the techniques of Soviet Communists who boasted of the inevitability and irrefutability of 'scientific socialism'; and perhaps he had learned a trick or two from the post-modernist intellectuals of the 1980s whose freestyle riffs about truth and reality were given a semblance of empirical rigour by being expressed in the language of advanced physics and mathematics. It might seem an unlikely influence, since the deconstructionists presented themselves as radicals bent on demolishing reactionary grand narratives such as the Clash of Civilisations.

But were they? As we shall see, these self-styled progressives had more in common with the conservatives than they would care to admit.

4

The demolition merchants
of reality

You propose then, Philo, said Cleanthes, to erect religious faith on philosophical scepticism; and you think that if certainty or evidence be expelled from every other subject of inquiry, it will all retire to these theological doctrines, and there acquire a superior force and authority. Whether your scepticism be as absolute and sincere as you pretend, we shall learn by and by, when the company breaks up: We shall then see, whether you go out at the door or the window; and whether you really doubt if your body has gravity, or can be injured by its fall; according to popular opinion, derived from our fallacious senses, and more fallacious experience.

DAVID HUME, *Dialogues Concerning Natural Religion* (1779)

Colin MacCabe, an obscure young Fellow of King's College, Cambridge, was denied a lectureship by the English faculty's appointments board in January 1981. Not the sort of news that would usually merit a paragraph in the university newspaper, let alone the national press: yet the rebuff to MacCabe, an expert on the novels of James Joyce and the films of Jean-Luc Godard, was reported on the front page of the *Guardian*. When MacCabe returned to England from a trip abroad a couple of days later, he found himself mobbed by reporters and photographers at Heathrow airport. His failure to gain tenure at the university provoked demonstrations in the streets of Cambridge and earnest debate on current affairs programmes. *Newsweek* cleared a page for the story (under the inevitable headline, 'Unquiet Flow the Dons'), which it described as 'one of the most extraordinary debates in the [university's] eight-century history':

> Dons who normally confine their disputes to sherry parties leak damaging rumours about each other and threaten libel suits. Charges of academic sleaziness and intellectual persecution fly back and forth. Television crews roam King's Parade to catch the carping of talkative academicians ... Angry students began seeking to have the entire English faculty board suspended, and MacCabe sympathisers spoke of breaking away to form their own department.

Even some of his enemies agreed that MacCabe was an excellent scholar and teacher; but he was also a 'post-structuralist' who believed in analysing literature through study of its linguistic rules and cultural assumptions. Although MacCabe argued that these methods were no great radical departure from the traditions established by earlier generations of Cambridge dons – I. A. Richards and William Empson both undertook close formal analysis of the language of literary texts, while F. R. Leavis and Raymond Williams attempted to place novels within the general cultural history of the country – he did admit that it was the 'enormous explosion of work in the mid-Sixties in Paris' by structuralist and deconstructionist pioneers such as Jacques Lacan, Jacques Derrida, Roland Barthes, Louis Althusser and Michel Foucault which had 'galvanised me and many others', thus confirming the suspicion among traditionalists that MacCabe was the carrier of a dangerous foreign germ which would infect the whole corpus of English teaching unless he were swiftly quarantined. In the words of the anti-structuralist don Christopher Ricks, 'It is our job to teach and uphold the canon of English literature.' Ricks's colleague Ian Jack added that 'one does want to keep the attention of students focused on the great writers'. On the other side of the barricades, Dr Tony Tanner described the treatment of MacCabe as 'the most unjust thing I have ever seen in academic life' and resigned from the faculty's degree committee in protest. Raymond Williams, the grand old man of Marxist criticism, was voted off the appointments board for defending MacCabe. So, more surprisingly, was Professor Frank Kermode; though not a structuralist or semiologist himself, he argued that the university ought to accommodate a plurality of critical styles and techniques.

Having succeeded in forcing out Colin MacCabe, the Cambridge conservatives continued to guard the gates against foreign barbarians for many years. (As a young lecturer observed, 'Cambridge is an island in some ways, cut off from the rest of the country. When I ran into a colleague in London once, he said: "Fancy seeing you in England."') At a degree-awarding ceremony in March 1992, three of them shocked the hundreds of proud parents assembled in Senate House by standing up and shouting 'non placet' – thus imposing a temporary veto on the proposal to give an honorary doctorate to Jacques Derrida, the sixty-two-year-old doyen of deconstructionism. But although Cambridge may have won the odd battle, it was the continental theorists who won the war. When Derrida came to speak in Oxford a few weeks before the Cantabrigian yell of 'non placet', he drew an audience of

1,800 – as against the 400 who turned up at the Oxford Union that month to hear the Hollywood star Warren Beatty. The success of the theorists' long march through the institutions can also be gauged by Colin MacCabe's career: immediately after his eviction from Cambridge a full-blown professorship was created for him at Strathclyde University; three years later he was appointed head of production at the British Film Institute and, for good measure, professor of English at the University of Pittsburgh.

By the end of the 1980s, deconstructionists and their allies – generically labelled 'post-modernists' – had established something of a hegemony (to use one of their own favourite terms) on campuses in the United States. They dominated the powerful American Modern Languages Association, whose conferences were attended by up to 10,000 academic critics. They controlled the recruitment of lecturers in many universities, a power they exercised with the same Stalinist intolerance displayed a few years earlier by the crusty conservatives of Cambridge. This time, however, the victims were those who could not recite the post-modern shibboleths. Even a don sympathetic to Derrida admitted that 'deconstruction, which began as a heresy, soon turned into a dogma, and hardened into a theology, sustained by a network of evangelists and high priests and inquisitors'. The Vatican of this new creed was Yale University, where the three 'boa-deconstructors' Jacques Derrida, Paul de Man and J. Hillis Miller reigned jointly as pontificating pontiffs, but the papal jurisdiction extended far beyond their own department of comparative literature. 'Students taking courses in literature, film, "cultural studies", and even, in some cases, anthropology and political science, were taught that the world is just a socially constructed "text" about which you can say just about anything you want, provided you say it murkily enough,' the left-wing American author Barbara Ehrenreich complained. 'One of my own children, whose college education cost about $25,000 a year, reported that in some classes, you could be marked down for using the word "reality" without the quotation marks.' A critical theory that rejoiced in a multiplicity of meanings thus acquired the status of doctrine, excluding all viewpoints but its own. Ehrenreich described it as 'one of the least lovable fads to hit American campuses since drinking-till-you-barf'.

Academic fashions, like literary texts, often have a greater ideological significance than is immediately apparent. English literature became a subject for study – not only in the universities, but in mechanics' institutes and workingmen's colleges – towards the end of the late nineteenth century, at a time when scientific advance and social change were eroding the dominance of religion as a source of moral guidance and timeless truths. One of the first occupants of the Merton professorship of English at Oxford, George Gordon, announced in his inaugural lecture that 'England is sick, and . . . English literature must save it. The Churches (as I understand) having failed, and social remedies being slow, English literature has now a triple function: still, I suppose, to delight and instruct us, but also, and above all, to save our souls and heal the State.'

The early structuralists and semioticians were therefore quite right to argue that literature couldn't be evaluated purely aesthetically or impressionistically, regardless of all historical and social context. A statement of the obvious, one might think; but sometimes, as with the emperor's new clothes, demystification can be achieved by pointing out what ought to be self-evident. As Terry Eagleton writes:

Loosely subjective talk was chastised by a criticism which recognised that the literary work, like any other product of language, is a *construct*, whose mechanisms could be classified and analysed like the objects of any other science. The Romantic prejudice that the poem, like a person, harboured a vital essence, a soul which it was discourteous to tamper with, was rudely unmasked as a bit of disguised theology, a superstitious fear of reasoned inquiry ... Meaning was neither a private experience nor a divinely ordained occurrence: it was the product of certain shared systems of signification ... Reality was not reflected by language but *produced* by it: it was a particular way of carving up the world which was deeply dependent on the sign-systems we had at our command, or more precisely which had us at theirs.

Yet structuralism, like its forebears and descendants, had its own ideological mission. The Russian Formalists, who emerged in the years before the 1917 revolution, were closely associated with the Bolsheviks, and their militant insistence on a 'scientific criticism' that would expose the 'material reality' of texts had a close kinship with the 'scientific socialism' of Marxism–Leninism. Similarly, post-structuralism – exemplified by Roland Barthes' *The Pleasure of the Text* – came into vogue soon after the Parisian eruptions of May 1968 had been comprehensively thwarted. 'Post-structuralism was a product of that blend of euphoria and disillusionment, liberation and dissipation, carnival and catastrophe, which was 1968,' Eagleton suggests, persuasively. 'Unable to break the structures of state power, post-structuralism found it possible instead to subvert the structures of language ... Its enemies, as for the later Barthes, became coherent belief systems of any kind – in particular all forms of political theory and organisation which sought to analyse, and act upon, the structures of society as a whole. For it was precisely such politics which seemed to have failed.' No systematic critique of monopoly capitalism was possible since capitalism was itself a fiction, like truth, justice, law and all other linguistic 'constructs'.

As post-structuralism morphed into deconstruction and then post-modernism, it often seemed a way of evading politics altogether – even if many of its practitioners continued to style themselves as Marxists. The logic of their playful insistence that there were no certainties or realities, and their refusal to acknowledge the legitimacy of value-judgments, led to a free-floating relativism that could celebrate both American pop culture and medieval superstition without a qualm. Michel Foucault visited Tehran soon after the fall of the Shah, and came back to Paris enraptured by the 'beauty' of the Ayatollah Khomeini's neanderthal regime. Asked about the suppression of all dissent, he replied:

They don't have the same regime of truth as ours, which, it has to be said, is very special, even if it has become almost universal. The Greeks had their own. The Arabs of the Maghreb have another. And in Iran it is largely modelled on a religion that has an exoteric form and an esoteric content. That is to say, everything that is said under the explicit form of the law also refers to another meaning. So not only is saying one thing that means another not a condemnable ambiguity, it is, on the contrary, a necessary and highly prized additional level of meaning. It's often the case that people say something that, at the factual level, isn't true, but which refers to another, deeper meaning, which cannot be assimilated in terms of precision and observation.

This is a magnificently Parisian method of avoiding a straight-forward question: with enough intellectual ingenuity, even the absence of free speech and promotion of mendacity can be admired as exercises in irony and textual ambiguity.

Despite their scorn for grand historical narratives, universalist ideologies and general laws of nature, many post-modernists seemed to accept the demise of socialism and the success of capitalism as immutable facts of life. Their subversive impulse therefore sought refuge in those marginal spaces where the victors' dominance seemed less secure. Hence the celebration of almost anything exotic or unincorporable, from Iranian theocracy to sado-masochistic fetishes. A fascination with the pleasures of consumption (TV soap operas, shopping malls, mass-market kitsch) displaced the traditional radical emphasis on the conditions of production. 'Culturalism' supplanted materialism, dialectic was ousted by discontinuity, reason yielded to random reflexivity. The consequence was, in Terry Eagleton's words, 'an immense linguistic inflation, as what appeared no longer conceivable in political reality was still just about possible in the areas of discourse or signs or textuality. The freedom of text or language would come to compensate for the un-freedom of the system as a whole.' One after another, academic disciplines took a 'linguistic turn' as the steering-wheel was grabbed by theorists who insisted that fact and fiction were indistinguishable. Everything from history to quantum physics was now a text, subject to the 'infinite play of signification'.

As Eagleton noticed, however, despite the post-modernists' keen eye for irony they seemed oddly oblivious to the contradictions of their own posture:

In pulling the rug out from under the certainties of its political opponents, this post-modern culture has often enough pulled it out from under itself too, leaving itself with no more reason why we should resist fascism than the feebly pragmatic plea that fascism is not the way we do things in Sussex or Sacramento. It has brought low the intimidating austerity of high culture with its playful, parodic spirit, and in thus imitating the commodity form has succeeded in reinforcing the crippling austerities of the marketplace.

Even the most striking irony of all somehow escaped their notice: that at the end of the 1980s, when post-modernists had contemptuously written off the possibility and indeed the desirability of collective political action, the citizens of Czechoslovakia, East Germany and other Stalinist bureaucracies took to the streets and overthrew their masters by sheer force of 'people power'.

Terry Eagleton's bracing left-wing critique of post-modernism, published by the *Monthly Review* in July 1995, noted yet another irony almost parenthetically: 'It believes in style and pleasure, and commonly churns out texts that might have been composed by, as well as on, a computer.' The truth of this quip was proved a year later when a mischievous Australian academic, Andrew Bulhak, designed a computer program 'to generate random, meaningless and yet quite realistic text in genres defined using recursive transition networks'. For the purposes of his experiment he needed a genre which employed 'context-free grammars'; and he found it. Anyone who visits the website of his 'post-modernism generator' will be rewarded with an apparently serious academic paper, complete with footnotes, on 'pretextual discourse that includes reality as a totality' or perhaps 'the subtextual paradigm of context'. In its first two years online, the generator delivered more than half a million such essays – each wholly original, and all utterly meaningless.

To the outsider, the babbling impenetrability of most post-modern texts arouses the suspicion that they are no more than atonal noise, signifying nothing – a fitting style, perhaps, for a theory that seeks to cast doubt on the very existence of 'meaning'. As long ago as 1968, in the early days of structuralism, the great scientist Peter Medawar protested that clarity had become a dirty word:

> A writer on structuralism in the *Times Literary Supplement* has suggested that thoughts which are confused and tortuous by reason of their profundity are most appropriately expressed in prose that is deliberately unclear. What a preposterously silly idea! I am reminded of an air-raid warden in wartime Oxford who, when bright moonlight seemed to be defeating the spirit of the blackout, exhorted us to wear dark glasses. He, however, was being funny on purpose.

The wilful opaqueness that distressed Medawar now seems almost pellucid beside what succeeded it. Here, for example, is a passage from the French theorist Gilles Deleuze:

> In the first place, singularities-events correspond to heterogeneous series which are organised into a system which is neither stable nor unstable, but rather 'metastable', endowed with a potential energy wherein the differences between series are distributed . . . In the second place, singularities possess a process of auto-unification, always mobile and displaced to the extent that a paradoxical element traverses the series and makes them resonate, enveloping the corresponding singular

points in a single aleatory point and all the emissions, all dice throws, in a single cast.

One can gaze at this paragraph for hours and be none the wiser. Read it back to front, break it up into constituent clauses, ingest a few hallucinogenic drugs to aid comprehension: it remains gibberish. Yet no less a figure than Michel Foucault praised Deleuze as 'among the greatest of the great', adding that 'some day, perhaps, the century will be Deleuzian'.

Although much post-modernism may be nonsense, it is nonsense with a purpose: by using quasi-scientific terminology the po-mo theologians intended to explode the 'objectivity' of science itself. The fact that they knew nothing about mathematics, physics or chemistry was no obstacle. Luce Irigaray, a high priestess of the movement, denounced Einstein's $E=mc^2$ as a 'sexed equation', since 'it privileges the speed of light over other [less masculine] speeds that are vitally necessary to us'. In similar vein, she protested at 'the privileging of solid over fluid mechanics, and indeed the inability of science to deal with turbulent flow at all', attributing this bias to the association of fluidity with femininity: 'Whereas men have sex organs that protrude and become rigid, women have openings that leak menstrual blood and vaginal fluids ... From this perspective it is no wonder that science has not been able to arrive at a successful model for turbulence. The problem of turbulent flow cannot be solved because the conceptions of fluids (and of women) have been formulated so as necessarily to leave unarticulated remainders.' Jacques Lacan, whose oracular pronouncements were received with awe on many British and American campuses, sought to give his deconstructionism a semblance of methodical rigour by transforming it into the following equation:

$$\frac{S \text{ (signifier)}}{s \text{ (signified)}} = s \text{ (the statement), with } S = (-1), \text{ produces: } s = \sqrt{-1}$$

Any mathematically competent schoolchild can recognise that this is unmitigated poppycock. For Lacan, however, there is nothing that can't be expressed algebraically: 'Thus the erectile organ comes to symbolize the place of *jouissance* [ecstasy], not in itself, or even in the form of an image, but as a part lacking in the desired image: that is why it is equivalent to the $\sqrt{-1}$ of the signification produced above, of the *jouissance* that it restores by the coefficient of its statement to the function of lack of signifier (-1).' What does it matter, Barbara Ehrenreich once asked, if some French guy wants to think of his penis as the square root of minus one? 'Not much, except that on American campuses, especially the more elite ones, such utterances were routinely passed off as examples of boldly "transgressive" left-wing thought.' Few progressives dared to challenge this tyranny of twaddle for fear of being reviled as cultural and political reactionaries – or, no less shamingly, ignorant philistines. 'For some years I've been troubled by an apparent decline in the standards of intellectual rigour in certain precincts of the American academic humanities,' Alan Sokal, a physics professor at New York University, wrote in 1996. 'But I'm a mere physicist: if I find myself unable to make head or tail of *jouissance* and *différance*, perhaps that just reflects my own inadequacy.'

Sokal's reluctance to make a fool of himself was, however, outweighed by his fury at the betrayal of the Enlightenment. As a socialist who had taught in Nicaragua after the Sandinista revolution, he felt doubly indignant that much of the new mystificatory folly emanated from the self-proclaimed left. For two centuries, progressives had championed science against obscurantism. The sudden lurch of academic humanists and social scientists towards epistemic relativism not only betrayed this heritage but jeopardised 'the already fragile prospects for a progressive social critique', since it was impossible to combat bogus ideas if all notions of truth and falsity ceased to have any validity. To test the prevailing intellectual standards, Sokal decided to perform a modest experiment: would the leading American journal of 'cultural studies' accept an article that made no sense whatsoever if it flattered the editors' ideological preconceptions? The answer was provided in the spring of 1996 when *Social Text* – whose editorial board included many of the starriest post-modern professors in the US – produced a special issue on 'Science Wars', whose purpose was to 'uncover the gender-laden and racist assumptions built into the Euro-American scientific method ... to talk about different ways of doing science, ways that downgrade methodology [and] experiment'. It included an unsolicited paper by Alan Sokal titled 'Transgressing the Boundaries: Toward a Transformative Hermeneutics of Quantum Gravity'.

Anyone outside the self-referential, self-satisfied cult could have rumbled the essay as a spoof straight away. In his opening paragraph Sokal derided the 'dogma imposed by the long post-Enlightenment hegemony', which he summarised thus:

> that there exists an external world, whose properties are independent of any individual human being and indeed of humanity as a whole; that these properties are encoded in 'eternal' physical laws; and that human beings can obtain reliable, albeit imperfect and tentative, knowledge of these laws by

hewing to the 'objective' procedures and epistemological strictures prescribed by the (so-called) scientific method.

Even the editors of *Social Text* must have noticed the supposedly imaginary 'external world' from time to time, not least when the sun rises every morning. Yet their bullshit detectors failed to sound the alarm – possibly, as Sokal had guessed, because they were flattered to find a bona-fide physicist paying homage to their superior wisdom. In the very next paragraph he praised post-structuralist critics for demystifying Western scientific practice and 'revealing the ideology of domination concealed behind the façade of "objectivity". It has thus become increasingly apparent that physical "reality", no less than social "reality", is at bottom a social and linguistic construct.' Not *theories* of physical reality, *nota bene*, but the reality itself. As Sokal commented when the hoax was revealed, recalling a joke made by David Hume more than two centuries earlier, 'Fair enough: anyone who believes that the laws of physics are mere social conventions is invited to try transgressing those conventions from the windows of my apartment. I live on the twenty-first floor.' (There's also an echo here of a famous passage from James Boswell's *Life of Johnson*: 'After we came out of church we stood talking for some time together of Bishop Berkeley's ingenious sophistry to prove the non-existence of matter and that everything in the universe is merely ideal. I observed, that though we are satisfied his doctrine is not true, it is impossible to refute it. I shall never forget the alacrity with which Johnson answered, striking his foot with mighty force against a large stone, till he rebounded from it, "I refute it thus."')

Sokal's article was littered with scientific howlers and absurdities. He claimed that Jacques Lacan's Freudian speculations had now been proved by quantum theory, and that Jacques Derrida's thoughts on variability confirmed Einstein's general theory of relativity:

> In mathematical terms, Derrida's observation relates to the invariance of the Einstein field equation $G_{\mu\nu} = 8nT_{\mu\nu}G_{\mu\nu} = 8nGT_{\mu\nu}$ under nonlinear space-time diffeomorphisms (self-mappings of the space–time manifold which are infinitely differentiable but not necessarily analytic) . . . The n of Euclid and the G of Newton, formerly thought to be constant and universal, are now perceived in their ineluctable historicity.

In truth, of course, n *is* constant and universal, a precisely defined number with the same value on the surface of the moon as in Outer Mongolia. It is beyond belief that a professor of physics would ever argue otherwise except for satirical purposes, but still the editors saw nothing amiss. Nor, incidentally, did they follow the usual procedure of scholarly journals by sending the article to an outside referee before publication. An assessor with some knowledge of mathematics would certainly have spared them the embarrassment of falling for tosh such as this:

> Just as liberal feminists are frequently content with a minimal agenda of legal and social equality for women and 'pro-choice', so liberal (and even some socialist) mathematicians are often content to work within the hegemonic Zermelo-Fraenkel framework (which, reflecting its nineteenth-century liberal origins, already incorporates the axioms of equality) supplemented only by the axiom of choice. But this framework is grossly insufficient for a liberatory mathematics.

The axiom of choice, as formulated by Ernst Zermelo in 1904, states that within any set of mutually exclusive and 'non-empty' subsets there is at least one subset which has exactly one element in common with each of the others. Some mathematicians find it useful, others do not; all, however, would be amazed to hear that it had some relevance to the debate on abortion law. Sokal's equally ludicrous assertion that it was a product of nineteenth-century liberalism led on to this hilarious political conclusion:

> A liberatory science cannot be complete without a profound revision of the canon of mathematics. As yet no such emancipatory mathematics exists, and we can only speculate upon its eventual content. We can see hints of it in the multidimensional and nonlinear logic of fuzzy systems theory; but this approach is still heavily marked by its origins in the crisis of late-capitalist production relations. Catastrophe theory, with its dialectical emphasis on smoothness/discontinuity and metamorphosis/unfolding, will indubitably play a major role in future mathematics; but much theoretical work remains to be done before this approach can become a concrete tool of progressive political praxis.

In May 1996, a week after publication of the 'Science Wars' edition of *Social Text*, Alan Sokal wrote a short essay for *Lingua Franca* magazine revealing the hoax and explaining his motives. Not since the MacCabe affair had a theoretical academic dispute provoked such journalistic sensation: the story was reported on the front page of the *New York Times*, and in dozens of newspapers from Bombay to Buenos Aires. In France, *Le Monde* ran at least twenty articles on 'l'affaire Sokal', including a contribution from Jacques Derrida huffily dismissing the prankster-professor as 'pas sérieux'. But the post-modernists' attempts to discredit Sokal were hampered by the fact that his article, like his subsequent book *Intellectual Impostures*, included dozens of genuine quotations from their own work. Julia Kristeva, who had often referred to differential calculus, algebraic geometry, predicate logic and 'infinite functional Hilbert spaces' in her writings about poetry, psychoanalysis and politics, was invited by *Le Nouvel Observateur* to answer Sokal's charge that she sought to dazzle readers with technical concepts which she manifestly didn't understand. 'Obviously,' she conceded, 'I'm not a real mathematician.'

The egg-spattered editors of *Social Text* could do little but splutter and grumble. One, displaying a fine deconstructionist contempt for authorial intention, insisted that 'Sokal's parody was nothing of the sort, and that his admission represented a change of heart, or a folding of his intellectual resolve'. Another, the sociologist Professor Stanley Aronowitz, accused Sokal of caricaturing post-modernism: 'He got it wrong. One of the reasons he got it wrong is he's ill-read and half-educated.' Which was pretty rich coming from someone whose journal had unblinkingly accepted an article strewn with obvious errors. Besides, if Aronowitz and his colleagues were successfully conned by an ignoramus, what did that imply about their own critical intelligence?

Predictably enough, Sokal was also accused of political betrayal. According to an editorial statement from *Social Text*, 'what Sokal's confession most altered was our perception of his own good faith as a self-declared leftist', because his stunt had exposed the journal to 'derision from conservatives'. No doubt they were thinking of gleeful comments from right-wing pundits such as George F. Will of the *Washington*

Post and Roger Kimball of the *Wall Street Journal*. Yet it was feminists and leftists – Katha Pollitt in the *Nation*, Barbara Ehrenreich in *The Progressive*, Barbara Epstein in *New Politics* – who led the applause for Alan Sokal. As Ehrenreich pointed out, the post-modernists were right about one thing: that many people subscribe to socially constructed 'realities' which flout common sense and experience, such as the belief that there is a Supreme Being who takes a personal interest in our careers, romances and efforts to lose weight. However, since the theorists also insisted that the whole world was nothing but a ghostly swarm of human-generated imaginings they had effectively opted out of the struggle against this fantasy.

To describe them as non-combatants or conscientious objectors would be too generous by half: while vilifying their left-wing critics as accomplices of conservatism, they themselves abetted some thoroughly rancid characters and ideologies. As a young man in Belgium during the early 1940s, the deconstructionist guru Paul de Man wrote columns for a Nazi-controlled newspaper, *Le Soir*, praising collaborationists and claiming that Jews had contributed nothing to European civilisation. ('A solution to the Jewish problem that would lead to the creation of a Jewish colony isolated from Europe would not have, for the literary life of the West, regrettable consequences. It would lose, in all, some personalities of mediocre worth.') After emigrating to the US in 1947 he never mentioned his wartime record, except occasionally to hint that he had fought for the Resistance, and when the articles eventually came to light in 1987, three years after his death, colleagues and disciples were flabbergasted. Unable (as ever) to face reality, some of them promptly set about deconstructing his wartime journalism to show that it didn't mean what it said: the selfsame theorists who usually rejoiced in the infinite variety of possible textual interpretation now maintained that, with these particular texts, there was only one 'correct' reading – their own. Derrida, having persuaded himself that de Man's Jew-baiting was somehow an implicit *repudiation* of anti-semitism, accused the professor's critics of using the same 'exterminating gesture' as the Nazis, since they wished – 'at least figuratively' – to censor or destroy his work.

In truth, of course, it was de Man himself who had sought to conceal the articles for *Le Soir*; if they really had been daring satires on Nazi attitudes to the Jews, why did he remain silent about them for the rest of his life? Yet he did leave a few clues to his guilty secret, if only someone had known how to decode them. He admired Julia Kristeva's *Powers of Horror* (1982), which included a defence of the anti-semitic writings of the novelist Céline. (The chapter, titled 'Ours to Jew and Die', quoted with apparent approval Céline's depiction of the Jew as 'a fecalised, feminised, passivated rot'. In a laudatory blurb for the book, de Man singled out these 'illuminating' and 'indispensable' passages for special praise.) In a famous essay on Nietzsche, he wrote of 'a past that . . . is so threatening that it has to be forgotten', adding that we 'try to give ourselves a new past from which we should have liked to descend'. There had also been this suggestive observation, from a critique of Rousseau in de Man's *Allegories of Reading*:

It is always possible to face up to any experience (to excuse any guilt) because the experience always exists simultaneously as fictional discourse and as empirical event, and it is never possible to decide which of the two possibilities is the right one. The indecision makes it possible to excuse the bleakest of crimes because, as a fiction, it escapes from the constraints of guilt and innocence.

This recalls a comment by Professor Stanley Fish (the model for the flamboyant deconstructionist Professor Zapp in David Lodge's comic novel *Changing Places*), who said that critical theory 'relieves me of the obligation to be right ... and demands only that I be interesting'. Harmless enough in a literature department, perhaps, where fictional discourse is an inescapable element of the syllabus anyway. By the 1990s, however, the post-modernists had also colonised many history faculties, teaching their students that 'facts' were a chimera: history consisted solely of competing narratives, none of which should be 'privileged' over another.

There is ample justification for questioning scientific pretensions to absolute and disinterested objectivity: one needn't be a deconstructionist to notice the political and economic imperatives that fuelled President Kennedy's determination to put an American on the moon, or President Reagan's spending on 'Star Wars' research. But the post-modernists' rampant subjectivism nurtured its own illusions, and aroused the most primitive monsters from their slumber. It took them some time to notice that their 'anything goes' motto chimed harmoniously with the arguments of Hitler apologists such as the British historian David Irving, who maintained that no Jews were gassed in Auschwitz. As Professor Richard Evans pointed out in his spirited retort to hyper-relativism, *In Defence of History*:

> There is in fact a massive, carefully empirical literature on the Nazi extermination of the Jews. Clearly, to regard it as fictional, unreal or no nearer to historical reality than, say, the work of the 'revisionists' who deny that Auschwitz ever happened at all, is simply wrong. Here is an issue where evidence really counts, and can be used to establish the essential facts.

Auschwitz was not a discourse. It trivialises mass murder to
see it as a text. The gas chambers were not a piece of rhetoric.
Auschwitz was indeed inherently a tragedy and cannot be seen
either as a comedy or a farce. And if this is true of Auschwitz,
then it must be true at least to some degree of other past
happenings, events, institutions, people, as well.

Fearful of being associated with Nazis, especially after the
de Man scandal, some relativists staged a tactical retreat by
accepting that 'the facts of the Holocaust closed off the possibility of using certain types of emplotment to describe it' –
while still reserving the right to treat almost everything else
as a fictional narrative. Others turned the tables on the traditionalists, arguing that because historians such as David
Irving adopted 'the most conservative possible protocols of
discovery, revelation and truth-telling' – footnotes, biblio-
graphical references – their work actually demonstrated the
bankruptcy of classical scholarly approaches to objectivity and
truth. 'Although historians often frame their criticisms of colleagues' work in terms of evidence – sources overlooked,
misplaced emphasis, inappropriate categorisation – such
criticisms cannot demonstrate the superiority of one interpretation or story-type over another,' two post-modernists
declared in the *Journal of Social History*. 'These debates over
evidence are largely diversionary.'

Not so. As Richard Evans wrote, the purpose of source
citations is to allow historical interpretations to be tested by
appeal to the evidence, 'and some of the time at least, it really
is possible to prove that one side is right and the other is
wrong'. This was borne out in the year 2000, when David
Irving sued the American historian Deborah Lipstadt for
describing him as a pro-Nazi who distorted facts to suit his

political purposes. Summoned as an expert witness, Evans
spent many months investigating the footnotes in Irving's
books and produced a 700-page report listing all the omis-
sions, misquotations and outright fabrications. Until then,
even some reputable academics had maintained that despite
Irving's unsavoury politics his diligence as a researcher
couldn't be faulted. What finally destroyed this reputation
was old-fashioned source-checking – the sort of exercise cus-
tomarily sneered at by post-modernists as 'fetishising the
documents'.

The gas-chambers at Auschwitz were not a fiction. Nor was
Stalin's Gulag, though official historians in the Soviet Union
affected to believe that it could be airbrushed from the
record. Yet even verifiable facts can acquire the dangerous
potency of myth in an intellectual climate where equal validity
is granted to any interpretation, however perverse, tenden-
tious or 'transgressive'. 'The most usual ideological abuse of
history is based on anachronism rather than lies,' the Marxist
historian Eric Hobsbawm said in 1993, in a lecture delivered
to an audience of students from the former Communist countries of Eastern and Central Europe who knew a thing or two
about these abuses. Hobsbawm pointed out that there was
indeed a battle of Kosovo in 1389 at which the Turks defeated
the Serb warriors and their allies, and it did leave deep scars
on the Serbian psyche – but 'it does not follow that this
justifies the oppression of the Albanians, who now form
90 per cent of the region's population, or the Serb claim that
the land is essentially theirs. Denmark does not claim the
large part of eastern England which was settled and ruled
by Danes before the eleventh century, which continued to
be known as the Danelaw and whose village names are still
philologically Danish.'

Nevertheless, Hobsbawm's distinction is not as straight-forward as he thinks. When facts are transmuted into myth for political and nationalistic purposes, as with the Battle of Kosovo, they can become both anachronisms *and* lies. In the spring of 1999, when the British parliament debated Nato's military campaign against Serbia, the veteran MP Tony Benn complained that 'the House suffers from its lack of knowledge of history' and then proved his own knowledge by declaring that 'Kosovo has been in Yugoslavia for centuries' – no mean feat, given that the state of Yugoslavia didn't exist until the twentieth century. The example given by Hobsbawm in his lecture was a study of the ancient civilisation of the Indus valley entitled *Five Thousand Years of Pakistan* – even though Pakistan was not even thought of until 1932–3, when the name was invented by student agitators, and has existed as a state only since 1947. There is, he said, 'no evidence of any more connection between the civilisation of Mohenjo Daro and the current rulers of Islamabad than there is of a connec-tion between the Trojan War and the [present] government in Ankara'.

To say that Elvis Presley is alive would be anachronistic and false; but in 1963 it was demonstrably true. To say that the world is flat *has always been untrue*, no matter how many people might once have believed it: a glance at a satellite photograph should settle any doubts. Yet the fractured logic of post-modernism misses this distinction, and leads to the con-clusion that any perception of 'reality' is as valid (or illusory) as another. In their book *Intellectual Impostures*, Alan Sokal and the Belgian physicist Jean Bricmont quote from an epis-temological primer written for high-school teachers in the mid-1990s:

What one generally calls a fact is an interpretation of a situation that no one, at least for the moment, wants to call into question . . . But a fact can be put into question. Example: for many centuries, it was considered to be a fact that the Sun revolves each day around the Earth. The appearance of another theory, such as that of the diurnal rotation of the Earth, entailed the replacement of the fact just cited by another: 'The Earth rotates on its axis each day.'

In saying that the sun's revolution around the earth was 'considered to be a fact', the author appeared to accept that it wasn't really a fact at all. In the next sentence, however, it reverted to the status of 'fact' again – albeit a fact that had been 'replaced' by another. As Sokal and Bricmont comment, 'Taken literally, in the *usual* sense of the word "fact", this would mean that the Earth has rotated on its axis only since Copernicus.'

All human knowledge is provisional, but it is also incremental: the sum of what we know is far greater today than thirty years ago, let alone three hundred years ago. 'I have no doubt that, although progressive changes are to be expected in physics, the present doctrines are likely to be nearer to the truth than any rival doctrines now before the world,' Bertrand Russell wrote in 1959. 'Science is at no moment quite right, but it is seldom quite wrong, and has, as a rule, a better chance of being right than the theories of the unscientific. It is, therefore, rational to accept it hypothetically.' For those who regard rationality itself as a form of oppression, however, there is no reason why scientific theories and hypotheses should be 'privileged' over alternative interpretations of reality such as religion or astrology. The philosopher Paul Feyerabend – author of the suggestively titled *Farewell to*

Reason, and one of the founding fathers of post-modern anti-scientific relativism – maintained that since all methodologies have their limitations the only rule should be 'anything goes'. In his influential book *Against Method* he saw the teaching of science in schools as nothing less than state tyranny:

> While the parents of a six-year-old child can decide to have him instructed in the rudiments of Protestantism, or in the rudiments of the Jewish faith, or to omit religious instruction altogether, they do not have a similar freedom on the case of the sciences. Physics, astronomy, history *must* be learned. They cannot be replaced by magic, astrology, or by a study of legends.
>
> Nor is one content with a merely *historical* presentation of physical (astronomical, historical, etc) facts and principles. One does not say: *some people believe* that the earth moves round the sun while others regard the earth as a hollow sphere that contains the sun, the planets, the fixed stars. One says: the earth *moves* round the sun – everything else is sheer idiocy.

Like his post-modern disciples, Feyerabend held that science was little different from myth: 'It is one of the many forms of thought that have been developed by man, and not necessarily the best. It is conspicuous, noisy and impudent, but it is inherently superior only for those who have already decided in favour of a certain ideology.' The sole purpose of rationality was 'to lend class to the general drive towards monotony', whereas relativism endorsed 'the phenomenon of cultural variety'. In short, those who tried to apply boring old reason to human affairs were pedantic, narrow-minded and unromantic.

It's a familiar complaint: if small children believe that

Father Christmas and the Tooth Fairy really exist, why spoil their pleasure? Most parents would probably agree, but they might begin to worry if a child reached the age of sixteen and remained convinced that Santa comes down the chimney on 24 December. Even so, many friends would no doubt reassure them that the endurance of the illusion was harmless and rather charming, while others would counsel against 'overreaction'. As Cleanthes said in David Hume's *Dialogues Concerning Natural Religion*, 'humorous sects' needn't be taken too seriously: 'If they be thoroughly in earnest, they will not long trouble the world with their doubts, cavils, and disputes: If they be only in jest, they are, perhaps, bad raillers; but can never be very dangerous, either to the state, to philosophy, or to religion.' Certainly that was the atittude of many amused outsiders to the academic turf wars over deconstructionism. Why worry if Luce Irigaray thinks $E=mc^2$ is a 'sexed equation'?

But loopiness is not confined to senior common rooms. In their assault on reason, the post-modernists had far more allies than perhaps even they had realised. A Gallup poll in June 1993 found that only 11 per cent of Americans accepted the standard secular account of evolution, that 'human beings have developed over millions of years from less advanced forms of life, but God had no part in this process'; 35 per cent thought that humans evolved over millions of years, but with divine guidance; and 47 per cent maintained that 'God created human beings pretty much in their present form at one time within the last 10,000 years or so' – the creation story as told in the Book of Genesis. Other polls at about the same time discovered that 49 per cent of Americans believed in demonic possession, 36 per cent in telepathy and 25 per cent in astrology; and that no fewer than 68 per cent approved of creationism being taught in biology classes. By then, however, few of creationism's advocates actually used the word any more. 'Religious America is awakening,' President Reagan had announced jubilantly in 1980, shortly before the states of Arkansas and Louisiana passed Bills obliging public schools to teach creationism in science lessons. But the laws were struck down by the Supreme Court, which ruled that because creationism was indeed a religious belief it could not be added to the biology curriculum without infringing the constitutional ban on promoting religion, and thereafter the fundamentalists adopted a more scientific-sounding phraseology – 'abrupt appearance theory', 'intelligent-design theory' – to disguise the fact that their only textbook was the Old Testament.

During his presidential campaign of 2000, George W. Bush often attacked the relativism that 'liberals' had inflicted on America – the idea that nothing was right or wrong, true or false. Yet only a few months earlier, when Christian fanatics on the Kansas board of education voted to remove evolution from the state's science curriculum, Bush paraded his own relativism by arguing that creationism should be taught alongside evolution since 'the jury is still out' and 'children ought to be exposed to different theories about how the world started'. Some theories, as George Orwell might have said, are more different than others. 'Science is about fact,' a Kansas newspaper, the *Topeka Capital Journal*, editorialised. 'But it's also about hypotheses; and creationism is as good a hypothesis as any for how the universe began.' To judge by the newspaper's letters page, many readers agreed. 'I am writing in response to the poor souls out there who believe that the state board of education has taken education back to the Dark Ages,' one wrote. 'I say it's about time! ... Take my children back to the Dark Ages, where truth was taught and they received the education they deserved.' No wonder some wags wondered if the Kansas board had decided to solve the Y2K problem by turning the clock back to Y1K. 'In one pan of the scales,' Salman Rushdie wrote in the Toronto *Globe and Mail*, 'we now have General Relativity, the Hubble Telescope and all the imperfect but painstakingly accumulated learning of the human race, and, in the other, the Book of Genesis. In Kansas, the scales balance.' And not only in Kansas. Even Al Gore, who had acquired a reputation as the 'Mr Science' of the Clinton administration, seemed reluctant to disturb this bogus equilibrium. A few months earlier one of his chief policy advisers had told the *Boston Globe* that 'the Democratic party is going to take God back this time', and on hearing the news from Kansas the candidate said that although he personally favoured the teaching of evolution, 'localities should be free to teach creationism as well'.

Gore thus maintained the ignoble tradition of politicians from Tennessee – the same state which made itself the laughing stock of the civilised world in 1925 by prosecuting a young high-school teacher, John Scopes, for teaching Darwinian theory in biology class. The great reporter H. L. Mencken, in one of his many lacerating despatches from the Scopes trial, suggested that Tennessee hillbillies 'are not more stupid than the city proletariat; they are only less informed'. Why, then, were even the most intelligent Tennesseans so reluctant to assist the cause of enlightenment by repudiating the antediluvian nonsense taught in local schools and endorsed by local nabobs? 'I suspect that politics is what keeps them silent and makes their state ridiculous. Most of them seem to be candidates for office, and a candidate for office, if he would get the votes of fundamentalists, must bawl for Genesis before he begins to bawl for anything else.' The 'typical Tennessee politician' was a man such as the then governor, Austin Peay, who sought to exploit the Scopes trial for his own political advantage before it had even begun. 'The local papers print a telegram that he has sent to Attorney-General A. T. Stewart whooping for prayer,' Mencken reported. 'In the North a governor who indulged in such monkey shines would be rebuked for trying to influence the conduct of a case in court. And he would be derided as a cheap mountebank. But not here.'

Al Gore, who might best be characterised as an expensive mountebank, was another great whooper for prayer. As vice-president, he had on his desk a placard with the toe-curling motto 'WWJD' – What Would Jesus Do? Apparently he never pondered a more pertinent question: what would the founding fathers think? The American presidential election of 1800, in which John Adams stood against his old friend Thomas Jefferson, also happened to be a contest between two men who were, at the time, the president of the American Academy of Arts and Sciences and the president of the American Philosophical Society. The historian Henry May described this as 'a coincidence very unlikely ever to be repeated in American politics', and his prediction looks increasingly solid. Exactly two centuries later, the main contenders for the presidency were George W. Bush, a genial chump, and Al Gore, a moderately intelligent liar and influence-pedlar – a choice summarised by one British newspaper as 'Dumbo vs. Pinocchio'.

The contrast between 1800 and 2000 went further than mere intellectual power and integrity. Adams and Jefferson, though flawed and complex characters, were both major figures of the American Enlightenment who believed that what the Europeans had merely imagined was being realised and fulfilled in the New World. Many of the European philosophers of the late eighteenth century thought so too: to the Marquis de Condorcet, America was of all nations 'the most enlightened, the freest and the least burdened by prejudices'; Diderot saw it as 'offering all the inhabitants of Europe an asylum against fanaticism and tyranny'. Tom Paine described the cause of America as 'the cause of all mankind', since political or clerical aristocracies would hold no sway in a state founded on secular reason and equal opportunity. Two hundred years later, the candidates Gore and Bush were respectively the son of a president and the son of a senator. (The one serious and substantial contender, Ralph Nader, was excluded from the televised debates and largely ignored by the mainstream media, perhaps for fear that he might show up his rivals as a couple of bozos. Liberal Democrats warned potential Nader supporters that unless they voted for Gore as 'the lesser of two evils' they would be responsible for letting Bush into the Oval Office, a counsel of despair and desperation likened by the columnist Alexander Cockburn to 'a man on a raft facing the decision of whether to drink seawater or his own urine'.)

In this light, Henry May might seem to have been right in arguing that the 1800 election 'marked the real end of the Enlightenment in America': thereafter, the idealistic rhetoric and practice of the 1770s and 1780s adjusted to the realities of popular democracy, and what came into existence was a nation radically democratic in its suffrage but moderately conservative in its institutions. 'The Secular Millennium gradually turned into Manifest Destiny . . . There was less and less disposition to dwell on political doctrines, including the political doctrines of the Enlightenment, closely associated with the increasingly different European world.'

One could appear to prove the point by marking further distinctions between the presidential candidates of 1800 and 2000. Jefferson commissioned for his library a composite portrait of Francis Bacon, John Locke and Isaac Newton, the English prophets of Enlightenment, hailing them as 'the three greatest men who ever lived, without any exception'. In his book *Earth in the Balance*, Al Gore described the same Francis Bacon as the greatest villain who ever lived: 'Bacon's moral confusion – the confusion at the heart of much modern science – came from his assumption, echoing Plato, that human intellect could safely analyse and understand the natural world without reference to any moral principles defining our relationship and duties to both God and God's creation.' Jefferson advised his nephew to 'question with boldness even the existence of a god; because, if there be one, he must approve the homage of reason rather than of blindfolded fear'; both Al Gore and George W. Bush, however, proudly proclaimed their blindfolded allegiance as born-again evangelical protestants. (At a hustings in December 1999, Republican hopefuls were asked 'what political philosopher or thinker do you most identify with and why?' Whereas Steve Forbes spoke of the enduring significance of John Locke, Bush replied simply: 'Christ, because he changed my heart.')

The influence of European Enlightenment ideals on American political institutions may have dwindled in the nineteenth and twentieth centuries; but the Enlightenment had never been a purely or even predominantly *political* movement in the first place. A more general respect for the secular, liberal humanism of the founding fathers – and for the spirit of scientific inquiry embodied by Benjamin Franklin, extravagantly depicted by the French Enlightenment philosopher Turgot as a liberating hero who 'seized fire from the heavens and the sceptre from the tyrant's hand' – endured far beyond the lifetime of Thomas Jefferson. 'Thank heaven I sat at the feet of Darwin and Huxley,' Theodore Roosevelt wrote in 1918, explaining how he became a naturalist. Woodrow Wilson, asked in 1922 for his thoughts on evolution, replied that 'of course like every other man of intelligence and education I do believe in organic evolution. It surprises me that at this late date such questions should be raised.' Only three years later, they were propelled on to every front page by the Scopes trial.

The small courtroom in Dayton, Tennessee, became the arena for an extraordinary joust between two national figures – William Jennings Bryan, a former presidential candidate who installed himself as 'associated prosecuting counsel', and Clarence Darrow, the country's most successful and famous attorney, who volunteered to represent Scopes. Each man saw the trial as nothing less than a battle between light and darkness, and it culminated in a direct showdown when Darrow called Bryan himself to the witness stand 'to show the people what fundamentalism is'. Although the judge protectively reminded Bryan that he was not obliged to endure this cross-examination, the elderly statesman seemed willing – indeed honoured – to appear as an expert witness on behalf of God. 'These gentlemen', he snarled, gesturing at the defence team, 'did not come here to try this case. They came here to try revealed religion. I am here to defend it and they can ask me any questions they please.' Darrow duly did so, eliciting a torrent of absurdities. 'If God had wanted a sponge to think,' Bryan declared, 'a sponge could think.' He also insisted, to incredulous hilarity from the defence benches, that humans were not mammals. Everything in the Old Testament – from Jonah and the whale to Noah and the ark – was literally true. God really did make the world 5,000 years ago.

'Do you say', Darrow asked, 'that you do not believe that there were any civilisations on this earth that reach back beyond five thousand years?'

'I am not satisfied by any evidence that I have seen.'

'Don't you know that the ancient civilisations of China are six or seven thousand years old, at the very least?'

'No, but they would not run back beyond the creation, according to the Bible.'

'Have you any idea how old the Egyptian civilisation is?'

'No.'

Metropolitan sophisticates all over the US, and far beyond, sniggered over the reports of Bryan's buffoonery. But metropolitan opinion counted for nothing in Dayton. Since the judge had ruled that Darwinism was inconsistent with the tale of Eve being created from Adam's rib (thus violating the state's law banning the teaching of anything that denied Genesis), and since the jury had to decide only whether Scopes had used a biology textbook explaining evolutionary theory – which he admitted – there could be only one verdict. He was convicted, and fined $100. Over the next few years, as other states copied Tennessee's anti-evolutionism statute, Darwin was removed from most school textbooks, not to return until the early 1960s.

The growing appeal of evangelical fundamentalism in America during the 1920s can most plausibly be interpreted as a quest for simple certainty by people who found the pace of change in society both bewildering and alarming. Mencken made the point with typical pugnacity in his article 'Homo Neanderthalensis', published a week or so before the Dayton hearings began in the summer of 1925:

The inferior man's reasons for hating knowledge are not hard to discern. He hates it because it is complex – because it puts an unbearable burden upon his meagre capacity for taking in ideas. Thus his search is always for short cuts. All superstitions are such short cuts. Their aim is to make the unintelligible simple, and even obvious. So on what seem to be higher levels. No man who has not had a long and arduous education can understand even the most elementary concepts of modern pathology. But even a hind at the plough can grasp the theory of chiropractic in two lessons. Hence the vast popularity of chiropractic among the submerged – and of osteopathy, Christian Science and other such quackeries with it. They are idiotic, but they are simple – and every man prefers what he can understand to what puzzles and dismays him.

The popularity of fundamentalism among the inferior orders of men is explicable in exactly the same way. The cosmogonies that educated men toy with are all inordinately complex. To comprehend their veriest outlines requires an immense stock of knowledge, and a habit of thought. It would be as vain to try to teach to peasants or to the city proletariat as it would be to try to teach them to streptococci. But the cosmogony of Genesis is so simple that even a yokel can grasp it. It is set forth in a few phrases. It offers, to an ignorant man, the irresistible reasonableness of the nonsensical. So he accepts it with loud hosannas, and has one more excuse for hating his betters.

Mencken was an unashamed snob, and his assumption that truth is beyond the comprehension of all but a small elite overlooks the indisputable fact that a partiality to bunkum is not confined to 'the lower orders' – unless one extends the definition of that phrase to include eminent grandees.

Mencken himself admitted elsewhere that superstition is often 'cherished by persons who should know better'. Recalling the surprise expressed by Woodrow Wilson in 1922 that anyone should still question organic evolution, one can imagine his astonishment had he known that Messrs Gore and Bush, the two men vying to become the first American president of the next century, would both flaunt their sympathy for the militant simpletons who were still fighting the good fight on behalf of the Book of Genesis.

Fortunately, as history confirms time and again, America is not dependent on presidents to protect its intellectual standards and values. It may be infested with flat-earthers and TV evangelists, but it also has more Nobel prizewinners than anywhere else – and plenty of citizens who will strenuously defend the legacy of Thomas Jefferson and Benjamin Franklin. For every populist moron such as William Jennings Bryan there is always at least one Clarence Darrow. After the Kansas vote in 1999, while the presidential wannabes were havering, the *Washington Post* struck a Menckenesque note by publishing this spoof memo from God to the Kansas board of education: 'Thank you for your support. Much obliged. Now, go forth and multiply. Beget many children. And yea, your children shall beget children. And their children shall beget children, and their children's children after them. And in time the genes that made you such pinheads will be eliminated through natural selection. Because that is how it works.' Even in Kansas itself, the state's Republican governor, Bill Graves, proved willing to take on the blockheads. 'This is a terrible, tragic, embarrassing solution to a problem that didn't exist,' he declared. 'I think this decision is so out of sync with reality that in some ways it minimises the credibility and the oversight that the state board is supposed to have on schools. What are they going to do, hire the evolution police?'

Why was the Kansas governor able to issue a more forth-right condemnation than either of the men hoping to occupy the office held by Thomas Jefferson? 'It's really not surprising, if you think about it,' the governor's press secretary told a reporter. 'If you're running for president, you have to be all things to all people. You don't want to alienate anybody.' In mitigation one could argue that George W. Bush, despite being an alumnus of both Yale and Harvard, was a bit of a goof who sincerely believed what he said about the jury still being out. The same indulgence cannot be permitted to Al Gore (Harvard, class of '69), who proudly paraded his scientific knowledge at every opportunity; nor to Tony Blair, the British prime minister, whose favourite word was 'modernisation'. These two clearly come into the category of 'persons who should know better'. Yet Blair, like Gore, took refuge in post-modern relativism to justify appeasing pre-modern zealots.

In March 2002 the *Guardian* revealed that Christian fundamentalists had taken control of a state-funded secondary school in north-east England and were striving to 'show the superiority' of creationist beliefs in their classes. 'As Christian teachers it is essential that we are able to counter the anti-creationist position,' the vice-principal of Emmanuel College, Gateshead, had advised colleagues. Another senior member of staff argued that Darwinians have 'a faith which is blind and vain by comparison with the faith of the Christian . . . A Christian teacher of biology will not or should not regard the theory of evolution as axiomatic, but will oppose it while teaching it alongside creation.'

In Britain, as elsewhere in Europe, creationism has little appeal. Both the Anglican and Roman Catholic hierarchies have long since accepted Darwin's theory: even Pope John Paul II said that it was 'more than just a hypothesis'. But Tony Blair had already announced his intention of building more 'faith-based schools', and the news from Gateshead strengthened the suspicion that some of these academies would proselytise rather than educate. Jenny Tonge MP asked if the prime minister was 'happy to allow the teaching of creationism alongside Darwin's theory of evolution in state schools'. A simple 'no' was surely the only possible answer, especially as he was due to deliver a speech to the Royal Society a few days later in which he would extol 'proper science' and warn against 'a retreat into a culture of unreason'. But it was not the answer he gave. Blair told Jenny Tonge that the creationists of Gateshead were doing a splendid job: 'In the end, a more diverse school system will deliver better results for our children.'

A few Labour backbenchers gawped in amazement as the significance of Blair's reply sunk in. Here was the leader of a supposedly secular, progressive government who, on being invited to assert that probable truth is preferable to palpable falsehood, pointedly refused to seize the opportunity – and indeed justified the teaching of bad science in the name of 'diversity'. He might just as well have trotted out the pernicious old maxim that ignorance is bliss, the last refuge of tyrants ever since God banished Adam and Eve from Eden for sampling the fruit of knowledge or the classical deities unleashed misery on the world through Pandora's box in revenge for Prometheus' heroic disobedience.

Had Tony Blair meant what he said when he told his party conference in 1996 that New Labour took its inspiration from 'the ancient prophets of the Old Testament'? A more likely explanation is that he had been infected (however unwittingly) by the cultural, moral and intellectual relativism of the post-modernists, and by the fashionable disease of 'non-judgmentalism'. As if to confirm the modishness of this affliction, his statement went largely unchallenged, even though it marked a new low in contemporary British political discourse. What if some schools informed their pupils that the moon was made of Swiss cheese, or that the stars were God's daisy-chain? Would that be officially welcomed as another healthy consequence of Blair's 'more diverse school system'?

This is the enfeebling legacy of post-modernism – a paralysis of reason, a refusal to observe any qualitative difference between reasonable hypotheses and swirling hogwash. At a time when countless loopy creeds were winning new converts it gave aid and comfort to the pedlars of nonsense. Even extra-terrestrial conspiracy theories were granted some academic respectability, notably through the publication in 1998 – by the reputable Cornell University Press – of *Aliens in America: Conspiracy Cultures from Outerspace to Cyberspace*, a post-structuralist study of UFO sightings and alien abductions. The author, Professor Jodi Dean, was not an astronomer but a political scientist who specialised in 'identity politics', and throughout the book's 242 pages she strenuously avoided any kind of judgment on the likelihood of what she described – unsurprisingly, given her insistence that reality no longer exists anyway. Or, to quote her own professorial prose, 'the fact that abduction accesses the stresses and excesses of mil-lennial technoculture doesn't get to the truth of abduction (as if getting to truth were still a possibility)'. Alien narratives, she argued, 'challenge us to face head-on . . . the dissolution of notions of truth, rationality and credibility'. If notions of truth were disintegrating, shouldn't a professor feel some duty to rescue them from the acid-bath? Not at all: Jodi Dean rejoiced at their destruction, since rational dispute was an instrument of oppression rather than a method of seeking some kind of verity. 'Argument, thought by some to be an important part of the process of democracy, is futile, perhaps because democracy can bring about Holocaust.'

While indicting anyone who clung to the discredited methods of reason and critical engagement as an accomplice in genocide, she had no such strictures for the ufologists, who were presented as heroic dissidents opposing the 'governmental–juridical discourse' and the 'elite, official "arbiters of reality"'. And, as she noted with pleasure, they were rapidly becoming a mass movement. According to one opinion poll in the 1990s, some 2 per cent of Americans said that they had been kidnapped by extra-terrestrials, which would translate into 3.7 million victims. ('Since many claim multiple kidnappings,' John Leonard wrote in the *Nation*, 'we are talking about an air-traffic control nightmare.') A 1996 poll for *Newsweek* found that 48 per cent of all Americans believed in UFOs and 27 per cent thought that aliens had visited the earth. If, as Dean argued, a belief in UFOs and alien abductions was a 'political act', since it 'contests the status quo', there must have been many more radicals in the United States than one might suppose; and although she categorised them as 'the oppressed', they included some of the most powerful people in the land.

5

The catastrophists

One day when Chicken Licken was scratching among the leaves, an
acorn fell out of the sky and struck her on the tail. 'Oh,' said Chicken
Licken, 'the sky is falling! I am going to tell the King.' So she went
along and went along until she met Henny Penny. 'Good morning
Chicken Licken, where are you going?' 'Oh, Henny Penny, the sky is
falling and I am going to tell the King.' 'How do you know the sky
is falling?' asked Henny Penny. 'I saw it with my own eyes, I heard
it with my own ears, and a piece of it fell on my tail!' said Chicken
Licken. 'Then I will go with you,' said Henny Penny.

OLD NURSERY TALE

The Griffith Observatory is one of Los Angeles's great landmarks, a classic Art Deco pile topped with three huge copper
domes. Perched on the southern slope of Mount Hollywood,
the building commands a panoramic view of the LA basin
below – and, through its telescopes, of the heavens above. It
attracts two million visitors a year.

Seldom if ever in its seventy-five-year history has the Griffith
drawn a bigger crowd than on 4 February 1962, when a rare
conjunction of five visible planets coincided with a partial
solar eclipse. By lunchtime, the approach-road was 'a solid

mass of cars lined up bumper-to-bumper for half a mile'. The astronomer Robert S. Richardson reported in the observatory's house magazine, the *Griffith Observer*, that two anxious questions were heard again and again: 'What is going to happen?', swiftly followed by 'What does it mean?' One woman he met was weeping hysterically.

> She was practically on the verge of collapse. 'I know it's silly to carry on in this way,' she gasped between sobs, 'but I can't help myself' . . . In talking to these 'alarmed' individuals, one gets the impression very strongly of an insecure personality, torn this way and that by vague doubts and fears. When confronted by a problem, they seem incapable of forming an independent opinion concerning it, but tend to rely on the judgment of others. They are so highly susceptible to suggestion that it would be very easy for anyone who has gained their confidence to take advantage of them. The barest hint that there might be something wrong could drive them to suicide or hysterics.

Since then, staff at the observatory have become wearily familiar with the symptoms. In February 1982, for instance, they were bombarded with calls from terrified LA residents asking if the world would come to an end on 10 March. The source of this panic was *The Jupiter Effect*, a book written by the British astrophysicists John Gribbin and Stephen Plagemann, who claimed that in March 1982 all the major planets would form an exceedingly rare 'grand alignment' on the same side of the sun – and that, as the earth passed between the sun and the massed rank of planets, it would be trapped in the middle of a gravitational tug-of-war. 'A remarkable chain of evidence . . . points to 1982 as the year in which the Los

Angeles region of the San Andreas fault will be subjected to the most massive earthquake known in the populated regions of the earth in this century,' they warned. 'In 1982, when the Moon is in the Seventh House and Jupiter aligns with Mars and with the other seven planets of the solar system, Los Angeles will be destroyed.'

The Jupiter Effect was published in 1974, and became a best-seller. It was soon discredited by scientists who pointed out that the essential premiss was wrong. Contrary to the impression given by Gribbin and Plagemann – and by the cover of their book, which showed Jupiter, Saturn, Uranus *et al.* as neatly aligned as a row of chorus girls – the major planets would not be in anything like a straight line. Even if they were, no storms or earthquakes would ensue: they are so small compared with the sun, and so distant from it, that their gravitational effect is negligible. By 1980 even Gribbin himself had retracted the prediction, conceding that he had been 'too clever by half'. As the dread day approached, however, the scare was revived and fanned by TV stations and tabloids. 'Astronomers and scientists are desperately worried that one of the most terrible disasters in the history of mankind may hit the United States,' one newspaper reported, 'killing untold millions and reducing the American west coast to rubble.' The story was picked up far beyond California. An American physics professor visiting Sri Lanka was handed a pamphlet, based on *The Jupiter Effect*, entitled 'The Great Tribulation – How Near?' In Beijing, the *People's Daily* felt obliged to reassure its millions of readers that 'there is no regular cause–effect relation at all between this astronomical phenomenon and natural disasters like earthquakes'.

About thirty quakes occur daily in Southern California, most too slight to be felt, and 10 March proved to be an utterly average day. But why had Gribbin and Plagemann chosen the San Andreas Fault for their seismic cataclysm anyway? Edward Upton, an astronomer at the Griffith Observatory, had both posed and answered the question in a review of *The Jupiter Effect* back in January 1975: 'Why this one-track emphasis on impending disaster in California, as if it were the only place on earth subject to major quakes? Why are there no similar predictions concerning Chile, Alaska, Japan, Indonesia, or a hundred other places? Could it be because in California, better than any other place on earth, one finds a fear of earthquakes combined with a proven market for sensational books?' And, he might have added, sensational films and TV programmes. In the early weeks of 1988 staff at the Griffith Observatory were puzzled by another spate of phone calls asking, 'When are the planets going to line up and cause that big earthquake?' It was *déjà vu* all over again. The culprit this time was a film about the sixteenth-century astrologer Nostradamus, *The Man Who Saw Tomorrow*, narrated by Orson Welles. The movie had been largely ignored on its initial release in 1981, but the reaction to its screening on cable TV seven years later was remarkably similar to that provoked by Welles's 1938 radio production of *War of the Worlds*, which had convinced thousands of New Yorkers that the Martians had landed. Whereas *War of the Worlds* had been pure science fiction, however, the producers of *The Man Who Saw Tomorrow* claimed that it was a serious docu-drama. Standing in an opulent, vellum-stuffed library, Welles revealed that a new planetary alignment would bring 'fire from the centre of the earth, the great earthquake' to destroy Los Angeles – and 'Nostradamus has given us the exact month and year: May 1988 . . . Incredible? Hrmmph. But true.'

Not true at all, actually. John Mosley, program supervisor

of the Griffith Observatory, discovered that Nostradamus' prediction was that 'hailstones would fall larger than an egg';
the film-makers had improved on this by splicing together
two lines from one quatrain with two lines from another. Nor,
as Mosley informed hundreds of callers, was any planetary
alignment due that spring; and such a line-up couldn't cause
an earthquake anyway. Perhaps he should also have pointed
out that Nostradamus himself had little faith in the com-
petence of most star-gazers. 'Let the profane and ignorant
herd keep away,' he warned in one of his verses. 'Let all
astrologers, idiots and barbarians stay far off.' In *The Prophecies
of Nostradamus*, which went through more than twenty editions
during the 1980s and 1990s, Erika Cheetham expressed her
pain and puzzlement at this incantation: 'Why does Nostradamus include astrologers among the people he damns? Is
this yet another example of his trying to bluff the authorities?'
Or, more likely, a sly admission that he knew his celestial
prophecies were all hooey? Even if judged on their own terms,
Nostradamus-fanciers often have only the haziest idea of what
they are talking about. Cheetham claimed in her book that
'when Saturn and Aquarius are in conjunction with Sagit-
tarius in the ascendant, towards the end of the century, we
should expect a great war'. Since Saturn is a planet and Aquarius a sign of the zodiac, such a conjunction is astronomically
impossible – a category mistake, as philosophers would call
it. In *Nostradamus: The Final Reckoning*, Peter Lemesurier
brooded on another of the old boy's forecasts – 'Once he for
17 years has held the see, They'll change the papal term to
five years' time' – and concluded that if Nostradamus was
right 'then we are faced with the distinct possibility that on
16 October 1995, or possibly 22 October, Pope John Paul II
will be asked to stay on for another five years'. A moment's

thought would show this 'distinct possibility' to be quite absurd, since popes – unlike British prime ministers or American presidents – are elected for life.

During the 1988 panic the Griffith Observatory set up a Nostradamus Hotline in the hope of dispelling the smog of nonsense that had descended on Los Angeles, but it attracted fewer customers than the local video stores which were renting out *The Man Who Saw Tomorrow*. 'Travel agents, moving company workers, bottled-water suppliers, real estate agents and earthquake preparedness specialists say they're observing a small but significant minority of Southern Californians either getting out of the area or getting prepared to survive the Big One,' the *Los Angeles Times* reported on 6 May. A real estate agent in Beverly Hills revealed that 'we're getting a lot of phone calls about people leasing out their homes for the month. I'm not worried personally. I'm going to stay behind and make money with all the people who are splitting.' A caller to a talk-show complained tearfully that his marriage was breaking up 'because of a fight over what to do about the earthquake'. Extend-a-Life, a Pasadena firm specialising in 'disaster supplies' such as first-aid kits and thermal blankets, reported a ten-fold increase in sales during the first week of May. 'Since Monday [2 May] the calls have become almost hysterical,' the company's chairman, Roberta Goldfeder, said. 'A gentleman called from Beverly Hills who said that most of the people on his street were going to Florida and he didn't know what to do.'

As writers of horror fiction have long known, many people take a perverse pleasure in being scared out of their wits – and resent anyone who tries to shatter their suspension of disbelief. A local TV weatherman, Fritz Coleman, was inundated with angry calls whenever he laughed at the Nostradamus craze.

'The thing that makes me mad', he grumbled, 'is that we have satellites and all this technology and people would rather believe this guy with a beret from the sixteenth century.'

These superstitious irrationalists included a certain ex-governor of California, who was now coming towards the end of his second term in the White House. The memoirs of the former presidential aide Donald Regan – published just as the latest earthquake deadline loomed – revealed that 'virtually every major move and decision the Reagans made during my time as White House chief of staff was cleared in advance with a woman in San Francisco who drew up horoscopes to make certain that the planets were in a favourable alignment for the enterprise'. Before the 1985 Geneva summit she had been commissioned to study the star-charts of the new Soviet leader Mikhail Gorbachev (a Piscean) for clues to his character and behaviour; she also fixed the exact time at which Reagan signed the Intermediate Nuclear Forces treaty in December 1987. Though Donald Regan didn't name her, the press quickly identified the mystery adviser as Joan Quigley, an upmarket astrologer from San Francisco. In mid-April she had left for a month's holiday in Europe – not to avoid the fall-out from Regan's book but because she had foreseen a major earthquake in California on 5 May. Returning home on 7 May to find her prophecy unfulfilled, she told reporters that 'she was confident any danger was past'.

Danger from earthquakes, that is. Saner citizens might have expected an eruption of scandalised outrage at the news that an astrologer held such sway over the most powerful man on planet earth. As with Nostradamus' earthquake, however, there was no great seismic shock. Although Donald Regan claimed that Nancy Reagan's dependence on Joan Quigley was 'the most closely guarded secret of the White House', most people seemed remarkably unsurprised. 'I have known since Reagan was elected that they [Ronnie and Nancy] went to astrologers,' the *Washington Post*'s style reporter Sally Quinn wrote, neglecting to add that she and her husband, Ben Bradlee, were private clients of the *Post*'s own resident astrologer, Svetlana Godilla. Others pointed out that back in the 1960s, when he entered politics, Reagan's circle of advisers included the famous mystic Jeane Dixon. Even the left-wing columnist Alexander Cockburn, a tireless critic of Ronald Reagan, declined to make a fuss this time. 'The image of two women, one of them peering into a crystal ball, guiding the policies of the United States, is irresistible in prompting coarse calumnies both on the termagant Nancy and on her pliant husband's abdication of executive responsibility,' he wrote in the *Nation*. 'But reflection should excite a more kindly analysis. For most of human history, leaders burdened with at least as many cares as Ronald Reagan have sought counsel from planets or entrails, and who now chastises the Emperor Augustus for his naivete?' Besides, why should anyone be astonished to learn that in his credulity, as in much else, Reagan was a fair representative of mainstream America? 'The United States retains, unusually for an advanced industrial society, about the same per capita level of religious superstition as Bangladesh. What one of Jimmy Carter's aides once referred to as the "abracadabra vote" is ample ... [Reagan] has been nurtured in the same rich loam of folk ignorance, historical figment and paranormal intellectual constructs as millions of his fellow citizens.' Astrology was entirely consonant with Reaganism and the twinkling penumbra of its faith in the 'free market' – an equally imaginary cosmic dispensation whose methods and purposes were beyond human understanding or challenge.

True enough, and all the more disconcerting for being so. A study of Wall Street stockholders found that 48 per cent used horoscopes when deciding what to buy or sell. Washington DC was second only to Berkeley, California – a famously wacky community – in the circulation figures for *Dell's Horoscope* magazine. Even the sober *Los Angeles Times* carried a daily horoscope column by another of Reagan's old soothsaying chums, Carroll Righter, the self-styled 'gregarious Aquarius' whose clients had included Marlene Dietrich, Princess Grace, Tyrone Power and Cary Grant. (Righter died in the week that Donald Regan's book was published, having correctly predicted that 'I will not make it out of the Taurean period.' Since he was eighty-eight and in poor health, however, no extra-terrestrial guidance would have been required for this particular prophecy.) Like so many manifestations of folly, horoscopes also enjoyed bipartisan support: Caroline Casey, Washington's leading astrological adviser to politicians, media figures, bureaucrats and Georgetown socialites, was the daughter of a former Democratic congressman. Liberals did it, conservatives did it: there seemed to be general acceptance of Nancy Reagan's mitigating plea that allowing one's life to be governed by mumbo-jumbo was a 'harmless little pastime'.

Astrology might appear an odd, even heretical hobby for a man who proclaimed himself a Christian and often cited the Book of Revelation (which had itself been dismissed by one of his predecessors, Thomas Jefferson, as 'the ravings of a maniac, no more worthy, nor capable of explanation than the incoherences of our own nightly dreams'). Here too, however, Ronald Reagan represented the spirit of the times. Over the past couple of decades many Westerners have acquired their own DIY faiths, hybrids comprising elements from Christianity, Hinduism, alchemy, geomancy, the teachings of the Dalai Lama, the ancient wisdom of Atlantis and much else. And, since we live in a 'non-judgmental' era, otherwise intelligent people will respect and even pander to these follies. When writing a regular column for the *Observer* in the early 1990s, I once sneered at a rival broadsheet, the *Sunday Times*, for introducing a weekly horoscope. You can guess the sequel: the *Observer*, Britain's most venerable liberal newspaper, acquired its own horoscope page soon afterwards. Not to be outdone, *The Times* announced in a leading article at Christmas 1995 that 'over our next 12 issues we shall consider what the next year holds in store for famous and less famous people born under each of the zodiac's signs'. Here's a sample of its editorials from the following fortnight: 'According to the mystic meteorological mirror, Peter Pans born under the sign of Virgo possess the secret of eternal youth . . . Librans are cocksure creatures. They know what they want and they usually get it . . . With Mars as its ruling planet, Aries is naturally the sign of soldiers and sportsmen – men and women of action and dynamic resolve. Their element is Fire. They tend to live in the here and now . . .'

Those who defend horoscopes as harmless fun never explain what is either funny or harmless in promoting a contrick which preys on ignorance and fear. Professor Richard Dawkins has pointed out that a pharmaceuticals manufacturer who marketed a birth-control pill with no demonstrable effect on fertility would be prosecuted under the Trades Descriptions Act, and sued by trusting customers who found themselves pregnant. 'If astrologers cannot be sued by individuals misadvised, say, into taking disastrous business decisions, why at least are they not prosecuted for false representations under the Trades Descriptions Act and driven out of business?' he demanded. 'Why, actually, are professional astrologers not jailed for fraud?' But why stop at professional astrologers? When *The Times* began its flirtation with star-gazing I wrote a brief, light-hearted feature suggesting that six months in the slammer might bring the editor to his senses. This provoked another editorial from the paper once known as the Thunderer, denouncing me as a po-faced killjoy. 'An arbitrary duodecimal division of the world's population according to the time of birth is just that: arbitrary. But it happens to be a favourite Western speculation: amusing because so patently irreverent of all that we know and hold dear in this rational world.'

Where was this rational world? It was clearly not the place inhabited by the editor of *The Times*, or by millions of other people in Britain. As if to prove the point, the same edition carried a leading article in praise of the National Lottery, that monument to irrationalism and imbecility, whose first winner was to be chosen that evening. 'The British puritanical heritage persists in finding a cloud before every silver lining,' it sighed. 'But for most of the nation tonight, a man is seldom as harmlessly employed as in fantasy about the pot of gold at the end of the rainbow.' It described the inaugural draw as 'the greatest national collective experience' since the end of the Second World War, adding proudly that 'nearly every adult in the land – 40 million – has bought a ticket'. Echoing *The Times*, the minister responsible for the lottery scolded those few heretics who declined to participate for their 'prudish' and 'sanctimonious' refusal to enjoy (here comes that word again) the 'fun' of having a flutter.

Not so. Even the great rationalist John Allen Paulos, professor of mathematics at Temple University in Philadelphia, confessed in his book *Innumeracy* that he plays blackjack in Atlantic City. (Blackjack is the only casino game where past occurrences affect future probabilities. In roulette, the likelihood of red on any given spin is always 18/37; in blackjack, the chance of drawing two aces in succession is not 4/52 × 4/52 but 4/52 × 3/51. The trick is to keep a careful count of what cards have already been drawn and increase your stake when the odds are slightly in your favour.) The objection to the National Lottery was not that it encouraged people to gamble but that it encouraged them to bet at such hopeless odds, heedless of Paulos's timely warning that there was an ominous and widening gap 'between scientists' assessment of various risks and the popular perception of those risks, a gap that threatens eventually to lead ... to unfounded and crippling anxieties'. The punters queueing desperately to buy their lottery tickets on the weekend of the first lottery draw were kindred spirits to the many Hollywood actors who cancelled their trips to the Cannes film festival during the first Gulf War for fear that they would be either blown up in mid-air or felled by an Iraqi Scud missile as soon as they set foot in Europe. These same stars never think twice before leaping into their limos to attend the Oscars ceremony. And yet, as Paulos noted, among the 28 million Americans who travelled abroad every year only about seventeen were murdered by terrorists – which works out at one chance in 1.6 million. Compare that with the probability of dying while riding a bicycle (one in 75,000), drowning (one in 20,000) or being killed in a car crash (one in 5,300). One didn't have to be a po-faced puritan to find it rather depressing that 40 million British adults were innumerate enough to succumb to odds of *13 million to one*. It may have been true, as *The Times* insisted, that 'of course, you are adult and mathematically unchallenged, and know you are not going to win'. But most punters still cherished, however secretly and shamefacedly, a tingling hope which had been encouraged by TV commercials showing a huge finger of fate descending from the stars to point at a random, anonymous citizen: 'It could be you . . .' The official 'expert' recruited to advise the public on the chances of winning the jackpot was not a professor of statistics but Mystic Meg, a tabloid astrologer. Britain's bestselling paper, the *Sun*, invited readers to rub their lottery tickets 'on our psychically charged red dot' to shorten the odds.

Those who lamented the decline of traditional Christianity in the twentieth century often quoted a line attributed to G. K. Chesterton (though there is no evidence of his authorship): 'When a man ceases to believe in God he does not believe in nothing; he believes in anything.' Like so many aphoristic clichés, it collapses after a moment's scrutiny – not least because nothing and anything are, in this context, effectively synonymous. A more telling version might be phrased thus: 'If you believe in God, you'll believe anything.' Even the no-nonsense Margaret Thatcher was a devotee of mystical 'electric baths' and Ayurveda therapy. But she was a mere dabbler compared with more recent inhabitants of Downing Street. Cherie Blair found her devout Catholicism no impediment to flirtations with New Age spirituality – inviting a feng-shui expert to rearrange the furniture at No. 10 and wearing a 'magic pendant' known as the BioElectric Shield, which has 'a matrix of specially cut quartz crystals' that surround the wearer with 'a cocoon of energy' to ward off evil forces. (She was, predictably enough, 'put on to the idea by Hillary Clinton'.) The catholicism – if not Catholicism – of her tastes was further demonstrated in 2002 by the revelation that she employed a former member of the Exegesis cult, Carole Caplin, as a 'lifestyle guru'. Through Caplin, the prime minister's wife was introduced to an eighty-six-year-old 'dowsing healer', Jack Temple, who treated her swollen ankles by swinging a crystal pendulum over the affected area and feeding her strawberry leaves grown within the 'electro-magnetic field' of a neolithic circle he had built in his back garden.

It was long assumed that Tony Blair, who wears his Christianity on his sleeve, did not share his wife's unorthodox enthusiasms. In 1999 he demanded the resignation of the England football coach Glenn Hoddle, who had told an interviewer that disabled people were paying off the bad karma they collected in previous incarnations. Blair thought this 'offensive', though it was not discernibly more offensive than the doctrine of original sin held by many of his fellow-Christians. From a Buddhist viewpoint, Hoddle was quite correct: no less a figure than the Dalai Lama confirmed as much, but added that 'if you live in a Christian country, you should keep these views to yourself. It is difficult to have a mish-mash of religions.' Not all that difficult, actually, as Blair confirmed when he and his wife underwent a 'rebirthing experience' under the supervision of one Nancy Aguilar while holidaying on the Mexican Riviera in the summer of 2001. *The Times*'s detailed account of the prime ministerial mud-bath is worth quoting at some length:

> The ceremony took place at dusk. Mr Blair and his wife, wearing bathing costumes, were led to the Temazcal, a brick-coloured pyramid on the south end of the beach ... Ms Aguilar told the Blairs to bow and pray to the four winds as Mayan prayers were read out. Each side of the building is decorated with Mayan religious symbols: the sun and baby lizards representing spring and childhood; a bird to signify adolescence, summer and freedom; a crab to represent maturity and autumn; and a serpent – the most sacred

in the Mayan Indian culture – to symbolise winter and transformation . . .

Within the Temazcal, a type of Ancient Mayan steam bath, herb-infused water was thrown over heated lava rocks, to create a cleansing sweat and balance the Blairs' 'energy flow'.

Ms Aguilar chanted Mayan songs, told the Blairs to imagine that they could see animals in the steam and explained what such visions meant. They were told the Temazcal was like the womb and those participating in the ritual must confront their hopes and fears before 'rebirth' and venturing outside. The Blairs were offered watermelon and papaya, then told to smear what they did not eat over each other's bodies along with mud from the Mayan jungle outside.

The prime minister, on holiday just a month before the 11 September attacks, is understood to have made a wish for world peace.

Before leaving, the Blairs were told to scream out loud to signify the pain of rebirth. They then walked hand in hand down the beach to swim in the sea.

Although Mayan rebirthing rituals are not yet available in Britain through the National Health Service, some of Cherie Blair's other peculiar obsessions have already been adopted as official policy. In January 1999 the government recruited a feng-shui consultant, Renuka Wickmaratne, for advice on how to improve inner-city council estates. 'Red and orange flowers would reduce crime,' she concluded, 'and introducing a water feature would reduce poverty. I was brought up with this ancient knowledge.' Two years later the government announced that, for the first time since the creation of the National Health Service, remedies such as acupuncture or Indian ayurvedic medicine could be granted the same status as conventional treatments. According to the *Sunday Times*, 'The inclusion of Indian ayurvedic medicine, a preventative approach to healing using diet, yoga and meditation, is thought to have been influenced by Cherie Blair's interest in alternative therapy.' An all too believable suggestion, since Cherie was a client of the ayurvedic guru Bharti Vyas and officiated at the opening ceremony for her holistic therapy centre in London.

The swelling popularity of quack potions and treatments in recent years is yet another manifestation of the retreat from reason and scientific method. According to a 1998 survey by the *Journal of the American Medical Association*, the use of homeopathic preparations in the United States more than doubled between 1990 and 1997. In Britain, by the end of the twentieth century the country's 36,000 general practitioners were outnumbered by the 50,000 purveyors of complementary and alternative medicine (CAM). When the British journalist John Diamond disclosed in the mid-1990s that he had cancer, he found himself bombarded with well-meant but batty advice, described in his final book *Snake Oil and Other Preoccupations*:

> Have you tried squid's cartilage? Establishment doctors scorn it, of course, but my aunt is still alive on squid's cartilage two years after her oncologist gave her only six months (well, yes, since you ask, she is having radiotherapy as well). Or there's this wonderful healer who practises the laying on of feet, with astonishing results. Apparently it's all a question of tuning your holistic (or is it holographic?) energies to the natural frequencies of organic (or is it orgonic?) cosmic vibrations. You've nothing to lose, you might as well try it. It's £500 for a course of treatment but what's money when your life is at stake?

The alluring adjectives 'complementary' and 'alternative' are essentially euphemisms for 'dud': there is only medicine that works and medicine that doesn't, medicine that has been adequately tested and medicine that hasn't. 'There isn't an "alternative" physiology or anatomy or nervous system,' Diamond wrote, 'any more than there's an alternative map of London which lets you get to Battersea from Chelsea without crossing the Thames.' In his introduction to Diamond's book, Professor Richard Dawkins pointed out that if a healing technique is shown to have curative properties in properly controlled double-blind trials, it ceases to be an alternative: it simply becomes medicine. 'Conversely, if a technique devised by the President of the Royal College of Physicians consistently fails in double-blind trials, it will cease to be part of "orthodox" medicine. Whether it will then become "alternative" will depend upon whether it is adopted by a sufficiently ambitious quack (there are always sufficiently gullible patients).'

It is a brave politician who risks incurring the wrath of those patients: 83 million Americans spend $27 billion a year on 'alternative' medicine, and most of them are entitled to vote. In 1992 the US government's National Institute of Health was awarded $2 million of public money to establish an Office of Alternative Medicine (later the National Centre for Complementary Alternative Medicine). Within eight years, thanks to strenuous lobbying, Congress had increased the budget to $90 million. A few months before the presidential election of 2000, in an overtly political gesture, Bill Clinton announced the creation of a White House commission to ensure 'that public policy maximises the benefits to Americans of complementary and alternative medicine'.

Even the sober *British Medical Journal* felt obliged to pander to the new quackery by running a series describing alternative therapies. 'Our readers wanted it,' the editor explained. 'They want to know more about it because their patients are interested in it and because they are wondering whether to refer people. They want to know what works and what doesn't.' Yet, as Richard Dawkins noted, the pedlars of complementary medicine are uninterested in proving that their remedies 'work'. Homeopathy has often been subjected to rigorous scientific testing since its 'discovery' by the German physician Samuel Hahnemann at the end of the eighteenth century, and it has always failed – most recently on a BBC *Horizon* documentary in 2003. This is scarcely surprising, as Hahnemann's perverse 'law of infinitesimals' (the smaller the dose of a drug, the stronger its effect) means that there is effectively nothing to test. Homeopathic products are diluted in 99 parts water (and/or alcohol) and shaken vigorously; a drop of the resulting solution is then added to more water, and so on until the original substance has been diluted many millions of times. A typical dilution is 30C, that is, one part cure to 100^{30} parts water: even if it contained only one molecule of the homeopathic ingredient, the amount of water required would be far greater than that in all the oceans of the earth. And, of course, no substance can be diluted beyond the point where one molecule remains without disappearing altogether. (An even more fantastic ratio of 200C is claimed for *Oscillococcinum*, a product for 'the relief of colds and flu-like symptoms', whose active ingredient is a duck's liver. If one molecule of the liver survived the dilution it would be mixed in 100^{200} molecules of water, more than the total number of molecules in the entire universe. *Oscillococcinum* had sales of $20 million in 1996, and all from a single duck's liver – prompting *US News & World Report* to describe the hapless bird as 'the $20-million duck'.) In a normal double-blind test, half the patients are given the 'remedy' while the rest take a placebo, but in the case of homeopathy the two doses are identical, since neither has any trace of the crucial ingredient. Hoist by their own law of infinitesimals, homeopaths argue that even if there is no molecule of the original substance in the medicine, the water somehow retains a metaphysical 'memory' of it. This idea has been promoted by the French scientist Jacques Benveniste, who submitted a paper to the journal *Nature* in 1988 claiming to have experimental proof. (When *Nature* sent a team of invigilators to the laboratory, he was unable to replicate his findings.) Benveniste has since extended his theory further, saying that not only can water 'remember' highly diluted substances, but that this memory can be taken electromagnetically from the water, stored digitally on a computer, emailed to the other side of the world and 'played back' via a sound card into new water – which instantly acquires the same properties as the original.

Like homeopathy, most alternative therapies are closer to mysticism than to medicine. This may explain their appeal to the British royal family, whose survival depends on another irrational faith – the magic of hereditary monarchy, which was so fiercely debunked by Tom Paine and other Enlightenment pamphleteers. Queen Elizabeth II carries homeopathic remedies with her at all times. Princess Diana was a devotee of reflexology, the belief that pressure applied to magical 'zones' in the hands and feet can heal ailments elsewhere in the body. Prince Charles has been a prominent champion of 'holistic' treatments since 1982, having been persuaded of their effectiveness by that absurd old charlatan Sir Laurens van der Post. In 1988 the Prince of Wales presided at the official opening of the Hale Clinic in London, which offers a choice of more than forty 'alternative therapies' such as acupuncture, aromatherapy, t'ai-chi, chakra balancing, colonic irrigation and bio-energy healing ('the healer acts as a channel allowing the positive energy to pass through the patient with one hand and extracting negative energy with the other hand'). Eight years later he set up the Foundation for Integrated Medicine, and in 2001 lent his support to a proposal for a new London hospital that would 'tap into the power of alternative therapy'.

Prince Philip, the Queen's robustly conservative consort, was often said to regard his eldest son's New Age interests with a mixture of hilarity and contempt. Yet he too had his eccentricities, having been an enthusiastic subscriber to *Flying Saucer Review* since the magazine began publication in the mid-1950s; and he was in good company. The founder-editor of *Flying Saucer Review*, the Earl of Clancarty, used his membership of the House of Lords to initiate a full-length parliamentary debate on UFOs in 1979, during which he revealed that not all aliens came from space: some emerged through tunnels from a civilisation beneath the earth's crust. 'I haven't been down there myself,' he said, 'but from what I gather [these beings] are very advanced.' He added that most visitors from other planets – and indeed from below the earth's crust – were friendly, but 'I'm told there is one hostile lot.' (One is reminded of Professor Roger Scruton's ingenious defence of the House of Lords as a more truly democratic chamber than the elected Commons: MPs would inevitably be brighter and more ambitious than the average citizen whereas hereditary peers, being selected by a mere accident of birth, were far more representative of the general population, including a few clever-dicks but also a fair proportion of blithering idiots.) Another peer, Admiral of the Fleet Lord Hill-Norton, contributed a preface to Timothy Good's 1991 book *Alien Liaison*, which reported that the US government had captured several 'alien spacecraft' and had been test-flying them at 'a super-secret base in the Nevada desert'. Describing Good as an 'honest and reliable' investigator, the former chief of the defence staff wrote that the allegations were 'impossible, certainly for me, to dismiss' unless they were 'publicly disproved'.

How could one disprove it? The simplest method would be to point out that Lord Hill-Norton had heard nothing about the extra-terrestrial alliance, officially or unofficially, even though he would surely have been party to the conspiracy as head of the British defence establishment from 1971 to 1974 and then chairman of Nato's military committee from 1974 to 1977. 'You'd think I would have known,' he agreed. 'But I hadn't the faintest bloody idea.' A damaging admission, surely? Quite the opposite: it showed that the cover-up was organised at a very high level indeed – 'as high as 38 levels above top secret', according to Timothy Good. 'I doubt', he told me, 'if anyone in the Cabinet is aware of what's going on.' To prove his bona fides, he brandished a letter sent to him a few years earlier by Prince Philip. 'There are many reasons to believe that they [UFOs] exist,' the prince wrote. 'There is so much evidence from reliable witnesses.'

One such witness was his own former equerry, Air Marshal Sir Peter Horsley, who later became deputy chief of RAF Strike Command. In his memoirs, published in 1997, Horsley claimed to have met an extra-terrestrial creature named Janus while working at Buckingham Palace in the 1950s. 'Prince Philip', the creature told him, 'is a man of great vision, a person of world renown and a leader in the realm of wildlife and the environment. He is a man who believes strongly in the proper relationship between man and nature, which will prove of great importance in future galactic harmony.' What did this interstellar royal-watcher look like? Alas, Horsley confessed, 'it is difficult to describe him with any accuracy; the room was poorly lit by two standard lamps and for the most part he sat in a deep chair by the side of a not very generous fire. In fact, I never really got any physical impression of him.' Rather surprisingly, Horsley never mentioned the encounter to anyone at the time. 'I was aged 33, very busy and had to get on with my job,' he explained.

'Oh God,' a senior officer at the Ministry of Defence groaned when Horsley's book appeared. 'How unfortunate that the public will learn that the man who had his finger on the button at Strike Command was seeing little green men.' Unfortunate, maybe, but not unusual. In the United States, two recent commanders-in-chief – Presidents Carter and Reagan – said they had seen UFOs. Indeed, it was impossible to live through the closing decades of the twentieth century without witnessing strange flying objects and alien visitors, often in one's own living room. From *Close Encounters of the Third Kind* and *ET* to *Independence Day* and *Men in Black*, filmmakers both stimulated and fed the public demand most lucratively. The top-rated television show for much of the 1990s, *The X-Files*, jostled in the schedules with *Third Rock from the Sun*, *Dark Skies* and *Millennium*. (There was no respite in the commercial breaks: UFO imagery appeared in advertising campaigns for Kodak film, Volkswagen cars, Hostess hotels, Quisp cereals and Breath-Rite Nasal Strips, lending cosmic enchantment to even the most mundane products of human industry.)

'The thing you have to remember about *The X-Files* is this,' the programme's creator, Chris Carter, told an interviewer. 'It's a fiction. If – and it's a big if – anyone does believe it is true, that merely suggests we are reflecting something wider in society.' Not all that big an if, as it turned out. By the mid-1990s the Internet was cluttered with websites which treated the tales of agents Mulder and Scully as gospel truth. A teacher in Ontario, Professor James Alcock, noticed that one of the 'information sources' most frequently cited in student essays was *The X-Files*. When he reminded them that it was fiction, they countered: 'Yes, but it's based on fact.' In an article for the *New York Times* in 1996, Professor Wayne Anderson of Sacramento City College reported that over half the students in his astronomy class believed that the government had concealed the truth about the arrival of UFOs; they too cited *The X-Files* as a source.

'I don't know that it's my responsibility to say that I've just created a fiction that is a fiction,' Chris Carter told the Committee for the Scientific Investigation of Claims of the Paranormal (CSICOP), a sceptical pressure-group which had proposed that each episode should be prefaced by such a disclaimer. But he acknowledged that his fiction invariably preferred supernatural explanations.

My intention, when I first set out to do the show, was to do a more balanced kind of storytelling. I wanted to expose hoaxes. I wanted Agent Scully to be right as much as Agent Mulder. Lo and behold, those stories were really boring. The suggestion that there was a rather plausible and rational and ultimately mundane answer for these things turned out to be a disappointing kind of storytelling, to be honest. And I think that's maybe where people have the most problems with my show ... But it's just the kind of storytelling we do, and because we have to entertain ... That's really the job they pay me for, and that's the thing I'm supposed to do.

This shoulder-shrugging defence was briskly rebutted by Richard Dawkins in his 1996 Dimbleby lecture:

> Soap operas, cop series and the like are justly criticised if, week after week, they ram home the same prejudice or bias. Each week *The X-Files* poses a mystery and offers two rival kinds of explanation, the rational theory and the paranormal theory. And, week after week, the rational explanation loses. But it is only fiction, a bit of fun, why get so hot under the collar?
>
> Imagine a crime series in which, every week, there is a white suspect and a black suspect. And every week, lo and behold, the black one turns out to have done it. Unpardonable, of course. And my point is that you could not defend it by saying: 'But it's only fiction, only entertainment.'

Another campaigner against junk science, Professor A. K. Dewdney, coined the phrase '*National Enquirer* syndrome' to evoke the pressure on media companies in a fiercely competitive market to come up with ever more sensational stories: 'The edge moves increasingly into the realm of the incredible.'

Incredible is certainly the *mot juste* for *Communion* (1987), sub-titled 'A True Story of Encounters with the Unknown', in which Whitley Strieber revealed that at Christmas 1985 he had been kidnapped by extra-terrestrials who subjected him to 'cerebral needle examinations and rectal probes'. Previously known as a horror-novelist, Strieber was a man who, by his own admission, had some difficulty in distinguishing fantasy from truth. For years he had told of how he was almost killed when a madman went on a shooting spree at the University of Texas, but in *Communion* he finally confessed that 'I wasn't there.' Nor did he witness *les événements* of May

1968 in Paris, as he had often maintained. 'Why do I need these absurd stories?' he wondered. 'They are not lies; when I tell them, I myself believe them.' Yet *Communion*, for which he received a $1 million advance, was marketed as non-fiction and soon topped the bestseller lists on both sides of the Atlantic, inspiring a whole new genre. In a London bookshop a few years later, I counted nearly 100 studies of alien abduction – of which only one, by the American space expert and *Aviation Week* journalist Philip J. Klass, was at all sceptical. These volumes used to emerge from small, eccentric New Age presses but after Strieber hit the jackpot even the most reputable publishers discovered the profitability of piffle, rushing in with *Cosmic Voyage: A Scientific Discovery of Extra-Terrestrials Visiting Earth* and *Alien Agenda: The Untold Story of the Extra-Terrestrials Around Us.*

Television programmes such as *Unsolved Mysteries* and *Sightings* were often scheduled after the network news, and the distinction between the two sometimes disappeared altogether, especially when famous anchormen were brought in to give spurious journalistic authority to the *National Enquirer* syndrome. In 1994 Larry King hosted *UFO Cover-Up?*, a two-hour 'special' broadcast live from Area 51, the USAF base in Nevada where UFO-fanciers believe extra-terrestrials work alongside air-force scientists developing secret aircraft and weapons. Although all four of his guests were conspiracy theorists, to create an illusion of balance King included brief pre-recorded interviews with Carl Sagan, the scientist, and Philip J. Klass, who has spent more than thirty years investigating and debunking yarns about flying saucers. 'During the two-hour show the audience was exposed to less than three minutes of sceptical views on UFOs, crashed saucers and government cover-up,' Klass wrote. 'And because Sagan and

I were taped many weeks earlier, neither of us could respond to the nonsense spouted by the four UFO promoters who appeared live.'

As the programme drew to a close, Larry King summed up: 'Crashed saucers. Who knows? But clearly the government is withholding something . . .' In fact it was King and his producer who were withholding information. Some weeks earlier, Klass had given them photocopies of formerly classified Pentagon documents from 1948 in which top intelligence officials proposed that 'UFOs' might be Soviet spy vehicles. If, as all ufologists believe, the US government captured several replicants following the crash of their spacecraft at the USAF base in Roswell, New Mexico, in July 1947, why did the directors of naval and air-force intelligence still not know about it more than a year later? The inescapable question arises, as with Lord Hill-Norton: if defence chiefs, Cabinet ministers and heads of government were too junior to be trusted with the information ('as high as 38 levels above top secret', no less), then who on earth – or in heaven, for that matter – *was* in on the conspiracy? Despite having two hours of airtime at his disposal, however, King omitted to mention Philip Klass's evidence.

In 1995 an exhibition called 'Alien Encounters and Extra-TERRORestrial Experience' opened at Disney World's new 'Tomorrowland' in Florida and was promoted on a one-hour show on ABC which began with a few blurry videos of alleged UFOs. 'This is not swamp gas. It is not a flock of birds. This is an actual spacecraft from another world, piloted by alien intelligence . . . Intelligent life from distant galaxies is now attempting to make open contact with the human race. Tonight we will show you the evidence.'

After a wholly uncritical recap of all the Roswell myths, an even more thrilling exhibit was produced with a flourish. When Jimmy Carter became president, 'his staff attempted to explore the availability of official investigations into alien contacts'. The camera panned swiftly down a typewritten document, zooming in on two words: 'no jurisdiction'. 'As this internal government memo illustrates,' the narrator declared, 'there are some security secrets outside the jurisdiction even of the White House.' Philip Klass recognised the document at once: it was a routine FBI reply to an inquiry from Carter's staff about UFO sightings, explaining that the Bureau had no jurisdiction to investigate such incidents and referring the White House to the air force. But most other viewers presumably concluded, as they were meant to, that even the head of state was denied access to UFO secrets. The commercial purpose of this sleight-of-hand became all too obvious as the narrator reached his conclusion: 'Statistics indicate a greater probability that you will experience extra-terrestrial contact in the next five years than the chances you will win a state lottery. But how do you prepare for such an extraordinary event? At Tomorrowland in Disney World, scientists and Disney engineers have brought to life a possible scenario that helps acclimatise the public to their inevitable alien encounters.'

In truth, the only inevitability was that television companies would continue to broadcast mendacious codswallop masquerading as investigative journalism. Their shamelessness is joyfully satirised in a 1997 episode of *The Simpsons*, in which Homer encounters a glowing, green homunculus in the woods outside Springfield. The 'alien' is eventually identified as his boss, the evil Montgomery Burns, who explains that 'a lifetime of working at a nuclear power plant has left me with a healthy green glow'. Before discovering the truth, however,

Homer suggests to Bart that they should go back and try to film the creature, in case it is 'the real thing'. Bart agrees: 'If it isn't, we can fake it and sell it to the Fox network! They'll buy anything!' 'Now, son,' Homer chides. 'They do a lot of quality programming.' Whereupon both father and son collapse in helpless laughter.

The extra joke here is that *The Simpsons* was itself a Fox show, and thus from the same stable as *The X-Files* and countless trashy 'reality programmes' about mystery spaceships. The irony was redoubled shortly afterwards when Fox transmitted *Opening the Lost Tombs: Live from Egypt*, a 'network special' introduced by Maury Povich which claimed that the pyramids were built by travellers from outer space. As if to prove that there were now no boundaries between fact and fiction, or journalism and entertainment, the network trailed the programme with a lengthy item in its main nightly news bulletin. Fox News correspondent David Garcia reported that although Egyptologists considered 'even the mention of UFOs or other-world intelligence as heresy', some people believed that the pyramids were indeed 'not of this earth'. He concluded his despatch thus: 'A higher intelligence, or merely dedicated hard work? Which theory is correct? Neither is proven. It is the mystery of Egypt.' Thus tabloid TV unwittingly echoed the argument of post-modernist philosophers such as Jean Baudrillard: that there is no such thing as reality – only a system of arbitrary signs, imagistic discourses and 'multiple refractions in hyperspace'. (In his book *The Gulf War Did Not Take Place*, Baudrillard coolly insisted that even the charred corpses of victims were not 'real'. No doubt their grieving friends and families were greatly consoled by the news.)

Paradoxically, despite their striking lack of interest in

empirical reality and their conviction that a wild conjecture carries as much evidential weight as decades of scholarly research, the purveyors of fantasy yearn passionately for objective proof that will vindicate them: like the heroes of *The X-Files*, they believe that the truth is out there, somewhere, if only they could find it. In August 1995, after almost half a century of sleuthing by dozens of diligent investigators, it surfaced at last – a hitherto 'secret' film of surgeons conducting an autopsy on dead aliens at the Roswell airbase in July 1947. More enticingly still, it included a fleeting appearance by a man in a long coat who was said to be President Harry S. Truman. The scratchy black-and-white footage was screened simultaneously on American, European and Japanese television, to a chorus of awestruck gasps. 'If that is a hoax, it a most elaborate and convincing one,' said Congressman Steven Schiff of New Mexico. Martin Walker, the well-respected Washington correspondent of the *Guardian*, filed a startlingly unsceptical 2,500-word despatch. 'This film is the first hard evidence to emerge from the most celebrated and best-documented UFO event of all,' he wrote.

> Forget about Whitewater and Watergate and even the unsettled issues of who shot President Kennedy. The biggest conspiracy of all, that earth has been visited by aliens and their bodies autopsied on film, is clambering out of the bizarre underworld of the cults and into the realm of the rational and verifiable world . . . This does not look like some creation of the Hollywood special effects labs. This seems convincingly to be the autopsy of some kind of being.

He was right on one point: Hollywood special effects wizards had nothing to do with it. The autopsy was shot in southern England during the summer of 1994, by two men who had previously produced karaoke videos and films of animals singing nursery rhymes. 'We found a barn in the quiet village of Ridgmont, Bedfordshire, through a farmer I knew,' one of the hoaxers, Andy Price-Watts, confessed four years later. 'I had an old paraffin lamp and we brought along a table, some sheets, overalls and rubber gloves. We filmed it in the evening to make it look as if it had been shot in the dark . . . We used a wig holder we bought for a few quid, which Eliot Willis, our tape operator, transformed using painted orange peel for the eyes. Elliot and the local butcher, Roger Baker, played the two medical staff. Roger got the part because he could supply the chicken guts we used as the alien's innards. We were thinking of using pig guts, but they looked too human.' Soon after the charade began, the farmer walked in to find out what was going on. 'I suddenly thought we could use him,' Price-Watts's partner recalled. 'There was an old scarecrow in the corner of the barn and we got the coat from it, put it on him and he had a little cameo as President Truman. We could hardly stop ourselves laughing as we shot the video, which took about an hour and a half to complete.' The film was edited down to six minutes, processed into monochrome and then transferred between different video formats several times to make it look as grainy as possible.

Yet more harmless fun? 'I want to believe' was one of the mantras of *The X-Files*, and the cut-price English japesters certainly performed a useful public service by showing how this intense yearning could overpower the critical faculties of otherwise intelligent people. 'Keep an open mind!' broadcasters pleaded when they screened the bogus Roswell video. The *Daily Telegraph*, one of the few newspapers which spotted

the film as a fake from the outset, had the best riposte: 'If
you open your mind too much, your brain may fall out.'

Myths are not static: they grow and spread like bindweed.
It is no coincidence that the first great UFO scare began in
1947, a year after Winston Churchill warned that an 'iron
curtain' had fallen across Europe, nor that the craze intensified in the 1950s – through sci-fi films such as *The Thing from
Another World, It Came from Outer Space* and *The Day the Earth
Stood Still* – at a time when Americans were building fall-out
shelters and Senator Joe McCarthy was seeking out Reds.
Warnings of an 'alien threat' to the United States provided
useful, if often subliminal, propaganda for Cold Warriors.
Similarly, the new surfeit of UFOria in the 1980s and 1990s,
for which Whitley Strieber's *Communion* was merely the *hors
d'oeuvre*, fed the paranoia of right-wing conspiracy theorists
who believed that their own government had now fallen
under the control of sinister aliens. Whether the aliens in
question were Jews, Bilderbergers, members of the Council
on Foreign Relations or visitors from a planet of Zeta 2 Retic-
uli scarcely seemed to matter. By the early 1990s, American
UFO magazines would often mention 'black helicopters'
arriving at the scene of an alien abduction, which were alleged
to be either cunningly disguised flying saucers or military
surveillance vehicles; another recurring theme was the
'implanting' of microchips in the skulls of abductees. As
Elaine Showalter pointed out in her book *Hystories: Hysterical
Epidemics and Modern Culture*, the same black helicopters
'appear in the literature of right-wing militia and paramilitary
groups; they link abduction narratives and other forms of
paranoid conspiracy. Implants and microchips also turn up
in the thinking of Timothy McVeigh.' To vary an old cliché:
the fact that ufologists are paranoid doesn't mean that they

aren't out to get us. On 19 April 1995, McVeigh delivered a bomb which killed 168 people at the Murrah Federal Building in downtown Oklahoma City. It was, until 11 September 2001, the worst terrorist attack on US soil.

Surveying the apocalyptic stew of religion, politics and militarism cooked up by modern American cults, the May Day 1995 issue of *Time* magazine concluded that nothing like it had ever been seen before: 'America has bred its own sort of new political monster.' A lengthy report on America's 'lunatic fringe', published the weekend after the Oklahoma bombing, noted that the 'new literature' of these groups includes 'a cult trilogy about a fantastical masonic group called the Illuminati . . . there is a belief that this occult elite is preparing to coincide a push for world domination with the advent of the third millennium'.

Fantastical, perhaps, but hardly new: the Illuminati – so named because they wanted to illumine the world with rational enlightenment – were founded in 1776 by Adam Weishaupt, a law professor at the University of Ingoldstadt who believed that 'princes and nations will disappear without violence from the earth, the human race will become one family and the world the abode of reasonable men'. Generations of conspiracy theorists have fingered the Illuminati as the evil masterminds behind the French Revolution and the subsequent Terror, and although there isn't a shred of evidence to support the case this is regarded merely as confirmation of how devilishly clever the plotters were at covering their tracks. By the end of the eighteenth century, Gothic novelists were already using the Illuminati to represent all the sinister forces that were scheming to undermine civilisation – rather like the KGB in cold-war thrillers, or Aunt Agatha in the Jeeves and Wooster stories. As Walter Scott wrote in *Waverley*, no author was 'so obtuse as not to image forth a profligate abbot, an oppressive duke, a secret and mysterious association of Rosycrucians and Illuminati, with all their properties of black cowls, caverns, daggers, electric machines, trap-doors and dark lanterns'.

Sherlock Holmes used to remind Dr Watson that when you have eliminated the impossible 'whatever remains, however improbable, must be the truth'. But the whole point of conspiracy theory is that nothing is impossible. What remains is everything, and so everything must be true: Shakespeare's plays were written by Francis Bacon, aided by four monkeys with typewriters; or, as the veteran American presidential candidate Lyndon LaRouche has long maintained, the global cocaine-smuggling industry is controlled by the Queen of England. In the 1960s, some superstitious obsessives even found a sinister synchronicity between JFK's death and the assassination of President Lincoln 100 years earlier: both men were shot in the head, on a Friday, in the presence of their wives; their alleged murderers were both killed before coming to trial; both Lincoln and Kennedy were succeeded by Southern Democrats called Johnson. What did it all add up to? No one could say, but it must mean *something*. 'Only connect' is the guiding principle of these inexhaustible gumshoes. Like Casaubon, who thought that a lifetime of research would yield up the key to all mythologies, they are convinced that by doggedly collating every scrap of fact or speculation they will eventually reveal the hidden hand behind the French Revolution, the assassination of President Kennedy and the Roswell UFO cover-up.

In his classic study *The Paranoid Style in American Politics*, Professor Richard Hofstadter explained that when discussing the 'paranoia' of conspiracy theorists, 'I am not speaking in

a clinical sense, but borrowing a clinical term for other purposes. I use the term much as a historian of art might speak
of the baroque or the mannerist style. It is, above all, a way
of seeing the world and of expressing oneself.' These people
are artists, creating a picture as teeming and nightmarish as
a canvas by Hieronymus Bosch. And they are artists in an old
tradition: the 'cult trilogy' which American right-wing militias
of the 1990s found so persuasive was the latest in a genre
whose lineage can be traced back at least as far as the Marquis
of Grosse's *Horrid Mysteries* (1796), a story about 'a band of
desperate Illuminati [who] strive for world dominion'.

Almost every contemporary cult, however weird, has its
forebears, though the ancestry is seldom acknowledged. A
sense of history is a handicap to apocalyptic fanatics: how can
you announce with a straight face that the end of the world
is nigh if you remember that people have been saying the
same thing for centuries, and that they have always been
wrong? In the late twelfth century, for instance, the Italian
mystic Joachim of Fiore found a 'concealed message' in the
Book of Revelation which proved that the Third Age – the
culmination of history – would start some time between AD
1200 and 1260. In November 1260, as the final deadline
approached, thousands of his desperate disciples began
scourging themselves violently and continuously with iron
spikes, having been assured that this would precipitate the
final catastrophe and usher in an era of eternal peace and
idleness. (In the Third Age, according to Joachim, every day
would be Sunday.) God was unmoved by this orgy of self-
flagellation: life went on, and they were left to lick their
wounds.

Joachim's failure to crack the scriptural code has not
deterred others from having a go. In the early 1980s, Ameri-

can fundamentalists persuaded themselves that the 'scarlet coloured beast' with ten horns which appeared in the Book of Revelation was the European Community, as the accession of Greece in 1981 brought the number of member states to ten. This ingenious idea was rather spoilt when two more countries, Spain and Portugal, joined the EC in 1986 – whereupon the scripture-sleuths shifted their attention to a passage from Chapter 12 of Revelation: 'After that there appeared a great sign in heaven: a woman robed with the sun, beneath her feet the moon, and on her head a crown of *twelve stars.*' Dan Fuller, a doom-monger from Idaho, informed *Time* magazine in 1995 that the 'mark of the beast' actually referred to Bill Clinton's fiscal policy, and the president himself must therefore be the Antichrist.

Clinton was in distinguished company. In England during the seventeenth and eighteenth centuries, the 'beast' was usually identified as the Church of Rome. After Britain's informal alliance with the Catholic powers in 1792, however, patriotic millenarians had to find a new candidate. Dr Johnson's great friend Hester Thrale Piozzi was one of the first to record the change: 'Here is an odd Idea now, that the Beast of the Revelation is this French democracy.' Mrs Thrale, who had a limitless and entirely credulous passion for portents and prophecies, was struck by the fact that the new French government had succeeded that of Louis XVI, whose name in Latin 'makes the number 666 exactly'. She added, for good measure, that the French Convention consisted 'at one time of 666 people'. A few years later, she came up with another exciting discovery: Napoleon's name in Corsican was N'Appollione – 'the Destroyer' – and his titles, when translated into roman numbers, added up to 666.

Although the wild baroque imagery of Revelation naturally

draws the starry-eyed gaze of those who seek hidden supernatural messages, the Hebrew text of the Pentateuch (the
first five books of the Bible) also has a magical allure, not
least because every word of it was supposedly dictated by
God to Moses. In May 1997 the following announcement was
splashed across the front page of the *Daily Mail*: 'Computers
have discovered a hidden code in the Bible that predicts every
event in history. Start reading this fascinating series today.'
The book from which the series had been extracted – *The Bible
Code*, by a former TV journalist named Michael Drosnin – sold
more than a hundred thousand copies in the next fortnight,
largely thanks to the *Mail*'s hysterical hype. (Although in its
editorials the *Daily Mail* poses as the voice of robust common
sense, unbeguiled by political snake-oil merchants, its appetite
for mystical gibberish is gluttonous. During the 1990s, scarcely
a week went by without an enthralled feature on the Turin
Shroud, the Knights Templar, the Ark of the Covenant,
Nostradamus, Mayan prophecies or the lost city of Atlantis.
'We had a UFO series recently,' a *Mail* reporter told the
Guardian, 'with an Alien Hotline number which people could
ring. The phone was jammed by thousands of readers claiming they had been abducted by Martians.')

Drosnin's main revelation was that a distinguished Israeli
mathematician, Professor Eli Rips, had discovered a cipher
in the Pentateuch which predicted the assassinations of John
F. Kennedy, Anwar Sadat and Yitzhak Rabin, the rise of Adolf
Hitler and the plays of William Shakespeare. The news caused
great excitement on the Internet, where fundamentalist
Christians of every hue proclaimed that God's existence had
now been proven beyond reasonable doubt. If so, however,
the God in question must have been a very odd character.
According to Drosnin, he foretold the arrival of the Shoe-

maker-Levy comet thousands of years before it actually appeared – and he named it, twice, in the scriptures. But since Messrs Shoemaker and Levy discovered the comet only in 1993, why should the Lord give them the credit that was rightly his?

Several mathematicians pointed out that the code-cracking method of 'equidistant letter spacing' could be applied to any large slab of text with similar results (or indeed to individual words: select every third letter from 'generalization' and you find 'Nazi'). Drosnin was unimpressed. 'When my critics find a message about the assassination of a prime minister encrypted in *Moby Dick*, I'll believe them,' he told *Newsweek*. Brendan McKay of the Australian National University took up the challenge: subjecting Melville's novel to the Drosnin technique, he elicited the phrase I GANDHI THE BLOODY DEED – obviously a reference to the assassination of Indira Gandhi, the Indian prime minister, in October 1984. More damning still was a statement issued by Professor Rips, the man who had supposedly endorsed *The Bible Code*: 'I do not support Mr Drosnin's work on the codes, or the conclusions he derives. The book gives the impression that I have done joint work with Mr Drosnin. This is not true . . . All attempts to extract messages from Torah codes, or to make predictions based on them, are futile and of no value. This is not only my own opinion, but the opinion of every scientist who has been involved in serious codes research.'

In short, even Michael Drosnin's 'expert source' admitted that the *Daily Mail* – and the thousands of customers who propelled his book to the top of the 'non-fiction' bestseller list – had been sold a pup. Yet the *Mail* returned to the story later that summer, on Saturday 30 August: 'BIBLE CODE: THE PROOF. When the *Mail* revealed evidence that all the major events in world history were encoded in the Bible, it caused an international sensation. Did the words of God really predict the rise of the Nazis . . . the atom bomb . . . the Gulf War? Now one of the scientists who cracked the code tells just how it was done . . . Start reading it on Monday – only in the *Daily Mail*.' Alas! Monday's edition of the paper carried a brief update: 'Due to pressure of space the new Bible Code series has been held over.' The divine author of the Pentateuch, who allegedly foresaw all the major events in history, had not known that on Sunday 31 August 1997 Princess Diana would die in a car crash.

Nor had anyone else, of course. Three weeks earlier, when the princess and her friend Dodi Fayed visited a soothsayer in Derbyshire, the *Mail* marked the occasion by commissioning two professional psychics to assess their romantic prospects. 'They'll marry, I'm sure of it,' wrote Jim Chivers. 'The wedding will take place in about a year's time and I think they'll be very happy.' Craig Hamilton-Parker, who conjured up visions of the future by 'allowing his mind to float', disagreed. 'The relationship will fizzle out soon after Christmas. It will be Diana who walks away from it, but Dodi won't give a damn when she does. The feeling will be mutual. In the meantime, though, they'll have some fun. I can see them going on a skiing holiday together.' Nine months after the accident, the *Mail* serialised a book by Rita Rogers, the Derbyshire psychic whose 'extraordinary powers' had so impressed Diana and Dodi. She disclosed that at her first meeting with Dodi Fayed the previous summer she immediately had 'a feeling of danger': she saw a black Mercedes and a tunnel, and 'felt there was a connection with France'. Extraordinary indeed: only the most mean-spirited sceptic could have wished for some sort of corroborative evidence, such as a letter from Fayed thanking Rogers for the warning about driving through French tunnels. Meanwhile, after two instalments of the book, the *Mail* printed a small apology: 'Due to pressure of space, the third part of our serialisation of psychic Rita Rogers's book was held out of Saturday's paper.' Yet again, one of the *Mail*'s crystal-ball readings had been postponed because of unforeseen circumstances.

Viewed from a safe distance, mysticism can seem quaintly amusing, even endearing: look at the fondness with which Marxist historians such as Christopher Hill and Eric Hobsbawm have depicted the Ranters, Muggletonians, Fifth Monarchists and other English cults that flourished in the 1650s, praising them for their 'generosity of emotion' and 'burning confidence in a new world'. True, these zealots may have spouted a lot of tosh about the Second Coming and the Antichrist – the Fifth Monarchists thought the world would end in 1666 (one thousand plus the number of the beast) and were prepared to 'resort to political action and, in the case of a minority, even violence' to attain the millennium, rather like some American cults of the 1990s – but they also yearned for a society with no war, no private property and no king except Jesus. Thanks to their 'revolutionary consciousness', the chiliastic sects of the seventeenth century were treated by twentieth-century left-wingers as a progressive force. Writing of his beloved Ranters, Christopher Hill warned fellow-historians 'to avoid the loaded phrase "lunatic fringe", since lunacy, like beauty, may be in the eye of the beholder ... and the "lunatic" may in some sense be saner than the society which rejects him'. Hobsbawm added that 'millenarians can ... readily exchange the primitive costume in which they dress their aspirations for the modern costume of Socialist and Communist politics'.

Yet there was little evidence of socialism among the Armageddon-awaiting cults of the 1990s, many of whom exchanged the primitive costume for army fatigues and AK-47s. Even milder New Age millenarians, who preferred cuddly toys to Great Beasts, were uniformly conservative. One of the more seemingly benign manifestations of eschatological craziness was the sudden reappearance of angels, heralded by Joan Wester Anderson's *Where Angels Walk* (1994), which sold more than half a million copies in the United States. In 1990 Malcolm Godwin had written a book with the gloomy title *Angels: An Endangered Species*, but only four years later the heavenly host was flourishing. One of Anderson's 'true stories' concerned a young woman who became nervous while walking through a park in Sydney, Australia, after dark. Suddenly she saw a large white Alsatian dog trotting along beside her. She tried to shoo it away, but without success; it accompanied her all the way to the other side of the park. Afterwards, the woman concluded that it must have been a guardian angel, sent to protect her from muggers: 'There was just no other explanation for his arrival, his behaviour.' William and Virginia Jackson once drove from Las Vegas to El Paso through Death Valley – and only later discovered that their car's fan belt hadn't been working. 'How had they managed to cross a treacherous desert without a vital piece of engine equipment? Virginia believes they were protected by spiritual beings.' Anderson's book cited dozens of instances of drivers having their engines fixed by celestial motor mechanics who disappeared as mysteriously as they arrived.

As with so much harmless nonsense, however, the angel-mania had a political sub-text. No less an expert than Billy Graham, in his book *Angels: God's Secret Agents*, noted that 'UFOs are astonishingly angel-like in some of their reported appearances.' But whereas the crews of flying saucers were thought by American fundamentalists to be servants of Lucifer, the fallen angel, the white-clad creatures in Joan Wester Anderson's stories operated a zero-tolerance policy on crime. An angel would help drivers swerve to avoid oncoming traffic only if they observed the speed limit. 'Angelic protection never seems to occur when people are deliberately breaking the laws of society,' she warned. But as long as we served God and kept to 30 m.p.h. in built-up areas, they would come to our aid if required.

Since angels cost the taxpayer nothing and are always on call, the state need not spend billions on social security, health care and unemployment benefit: God will provide. This message was made explicit in another collection of seraphim-sightings, H. C. Moolenburgh's *A Handbook of Angels*. 'The welfare state has made "spiritual lazybones" of us all,' Dr Moolenburgh lamented, since those of us accustomed to 'being served our every wish' have no incentive to pray. If we break free of our welfare dependence, however, 'then God sends his servants and man is helped in the most remarkable ways'.

6

With God on our side

> Take up the White Man's burden –
>   Ye dare not stoop to less –
> Nor call too loud on Freedom
>   To cloak your weariness;
> By all ye cry and whisper,
>   By all ye leave or do,
> The silent, sullen peoples
>   Shall weigh your Gods and you.
>
> RUDYARD KIPLING 1899

God arrived in America with the *Mayflower*, and has been a permanent resident ever since. The words of the first US president are displayed on a monument in New York's Washington Square: 'We must raise a standard to which the wise and the honest can repair. The event is in the hands of God.' Nevertheless, the self-evident truths of the American constitution – which guaranteed not only freedom of religion but also freedom *from* religion – also represented a defiant challenge to the Divine Right of Kings. As the historian Frances Stonor Saunders points out, it was only during the Cold War that 'America discovered how useful the invocation of the highest hosanna could be'. President Truman announced that 'the issue which confronts the world today' – tyranny versus freedom – was also a crusade against atheism, since 'Communism denies the very existence of God'. Congress added the words 'one nation under God' to the pledge of allegiance in 1954; 'In God we trust' became the nation's official motto two years later. No wonder the inquisitorial antics of Senator Joe McCarthy were so often described as a witch-hunt. The preacher Billy Graham warned that 'Communism is inspired, directed and motivated by the Devil himself . . . Will we turn to the left-wingers and atheists, or will we turn to the right and embrace the cross?' Another hot-gospeller, Richard Wurmbrand, wrote *The Answer to Moscow's Bible* and *Was Karl Marx a Satanist?*

This theme was replayed *fortissimo* during the presidency of Ronald Reagan. As long ago as 1961 Reagan had addressed a rally of Dr Fred Schwarz's Christian Anti-Communist Crusade, and in a speech on behalf of Barry Goldwater three years later he criticised politicians who advocated an 'accommodation' with the Soviet Union: 'We are being asked to buy our safety from the threat of the Bomb by selling into permanent slavery our fellow human beings enslaved behind the Iron Curtain . . . If we are to believe that nothing is worth the dying, when did this begin? Should Moses have told the children of Israel to live in slavery rather than dare the wilderness? Should Christ have refused the Cross?' When challenging Gerald Ford for the Republican nomination in 1976, he summarised his foreign policy thus: 'Honestly, openly, and with firm conviction, we shall go forward as a united people to forge a lasting peace in the world based upon our deep belief in the rights of man, the rule of law, and guidance by the hand of God.' In the election of 1980 even Southern evangelical voters deserted President Carter, although in most ways he reflected their background far more closely than Reagan. 'Jimmy Carter was more devout by ordinary standards (like church attendance), better acquainted with the Bible, far more active in church affairs (like doing missionary work), more willing to talk about his born-again experience,' Garry Wills wrote. 'Despite all these discrete points of contact between his experience and theirs, religious voters found that Carter lacked the higher confidence in man, man's products, and America. He talked of limits and self-denial, of tendencies toward aggression, even in a sacred or "saved" nation like America. He believed in original sin.'

For Reagan, by contrast, there had been no Fall of Man, no permanent exile from Eden. 'Our optimism has once again been turned loose,' he said during the 1980 campaign. 'And all of us recognise that these people who keep talking about the age of limits are really talking about their own limitation, not America's.' It was while addressing the National Association of Evangelicals in 1983 that he first characterised the Soviet Union as an evil empire. 'Let us pray for those who live in that totalitarian darkness, pray that they will discover the joy of knowing God. But, until they do, let us be aware that . . . they are the focus of evil in the modern world.' Paradise could be regained only if the Christian soldiers of the 'moral majority' marched onward as to war: 'I believe that Communism is another sad, bizarre chapter in human history whose last pages are even now being written.' Inspired by his millenarian rhetoric, some born-again fundamentalists came to believe that the 'mark of the beast' was almost certainly the wine-coloured birthmark on Mikhail Gorbachev's forehead.

The Moral Majority, founded by the TV evangelist Jerry

Falwell, canvassed energetically for Ronald Reagan in the 1980 campaign, and thereafter enjoyed the priceless Washington gift of 'access' to the Oval Office. In February 1985, when the president declined an invitation to address the National Religious Broadcasters, one phone call from Falwell was enough to change his mind; to prove his penitence, Reagan promised a speech from Vice-President George Bush as well. On the home front, nevertheless, Reagan often disappointed his chiliastic cheerleaders: he did not outlaw abortion or end the prohibition on prayer in schools. The Christian right consoled itself by fighting the good fight abroad, offering spiritual and financial support to Reagan's anti-Communist footsoldiers in Central and South America. The Rev. Pat Robertson's Christian Broadcasting Network raised several million dollars for the Nicaraguan Contras (guerrillas opposed to the Sandinista regime), and offered hosannas to the outstandingly brutal Guatemalan despot General Rios Montt, a Pentecostal Christian who justified his massacres of tribespeople by maintaining that they were agents of the devil. (Further afield, Robertson befriended the legendarily corrupt Mobutu Sese Seko of Zaire and was rewarded with valuable diamond-mining concessions – proof, as if any were needed, that God and Mammon could coexist quite happily.)

Many Reaganite evangelists were also stalwart defenders of Israel, thus seemingly ditching the Christian conservative tradition represented by figures such as Father Charles Coughlin of Detroit, the 'radio priest' whose anti-semitic rants in the 1930s had reached an audience of 30 million listeners. Soon after founding the Moral Majority in 1979, the Rev. Jerry Falwell said that 'whoever stands against Israel stands against God'. But the shift to philo-semitism was more apparent than real. In Falwell's pre-millennialist creed, the rebuilding of the nation of Israel was a necessary precondition for the mass conversion of Jews to Christianity that would coincide with the Second Coming.

For those religious reactionaries who lacked Falwell's eschatological enthusiasm, it was business as usual. On the eve of the 1991 Gulf War, the Catholic populist Pat Buchanan complained that 'kids with names like McAllister, Murphy, Gonzalez and Leroy Brown' would be fighting and dying at the behest of the Israeli defence ministry 'and its amen corner in the United States'. Four members of the amen corner were named: Henry Kissinger, Richard Perle and the journalists A. M. Rosenthal and Charles Krauthammer. All were Jewish. Why did Buchanan neglect to mention Alexander Haig, or George F. Will, or other public figures of an equally hawkish temperament who happened to be Christians? Even the right-wing editor William F. Buckley, a political soulmate, observed with distaste that 'there is no way to read that sentence without concluding that Pat Buchanan was suggesting that American Jews manage to avoid personal military exposure even while advancing military policies they (uniquely?) engineer'. Jewish commentators heard in Buchanan's rhetoric a direct echo of Father Coughlin's pre-war diatribes against the influence of 'godless capitalists, the Jews, communists, international bankers and plutocrats' on American foreign policy – and of Charles Lindbergh, the pro-fascist aviator, who in 1941 had announced that 'the three most important groups who have been pressing this country to war are the British, the Jewish and the Roosevelt Administration'.

Straightforward anti-semitism may have limited appeal in the United States, but there is a far more potent and resonant sub-text to these outbursts: they play on the hostility of 'ordinary folks' to sophisticated metropolitans – Wall Street dealers, Hollywood producers, Washington fixers. To much of the outside world, Manhattan may seem the epitome of American energy and pluralism; but for many in the Midwest and deep South it is a latter-day Sodom or Gomorrah, a godless carnival of feminism, homosexuality, hedonism and ill-gotten wealth. The Christian right had no quarrel with, say, Hassidic Jewry; the real divide which they sought to define and exacerbate was between 'secular' citizens (including reform Jews, liberal Catholics, mainstream Protestants) and fundamentalists of any and every creed – including both Judaism and Islam.

One test of allegiance for the religious right was the fatwa against Salman Rushdie, pronounced by the Ayatollah Khomeini on St Valentine's Day, 1989. The United States is, at least ostensibly, a polity so devoted to free speech that the American Civil Liberties Union has on occasion gone to court to uphold the right of neo-Nazis to expound their ideas. Besides, the death-sentence against Rushdie had been promulgated by a government which demonised the US as 'the great Satan' and had held dozens of Americans captive after the Islamic revolution of 1979. The issue ought to have been, in American parlance, a no-brainer. Yet Pat Buchanan sprang to the barricades on the Ayatollah's side without hesitation, damning *The Satanic Verses* as 'a blasphemous assault on the faith of hundreds of millions'. President George H. W. Bush's only comment on the fatwa was that Iran would be held responsible 'should any action be taken against American interests', implying that America no longer had any general interest in defending freedom of expression.

Even in England, where ostentatious religious zeal is generally regarded as bad form, the international solidarity of spiritual chieftains proved stronger than loyalty to a compatriot under threat of murder. 'The book contained an outrageous slur on the Prophet [Mohammed] and so was damaging to the reputation of the faith,' said George Carey, an evangelical dimwit who had been appointed Archbishop of Canterbury by Margaret Thatcher because she deduced from the title of his book *The Church in the Market Place* that he must be economically sound. 'I well understand the devout Muslims' reaction, wounded by [an attack on] what they hold most dear and would themselves die for.' Carey offered no word of protest against the fatwa, nor any recognition that the essential point was not the preparedness of Muslims to die for their beliefs but the preparedness to kill.

Those defenders of Rushdie who expressed shock and surprise at this *trahison des clercs* had, perhaps, not been paying enough attention. Reagan and Oliver North happily sold arms to the Ayatollahs and used the proceeds to fund the Contras' war in Nicaragua, even though the Sandinista regime included several Catholic priests. Reactionary Islam was clearly preferable to left-wing Christianity – and of course *vastly* preferable to secular atheism. Hence Margaret Thatcher's admiration for the mujahedin in Afghanistan, and the unwillingness of Tory ministers and Archbishop Carey to condemn the fatwa against Rushdie.

'Not the least fundamental of divisions among theories of society', R. H. Tawney wrote in *Religion and the Rise of Capitalism*, 'is between those which regard the world of human affairs as self-contained, and those which appeal to a supernatural criterion. Modern social theory, like modern political theory, developed only when society was given a naturalistic instead of religious explanation.' In which case modern social and political theories would now seem to be dead. Even after

11 September 2001, Tony Blair claimed that religion was the solution and not the problem since 'Jews, Muslims and Christians are all children of Abraham' – unaware that the example of Abraham had also inspired Mohammed Atta, chief hijacker of one of the planes that shattered the New York skyline. In his last will and testament, after a series of grimly hilarious instructions for the organisers of his funeral ('women should neither be present at my burial nor at any later date should visit my grave . . . Those who touch my body in the area of my genitalia should wear gloves so that I remain undisturbed in that region'), Atta concluded with the wish that 'my family and anyone who reads what is written here is fearful of the almighty God, and does not allow himself to be distracted in life. In remembrance of me, they should act according to the example of Abraham who, as a good Muslim, offered his son to die.' Abraham was no more a Muslim than he was a fan of *The Simpsons*, of course, but he is indeed regarded as a common ancestor by Jews, Christians and Muslims alike. 'It is only the civilised who would be ashamed to have him in their family,' Nick Cohen wrote in the *Observer*. 'Abraham's readiness to obey the order of a jealous, not to say psychopathic, God to "take now thy son, thine only son Isaac, whom thou lovest, and get thee into the land of Moriah; and offer him there for a burnt offering" is divine justification for murderous servility. A servant who will slaughter his son on the whim of the Lord will do anything.'

In 1991, after the swift rout of Iraqi forces in the Gulf War, General Colin Powell had complained: 'I'm running out of demons. I'm running out of villains.' By the time replacements arrived in 2001, Powell was a senior member of George Bush Junior's administration prosecuting the 'war on terrorism'. There had been plenty of terrorism in the 1970s (not least in Northern Ireland, where the Provisional IRA was partly bankrolled by donations from Irish Americans), but even in the Middle East it had been mainly secular and political: the Public Enemy Number One was Carlos the Jackal, a boozy playboy in a cravat. Osama Bin Laden, by contrast, was manifestly not an atheist, still less a Communist. A God-fearing, teetotal, anti-gay traditionalist who believed that a woman's place was in the home and crime should be punished severely – what kind of enemy was this?

7

Us and them

When I was coming up, it was a dangerous world, and we knew exactly who the they were. It was us versus them, and it was clear who them was. Today, we are not so sure who the they are, but we know they're there.

Speech by GEORGE W. BUSH in Council Bluffs, Iowa,
21 January 2000

'You have to worry: has the world slipped off its hinges?' the *New York Times* columnist Russell Baker wrote in 1989. 'Where can we look for assurance that it's still the same reliably inevitable old world we loved to hate?' Baker, one of America's wisest political satirists, may have been kidding; but he was kidding on the level, reflecting what *Newsweek*, later that summer, called 'the general unease' at the disappearance of Cold War attitudes. Academic experts from the modish new discipline of 'political psychology' were much in demand over the next couple of years to explain the lack of rejoicing. 'There is no "us" without there being a corresponding "them" to oppose,' said Professor Howard Stein, editor of the *Journal of Psychoanalytic Anthropology*. 'We need the bad guys, the people who embody all that stuff we want to get rid of – our greed, anger, avarice.' Vamik Volkan, a sometime president of the International Society of Political Psychology, published a book called *The Need to Have Enemies and Allies*. At a seminar on the New World Order hosted by the American Psychiatric Association, Stein argued that with the crumbling of Communism 'we've had a hard time finding an enemy to glom onto'. He believed that politically, as well as personally, 'you hate somebody who embodies what you most envy' (though how this applied to the decades of Soviet-hating was not divulged), and therefore 'the next evil empire is going to be our economic competitor, Japan'.

The idea seemed plausible enough. A Gallup poll conducted by the Chicago Council on Foreign Relations in 1990 found that 60 per cent of respondents regarded Japanese economic power as the 'critical threat' to American interests over the next decade – almost twice the 33 per cent who cited the Russian military menace. The scare was fanned by *The Coming War with Japan*, a bestseller in both Washington and Tokyo, in which the right-wing academics George Friedman and Meredith Lombard argued that competition for Pacific markets would almost certainly end in military combat. A CIA-sponsored report, leaked in June 1991, described the Japanese in terms pillaged from the anti-semitic lexicon – 'creatures of an ageless, amoral, manipulative and controlling culture' who had 'a shared national vision for world economic domination'. Although some members of congress suspected that the CIA was trying to replace the Red Peril with the Yellow Peril merely to avoid budget cuts, many officials in Washington privately agreed with the agency's assessment that Japan was now the great menace to American national security. The hysteria crossed the Atlantic later that month, when the French prime minister Edith Cresson characterised the

Japanese as 'yellow dwarfs who sit up all night thinking of ways to screw the Americans and the Europeans'. (Cresson, it should be said, had quite a talent for giving offence: she also described her Cabinet colleagues as 'creeps' and announced that one Englishman in four was homosexual, a statistic inferred from the fact that no one wolf-whistled her in the streets of London. 'You cannot imagine it in the history of France,' she wailed. 'Frenchmen are much more interested in women; Anglo-Saxon men are not, and this is a problem that needs analysis.')

By the end of 1991, with election primaries looming in the United States, American politicians of all parties were blaming unfair Japanese competition for the recession at home: Virginia governor Douglas Wilder adopted the campaign slogan 'Put America First'; Senator Tom Harkin delighted an audience of labour activists in Maine by boasting that 'I'm proud of being accused of being a protectionist!' Never mind that Japan's average tariff on industrial products – 2.6 per cent – was actually *lower* than the US average, of 3 per cent; nor that World Bank figures showed Japanese and American non-tariff barriers to be roughly equal. Why let facts intrude on the hustings? Soon after announcing his intention of challenging President Bush for the Republican presidential nomination, the hoarse right-wing demagogue Pat Buchanan was asked about his attitude to Japan by a reporter from a Tokyo newspaper. 'You and I may be friends,' Buchanan replied, 'but we're not going to tolerate dumping of computer chips, which take out a couple of American industries, and then sudden shortages . . . This is the kind of stuff that is not going to go on. We're going to play hardball with you. If we think that you folks are going for economic hegemony in the twenty-first century . . . we Americans have not yet begun to fight.'

Another of Bush's Republican rivals, the former Ku Klux Klansman David Duke, was even blunter: 'I'm from Louisiana. We produce rice. We must go to the Japanese and say, "You no buy our rice, we no buy your cars."' ('Duke later denied his remarks were a slur on the Japanese,' a deadpan report in the *Chicago Tribune* added.)

Meanwhile, in California, a prominent local official fired a rhetorical fusillade at a ceremony to mark the fiftieth anniversary of the attack on Pearl Harbor. 'I'm getting sick and tired of these Japs trying to take this country over,' yelled James Bucher, chairman of the Imperial County board of supervisors. 'They'll do it one way or the other . . . through their sneak attacks or through their dollars. It's about time this country wakes up and puts this country back on its feet. If we rely totally on these Japs we're going to pay the price. We've already paid the price and I'm not willing to pay it a second time.' When the Japanese-American Citizens' League demanded an apology Bucher tried to clarify his remarks by saying that the insults were directed not at Americans of Japanese descent but at 'the damn Japs as a nation'. Delta Press Ltd, an Arkansas company, commemorated the Pearl Harbor anniversary by placing advertisements in *USA Today* for a 'revenge t-shirt' in red, white and blue, which carried a picture of a mushroom cloud with the words: 'Made in America, Tested in Japan'. The owner of Delta Press, Billy Blann, seemed surprised by all the fuss. 'It really is a joke, OK?' he told the *Los Angeles Times*. 'All I did was put something in print that's behind every door in America.'

As soon became obvious, however, the damn Japs were unable to live up to their billing as bogeymen. While Americans prospered in the 1990s, Japan's economy was floored by its sumo-sized debts: by the end of the decade, shares on the Tokyo stock exchange had lost three-quarters of their value, thousands of companies were bankrupt and the *Los Angeles Times* was duly recording 'a national epidemic of indifference toward our closest Asian ally ... American interest in Japan is the lowest it has been in two decades.' In the absence of the Yellow Peril, American politicians were obliged to exhume older and more dependable ogres such as Saddam Hussein, or even occasionally that barmy old crowd-pleaser Colonel Gadafy. 'It is human to hate,' Samuel Huntington explained, with apparent relish. 'For self-affirmation and motivation people need enemies: competitors in business, rivals in achievement, opponents in politics ... The resolution of one conflict and the disappearance of one enemy generate personal, social and political forces that give rise to new ones.'

A visiting Martian – or indeed any intelligent child – might reasonably wonder why the leaders of the most powerful nation ever to bestride the globe should be so jumpy and insecure, especially since the only serious threat to its hegemony had disappeared with the collapse of the Soviet Union. 'It's a cycle that has repeated itself in American politics for centuries, and it's in direct relation to how badly off people are economically,' Robert Beckel, a Democratic Party consultant, suggested in November 1991. 'Right now, the American voter is being driven by nothing but fear.' True enough, up to a point: financial anxiety would account for the foamy tide of protectionism on which many candidates surfed during the 1992 presidential campaign. But it does not begin to explain why some of the most economically insignificant republics on the planet were periodically promoted to head the list of America's Most Wanted.

Despite the vapourings of political psychologists, there is

no reason to suppose that people cannot enjoy life, liberty and the pursuit of happiness without having an enemy 'to glom onto'. However, there are powerful interests in the United States which do require a constant supply of threats and villains – sometimes real, to be sure, but often exaggerated or simply invented. (Hence the resonance of the film *Wag the Dog*.) These interests are usually known as 'the military–industrial complex'. One might imagine that this shorthand was invented by peaceniks or left-wing malcontents: that was also the assumption of Ronald Reagan, who in his 1985 State of the Union speech asked congress to sanction a huge budget for his two pet projects, the MX missile and the 'Star Wars' Strategic Defence Initiative. 'We must not relax our efforts to restore military strength,' he said. 'You know, we only have a military–industrial complex until a time of danger; and then it becomes the arsenal of democracy. Spending for defence is investing in things that are priceless: peace and freedom.' Yet the man who first used the phrase was President Dwight D. Eisenhower, a four-star general and war hero. 'This conjunction of an immense military establishment and a large arms industry is new in the American experience,' he warned in a farewell speech on 17 January 1961, four days before handing over the White House to John F. Kennedy. 'The total influence – economic, political, even spiritual – is felt in every statehouse ... In the councils of government, we must guard against the acquisition of unwarranted influence, whether sought or unsought, by the military–industrial complex.' Scarcely anyone heeded him; least of all President Kennedy, who had repeatedly attacked the Republicans for allowing a 'missile gap' to develop between the Soviet Union and the USA. (There was indeed a gap – but it was overwhelmingly in America's favour.)

In the draft of his valedictory speech Eisenhower referred to the 'military–industrial–congressional complex', but he removed the third adjective because it was 'not fitting . . . for a President to criticise Congress'. Admirably courteous of him, no doubt, yet the unexpurgated phrase makes far more sense. Defence contractors' success in forcing up the military budget depends on politicians who have debts to pay and constituents to placate. During the 2000 election cycle, the four biggest arms manufacturers invested more than $11 million in campaign contributions; far more important, however, is the leverage they exert when deciding where to spend the taxpayers' bounty which congress has so generously bestowed upon them. Republicans and right-wing Democrats who are instinctively mistrustful of publicly financed welfare programmes will do almost anything to protect and nurture this particular welfare scam from the laws of the market. Between 1978 and 1998, for instance, the US Air Force requested five Lockheed Martin C-130 transport aircraft; but members of congress, several of whom had been employed by Lockheed Martin as consultants, approved funding for the purchase of no fewer than 256 C-130s. At this rate, as Senator John McCain pointed out, there would eventually be enough of these surplus planes to park one in every schoolyard in America.

US procurement policy is so flabbergastingly corrupt, and so wholly divorced from questions of military requirement or operational efficiency, that only a satirist could really do justice to it. Even the men clinging to the pork-barrel regard it as a joke. When the Senate Republican leader Trent Lott visited Georgia in 1999 to campaign for his friend Mack Mattingly, a former senator attempting to regain his seat, he told voters that if they chose 'good old Mack' he would personally ensure that production of the F-22 fighter (a notorious cash-guzzler, with a price-tag of $200 million per plane) remained at Lockheed's local plant; if they elected a Democrat, production might be transferred to Lott's own state of Mississippi. As the defence analyst William Hartung noted: 'Given Lott's proclivity for shovelling defence dollars to his own state for everything from a $1.5 billion Marine helicopter carrier to a space-based laser project, it took a moment for Georgians to realise that this was a joke. The irony of Lott's remark was heightened by the fact that Mattingly had just completed a stint as paid lobbyist for Lockheed Martin.'

Just occasionally, someone with the courage of his *laissez-faire* convictions tries to halt the boondoggle. As long ago as 1989, George H. W. Bush's defence secretary Dick Cheney horrified the military–industrial complex by scrapping Boeing's V-22 Osprey, an accident-prone flying machine – half-aeroplane, half-helicopter – which Boeing had been striving to perfect for several years with no visible success. Since Boeing had cunningly spread work on Osprey around twenty states, however, almost half the legislators on Capitol Hill had a direct local interest in saving the project. By the time the defence budget emerged from congress, Osprey had been reinstated.

Cheney learned his lesson: thirteen years later, as vice-president to George Bush Junior, he supported a defence budget that included a further $2 billion for the Osprey – which was *still* in its 'experimental stage' and had been described in a Pentagon report as 'not operationally sustainable'. (Over the previous decade four more prototypes had crashed in trials, killing thirty marines.) The same procurement estimates included an extra billion dollars for the army's Comanche helicopter, which was 'initiated' in 1983 but had not yet gone into production by 2002 despite an investment of $48.1 billion. One senior Pentagon analyst was prompted to wonder if 'this money can be followed and frozen by law enforcement as part of the war on terrorism, as the programme is clearly as much a threat to the US military as any marauding armed force in the world'.

President George W. Bush appeared at the Elgin air force base in Florida on 4 February 2002, clad in a leather bomber jacket, to announce his plan for a huge hike in military spending over the next five years. The proposed *increase* for 2003 alone – $48 billion – was itself higher than the entire defence budget of the United Kingdom, and the overall annual figure of $396 billion would be more than the combined total of the next fifteen highest-spending countries, including Russia and China. As retired Admiral Eugene Carroll commented: 'For 45 years of the Cold War, we were in an arms race with the Soviet Union. Now it appears we're in an arms race with ourselves.'

Many beneficiaries of the spending spree had no discernible connection with the war against terrorism. Almost $500 million was allocated to the Crusader self-propelled artillery system (cost so far: $9 billion), an ungainly 42-ton monster which was designed for fighting land battles against the Soviet Union and is so big that not even the most capacious cargo plane in the military fleet can actually carry it. Yet Bush's speech, delivered against a backdrop of F-15 and F-16 fighter planes, was salted and peppered with topical references to 'a new security environment'. For the American defence industry, which had spent the past decade fretfully calculating the consequences of a 'peace dividend', the identification of Islamic terrorism as the latest globe-threatening force was very good news indeed.

Our visiting Martian might note, with some puzzlement, a certain capriciousness in the official demonology. After the seizure of the US embassy in Tehran, in November 1979, Iran was public enemy number one; only a few years later, emissaries from Washington were selling arms to the Iranian mullahs and using the proceeds to finance a guerrilla war against the new adversary-in-chief, the Sandinistas of Nicaragua – even while both Britain and the United States were helping Saddam Hussein prosecute his own battles against the Iranians. Washington applauded Saddam's invasion of Iran in September 1980, which precipitated a decade of war, yet when he tried the same trick in Kuwait ten years later the full might of Nato was mobilised against 'the Hitler of the Gulf'.

Thus is the great game of Realpolitik played. Perhaps the most eloquent summary of its rules can be found in the report of the Pike Commission, which investigated covert intervention by the US in Iran and Iraq during the 1970s. The committee members found that in 1972 Henry Kissinger and Richard Nixon had told the Shah of Iran that Iraq was upsetting the 'balance of power' in the Gulf, and that this could best be remedied by exhorting the Kurds in northern Iraq to revolt against the Baathist regime. As the Pike report revealed: 'Documents in the committee's possession clearly show that the President, Dr Kissinger and the foreign head of state [the Shah] hoped that our clients [the Kurds] would not prevail. They preferred instead that the insurgents simply continue a level of hostilities sufficient to sap the resources of our ally's neighbouring country [Iraq]. This policy was not imparted to our clients, who were encouraged to continue fighting.' But it was imparted to Saddam Hussein, then the deputy leader in Baghdad, who eventually took the hint. He and the Shah signed a treaty in 1975 ending their border dispute and restoring the region's 'balance': on the very same day Washington abruptly cut off aid to the Kurds, and Saddam began his long *Blitzkrieg* against Kurdistan.

Henry Kissinger and other modern heirs to the tradition of Palmerston and Metternich like to repeat the old nineteenth-century dictum that great states have no permanent friends or principles, merely permanent interests. They maintain that this deadly cynicism – which they prefer to regard as worldly-wise realism – can be justified both practically and morally. It is idealism that destroys, as in the Gulag or Pol Pot's killing fields; the practitioners of Realpolitik or *raison d'état*, with their constant 'tilts' and 'shifts', may seem devious or even downright wicked to the untutored eye, yet by preserving a geostrategic equilibrium they are the true (if unacknowledged) peacemakers. The British foreign secretary Douglas Hurd proffered a fine example of this self-congratulatory style in April 1993, when explaining why the arms embargo against Bosnia should not be lifted: although 'at first sight it seems an act of justice', he said, in practice it would create a 'level killing field'.

To which one can only reply with Tacitus' resonant line: where they make a desert, they call it peace. The inference to be drawn from Hurd's logic was that he preferred an uneven killing field, on which Slobodan Milošević provided the Bosnian Serbs with troops and weapons while the Bosnian government had to make do with whatever equipment it could buy on the black market or grab from captured enemy soldiers. Confirming this interpretation, Hurd said that allowing the Bosnians to defend themselves would 'only prolong the fighting'. Yet the idea that lives are saved by such lofty pragmatism is not borne out by the record. The Iraqi

Kurds, who endured massacres galore after being abandoned by the Americans in 1991, might not agree that Washington's wily manoeuvring was essentially benign; nor, one guesses, would the dependants of the *half-million* corpses created by the Iran–Iraq War. The fruit of American Realpolitik in the region over recent decades has been war, and the seeds of future war – and further setbacks for the cause of secularism and democracy.

There is a useful American word for this – 'blowback', a term coined by the CIA to describe the unintended and usually disastrous consequences of the agency's activities. It was first used soon after the 1953 coup in Iran, secretly orchestrated by the CIA, which toppled Mohammed Mossadegh. (The blowback from this particular 'covert operation' was a quarter-century of flamboyant tyranny and increasingly brutal repression by the Shah, which in turn created the conditions for the Ayatollah Khomeini's triumphant return – and the subsequent seizure of American hostages.) Perhaps the most sublime instance of blowback was the despatch of US troops to Panama by President George Bush in 1989, for the sole purpose of arresting President Manuel Noriega and hauling him off to a Florida courtroom on charges of racketeering and drug-running. While awaiting trial, Noriega was approached by American prosecutors with an extraordinary plea-bargain: he could use cash from his foreign bank accounts (which had been frozen) to hire the best lawyers that dollars could buy, if in return he agreed not to mention that he had been on the payroll of the CIA since the 1970s. As they explained, rather unnecessarily, such an admission could be embarrassing, not least because the director of the CIA at the time of Noriega's recruitment, in the days of the Ford administration, had been a certain George Bush – who, as president, was now pursuing a 'war on drugs'. As R. M. Koster and Guillermo Sanchez Bourbon write in their lively, angry book *In the Time of the Tyrants: Panama 1968–89*:

> The very concept of a war on drugs became meaningless with Black Eagle and Supermarket, the CIA operations whereby weapons were secretly supplied to the Contras [in Nicaragua] in contravention of congressional strictures. In Black Eagle, Israeli stocks of captured PLO weapons were moved from Texas to Central America by means of Noriega's network of hidden airstrips . . . Instantly grasping that drug pilots would be sitting in the cockpits of empty planes for the return flights, Noriega alertly filled the void by arranging for them to carry narcotics. The CIA, of course, was buying the gas, as well as protecting the whole operation against the impious meddling of law-enforcement organisations, which put the US government in the cocaine trade – that is, in the war against drugs but on the wrong side.

Incidentally, the American invasion of Panama in 1989 was named Operation Just Cause. No irony was intended.

Noriega's entrepreneurial flair compels a certain admiration. Nor should one overlook the CIA's ingenuity in devising a scheme whereby weapons would be seized from Palestinian fighters by Israel, transferred to the US and then forwarded to the Contras via the agency's chief 'asset' in Panama. Something similar had been practised in the early 1980s, when Ronald Reagan wanted to assist the raggle-taggle army of Islamic fighters in Afghanistan while retaining 'deniability'. Although the US spent about $5 billion funding the various mujahedin armies, until 1985 it provided them with Eastern-bloc weapons which would look as if they had been captured from Russian soldiers rather than despatched from Washington. To distance itself further from the fray, it sub-contracted the day-to-day supervision of the rebels to its allies Saudia Arabia and Pakistan. The greatest beneficiary of this policy was a young construction engineer named Osama Bin Laden.

The declared purpose of President George W. Bush's Afghan War in the autumn of 2001, beyond the obvious and immediate aim of destroying al-Qaeda and the Taliban, was to install a regime in Kabul that would respect women's rights, promote secular education and lead the nation out of the middle ages. Yet throughout the 1980s Ronald Reagan and Margaret Thatcher had offered both financial and political support to fundamentalists – or 'freedom fighters', as they were styled – whose sole intent was to dislodge a government committed to just such a programme. 'The blowback theory is dead wrong,' a writer in the *New Republic* insisted. 'American intervention in the Afghan war didn't create Osama bin Laden. In fact, if the United States bears any blame for bin Laden's terrorist network today, it's because in the 1980s and 1990s we didn't intervene aggressively enough.' There are echoes here of the line still occasionally heard from dis-gruntled veterans who have seen *Rambo* rather more often than is good for their sanity: that the Vietnam War could also have been 'won' if only politicians in Washington hadn't been so feebly pusillanimous. Inspecting the corpse-strewn landscape of Vietnam during the 1960s and 1970s, and Afghanistan in the 1980s, one wonders just how much more aggression or intervention was required. Successive American administrations bankrolled and trained more than 25,000 zealots from thirty Islamic countries to join the anti-Soviet struggle in Afghanistan (without ever pausing to wonder if these militants might eventually turn the jihad against their paymasters). Even after the withdrawal of the last Russian troops in February 1989 – under the terms of the Geneva agreement signed the previous year – the US, Britain and Pakistan continued to arm the Islamic counter-revolutionaries, urging them to fight on until total victory was achieved. As Professor Fred Halliday wrote at the time, 'it was an irony indeed that in the middle of February 1989, when the Western world was united in outrage at Islamic fundamentalists' calls for the death of Salman Rushdie, protagonists of that very same fundamentalism should, in the guise of freedom fighters, be mustering at the gates of Kabul, incited by the whole of the Western world and brandishing missiles supplied by Ronald Reagan and Margaret Thatcher. Few bothered to ask what the Islamic state propounded by these mujahedin entailed.'

Though unasked, the question was answered soon enough. In 1990 the ever-helpful CIA provided the blind Muslim cleric Sheikh Omar Abdel-Rahman with a visa to enter the USA. Abdel-Rahman, whose son Mohammed was to become one of Osama Bin Laden's senior lieutenants, repaid the agency's generosity by preaching jihad from his base in New Jersey, and in 1996 was convicted of plotting to bomb the UN building and other New York landmarks – including the World Trade Centre.

Historical irony is, of course, the essence of blowback. Thus, after 11 September 2001, Margaret Thatcher chided British Muslim leaders for not having been sufficiently robust in their condemnation of Afghan terrorism. 'Passengers on those planes were told that they were going to die and there were children on board,' she raged. 'They must say that is disgraceful.' Yet in 1986 she had invited the young Afghan resistance leader Abdul Haq to fly to London at the British taxpayers' expense and be entertained in Downing Street. Haq was a self-confessed terrorist who in September 1984 had planted a bomb at Kabul airport, killing twenty-eight people – most of them schoolchildren who were preparing to fly to Moscow. His purpose, he explained, was 'to warn people not to send their children to the Soviet Union'. He also defended the firing of long-range rockets at Kabul, which had killed many civilians and children. 'We use poor rockets, we cannot control them,' he shrugged. 'They sometimes miss. I don't care . . . if I kill 50 civilians.' Did Thatcher – who was leading a crusade of her own at the time to deny Irish terrorists the oxygen of publicity – rebuke Haq for his 'disgraceful' callousness? Far from it: she exhorted him to persevere with 'one of the most heroic resistance struggles known to history'.

The blowback theory is not 'dead wrong'; nor is it new. Karl Marx identified the phenomenon as long ago as 1857 when reporting on the violent mutiny by Sepoys, native soldiers in the Anglo-Indian army: 'There is something in human history like retribution, and it is a rule of historical retribution that its instrument be forged not by the offended, but by the offender. The first blow to the French monarchy proceeded from the nobility; not from the peasants. The Indian revolt does not commence with the Ryots, tortured, dishonoured and stripped by the British, but with the Sepoys, clad, fed, petted, fatted and pampered by them.' Or, as Marx's friend Friedrich Engels said, 'those who unleash controlled forces also unleash uncontrolled forces'.

The Cambridge historian Christopher Andrew has calculated that in the 1960s there was not a single religious or cult-based terrorist group anywhere, and as recently as

1980 only two of the world's sixty-four known terrorist groups were religious. Since then, however, Shi'a extremists alone have been responsible for more than a quarter of the deaths from terrorism. 'We are not fighting so the enemy will offer us something,' the former Hezbollah leader Hussein Massawi said. 'We are fighting to wipe out the enemy.' Whereas groups such as the Palestine Liberation Organisation or the Provisional IRA spread terror for a specific and limited political purpose, their religious successors raised mass slaughter to an end in itself. The intelligence chief of the Japanese cult Aum Shinrikyo, which released nerve gas on the Tokyo subway in 1995, explained that 'we regarded the world outside as evil, and destroying the evil as salvation'.

Bruce Hoffmann, the author of *Inside Terrorism*, argues that this marked a return to an old tradition that had been only briefly interrupted by modern secularism. Until the late nineteenth century all terrorism was essentially religious, bent on annihilation of infidels. The leaders of Hezbollah and al-Qaeda thus had far more in common with the Christian fanatics of early modern Europe than with their immediate predecessors such as Abu Nidal or Carlos the Jackal – as some Christians, at least, appeared to recognise. Two days after the 11 September attacks in 2001 the Rev. Pat Robertson and the Rev. Jerry Falwell, America's best-known TV evangelists, appeared on *The 700 Club*, a religious chat-show. 'What we saw on Tuesday, as terrible as it is, could be minuscule if, in fact, God continues to lift the curtain and allow the enemies of America to give us probably what we deserve,' Falwell opined. The carnage was an expression of God's wrath at 'the pagans and the abortionists and the feminists and the gays and the lesbians ... the ACLU [American Civil Liberties

Union], People for the American Way, all of them who try to secularise America'. To which Robertson replied: 'I totally concur.'

8

Candles in the wind

Ours is an evangelical culture. So many people convinced that they've been saved by Jesus, cured by homeopathy or the laying on of hands, abducted by aliens or protected by angels seek public acknowledgement that their convictions are true. Imbued with messianic fervour, or simply seeking 'validation', they are not content to hoard the truth; they are compelled to share it and convert the unenlightened, relying on the force of their own intense emotions. Generally, the only proof offered for a fantastic belief is the passion it inspires.

WENDY KAMINER, *Sleeping with Extra-Terrestrials* (1999)

In September 1981, a few months after Ronald Reagan's arrival in the White House, the University of Notre Dame Press published *After Virtue*, a short philosophical tract by the British academic Alasdair MacIntyre – and suddenly found that it had a bestseller on its hands, thanks to an ecstatic article in *Newsweek* magazine praising this 'stunning new study of ethics' which 'projects a conservative revolution far more radical than any imagined by the men who rule America today'. As *Newsweek* reported, 'His slogan, he quips in conversation, is "forward to the twelfth century" – but he's not joking about the chaos and decay of modern society.'

MacIntyre argued that the Enlightenment had been 'a catastrophe' for ethical discourse: by substituting its idea of universally available and necessary moral principles for older notions of virtue ordained by divine authority, and by abandoning religious teleology (the belief that there is an ultimate purpose in life), it had ushered in a 'new dark age' of barbarism and nihilism. 'What, then,' he asked, 'is to be done in the face of such wholesale moral collapse?' The answer, bizarrely, was to take refuge in medieval monastic orders such as the Benedictines.

> What matters at this stage is the construction of local forms of community within which civility and the intellectual and moral life can be sustained through the new dark ages which are already upon us. And if the tradition of the virtues was able to survive the horrors of the last dark ages, we are not entirely without grounds for hope. This time however the barbarians are not waiting beyond our frontiers; they have already been governing us for quite some time. And it is our lack of consciousness of this that constitutes part of our predicament. We are waiting not for a Godot, but for another – doubtless very different – St Benedict.

MacIntyre was a former Marxist, whose intense anti-liberalism facilitated his transfer of allegiance from Leon Trotsky to Thomas Aquinas. Ex-Trotskyists who have been 'mugged by reality' (in the words of one such apostate, Irving Kristol) usually become enthusiastic cheerleaders for liberal capitalism. Not so MacIntyre, who remained wholly unreconciled to modernity. The natural rights and self-evident truths proclaimed in the American declaration of independence were tantamount to 'belief in witches and in unicorns'; Edmund

Burke, a hero to most conservatives, was 'an agent of positive harm'. Since writing *After Virtue* MacIntyre has formally converted to Catholicism, and continues to propose a revival of the Thomist tradition as the only way of 'defeating' Enlightenment liberalism.

This might sound like merely another lament from a nostalgic old grump who thinks the world is going to the dogs. But it clearly strikes a chord. In 1999 the *Weekly Standard* described Alasdair MacIntyre as 'possibly the greatest moral philosopher of the last fifty years', and *After Virtue* as 'the most widely discussed book of philosophy in English – not just among philosophers, but among general readers across America'. Where he led, many other intellectuals have followed: conservatives, Marxists, post-modernists and pre-modernists have queued up to take a kick at the bruised ideas of the eighteenth century. The most vicious of these boot-boys is John Gray, professor of European thought at the London School of Economics, who has published dozens of increasingly apocalyptic books and articles on the need to end the Enlightenment project forthwith. Whereas MacIntyre seeks sanctuary in twelfth-century monasteries, for Gray our only hope of salvation is to embrace Eastern mysticism: 'Any prospect of cultural recovery from the nihilism that the Enlightenment has spawned may lie with non-Occidental peoples, whose task will then be in part that of protecting themselves from the debris cast up by Western shipwreck.' Taoism seems to be his favoured creed but it is hard to interpret Gray's prescriptions with any certainty, partly because of his wild scattergun style but mostly because he changes his mind so often. A line on the dust-jacket of *Enlightenment's Wake* (1995), which says that the book 'stakes out the elements of John Gray's new position', could just as well be appended to everything he writes.

'One of the strange features of Gray's writings', an Australian commentator notes, 'is that he frequently offers us criticisms of various positions which he himself seems to have held until fairly recently, but which are then characterised in the most pejorative of terms, and as if only a fool or a knave could hold them.' Having been a long-haired socialist in 1968, in the 1970s he became a Thatcherite almost before Margaret Thatcher herself. His book *Hayek on Liberty*, published in 1984, was described by Friedrich von Hayek as 'the first survey of my work which not only fully understands but is able to carry on my ideas beyond the point at which I left off'. Thatcher sought his advice, as did many of the new right-wing think-tanks in London and Washington. By the mid-1990s, however, he was denouncing his hero Hayek as a 'neo-liberal ideologue' whose creed elevating 'the impersonal nexus of market exchange' threatened the very fabric of human civilisation.

'Whatever happened to John Gray?' Margaret Thatcher asked the economic historian Lord Skidelsky a few years ago. 'He used to be one of us.' She might well have been puzzled. Gray's *Beyond the New Right* (1993) offered a 'radical critique' of neo-liberalism 'from a standpoint which I believe to be that of traditional conservatism . . . It is by returning to the homely truths of traditional conservatism that we are best protected from the illusions of ideology.' But in *Endgames* (1997) he announced that 'Tory politics has reached a dead end . . . There is and can be no coherent form of conservative thought, and no effective mode of conservative practice, in a late modern culture.' The second edition of his book *Liberalism* (1995) warned that since the first edition in 1986 'the author's views have changed significantly'. They have been in perpetual motion ever since: his political affiliation now is with the animal liberationists and the New Age wing of the Green movement. Liberalism, rationalism and all other manifestations of the Enlightenment spirit are discredited and dying, he says – and about time too.

The charge-sheet against the Enlightenment produced by Gray, MacIntyre and others seems formidably damning. One of its crimes was to promote the idea of universal values – a camouflage, if the critics are to be believed, for a brutal imperialistic project to subjugate other cultures and impose Western hegemony. But of all the likely suspects who could be arraigned for this offence, why single out the Enlightenment philosophers, who actually made some effort to understand distant peoples and free them from subjugation? See, for example, Voltaire's denunciation of slavery in *Candide*, or the Abbé Raynal's tract *Histoire philosophique des établissements et du commerce des Européens dans les deux Indes*, one of the earliest and most powerful polemics against the slave trade: the Enlightenment provided much of the political language and principles that were to be used by anti-slavery campaigners in the nineteenth century, when the immorality of slave-owning became commonly – though not universally – accepted. Those who routinely deplore the 'imperialism' of Enlightenment attitudes cannot have read Reynal, Diderot, Kant, Condorcet or Adam Smith. 'When America, the Negro countries, the Spice Islands, the Cape and so forth were discovered,' Kant wrote in *Towards Perpetual Peace*, 'they were, to [the Europeans], countries belonging to no one, since they counted the inhabitants as nothing.' For these authors, moral universalism was not incommensurate with cultural pluralism. Quite the opposite: an insistence on universal standards of morality, freedom and human dignity was what inspired their defence of indigenous peoples against invaders who trashed 'inferior' cultures. As Diderot complained, 'the Spaniard, the first to be thrown up by the waves on to the shores of the New World, thought he had no duty to people who did not share his colour, customs or religion'.

No doubt the Enlightenment's give-and-take with other cultures was sometimes tainted by what is now called Orientalism – a fondness for exotic stereotypes – even if these were usually positive rather than negative. One thinks of Voltaire's reverence for the wisdom and decency of Confucian civilisation ('the best that the world has ever seen'), or the sarcastic observations on Parisians and their strange customs from the sophisticated Persian travellers Usbek and Rica in Montesquieu's novel *Persian Letters*. ('This king [Louis XV] is a great magician . . . If there are only a million crowns in the exchequer, and he needs two million, all he needs to do is persuade them that one crown is worth two, and they believe it.') But in contrast with the eighteenth century, as the historian Robert Darnton has pointed out, other ages were all take and no give:

> Byron and Kipling, Delacroix and Ingres, Verdi and Puccini outdid the artists of the eighteenth century by far in creating exotic Orientals. Moreover, the exoticising began long before the Enlightenment, and it often took the form of demonising. Cruel Saracens, Oriental despots, and 'têtes de Turcs' have proliferated in the Western imagination since the early wars against the Ottoman Empire. Older prejudices date from the Crusades. They developed over centuries, accompanied, it must be said, by Eastern prejudices against the West . . . To pin Orientalism on the Enlightenment is to confuse the thought of a few intellectuals in the eighteenth century with the entire course of Western civilisation.

But the Enlightenment stands accused of even more heinous crimes than Orientalism: its cavalry charge against mystification and unreason is said to have led to the fanaticism of the French revolutionary terror, the Nazi gas-chambers and the Soviet Gulag. In their celebrated work on 'the dialectic of Enlightenment', Theodor Adorno and Max Horkheimer argue that, by replacing myth with science and treating the natural world as an object to be dominated and exploited, modernist thinkers created a repressive new system of power relations, uninhibited by any external morality, in which man himself acquired the characteristics of God. They cite the Marquis de Sade as a typical specimen of 'the bourgeois individual freed from tutelage', revelling in barbarism and cruelty. The merciless tendency exemplified by de Sade, and later celebrated in Nietzsche's worship of the will-to-power and the super-man, reached its logical culmination in Adolf Hitler. Thus, by a 'negative dialectic', the supposedly progressive Enlightenment gave birth to genocidal tyranny.

One should make allowance for the fact that Adorno and Horkheimer were refugees from Nazi Germany, but their dialectic is so outrageously flawed that polite disagreement is impossible. Nietzsche was indeed Hitler's favourite philosopher, but he was not a philosopher of Enlightenment: he belonged to the Romantic tradition, a reaction *against* demythologising rationalism. Hitler was a fanatical nationalist, a man of blood and soil – whereas the *philosophes*, in Robert Darnton's words, 'lived in a Republic of Letters that was truly cosmopolitan. It had neither borders nor police.' More astonishing still, in a book which purports to debunk the Enlightenment, is the fact that few of its most prominent thinkers earn a mention. (The Marquis de Sade is, to be sure, an interesting figure, but scarcely a representative one.) The omission is understandable, if dishonest: Adorno and Horkheimer could not discuss Voltaire or Diderot or Rousseau without conceding that they opposed despotism and argued passionately for justice, liberty and respect for the individual. Why, after all, are we so shocked by Nazi atrocities? Because they are an outrage against human rights. And who developed this concept of human rights, which has been proclaimed again and again to the great benefit of mankind, whether by the American founding fathers or Amnesty International? To quote Robert Darnton again:

> True, the Enlightenment was time-bound as well as culture-bound. It took place in a world where some causes of the twentieth century remained unthinkable . . . The point is not to make an inventory of ideas, crossing some off the list and adding others. It is to adopt an intellectual position that will serve when lines are drawn and one's back is to the wall. When challenged to condemn torture in Argentina, war in Vietnam, or racism in the United States, where can we make our stand if not on principles enshrined in the Declaration of Independence and the Declaration of the Rights of Man and of the Citizen?

By the end of the twentieth century, however, the reassertion of these values had become increasingly unfashionable. There were countless indications of a general retreat from reason – the search for millennial portents, the revival of interest in Nostradamus (a bestseller after 11 September 2001), the appearance of horoscopes in even serious broadsheets, the flood of books about angels, fairies, Inca secrets, Egyptian rituals and secret Bible Codes. A coven of witches protesting against the World Trade Organisation in Seattle at the end of

1999 carried banners advocating salvation through wizardry, inspired by the Harry Potter novels: 'Wake Up, Muggles!'

The new irrationalism is an expression of despair by people who feel impotent to improve their lives and suspect that they are at the mercy of secretive, impersonal forces, whether these be the Pentagon or invaders from Mars. Political leaders accept it as a safe outlet for dissent, fulfilling much the same function that Marx attributed to religion – the heart of a heartless world, the opium of the people. Far better for the powerless to seek solace in crystals, ley-lines and the myth of Abraham than in actually challenging the rulers, or the social and economic system over which they preside. Ever since idealist philosophers such as Hegel and Schopenhauer denounced the demythologising spirit of modernity, empirical analysis has always been opposed by those who fear that the stripping away of illusions can only end in miserable disillusion.

But superstition is not the only enemy of rational thought and action. Jean-Jacques Rousseau, though often bracketed with other founders of the Enlightenment because of his progressive politics, may also be regarded as the first Romantic because of his exaltation of feeling over reason. Herder, another figurehead of the early Counter-Enlightenment, once said that 'I am not here to think, but to be, feel, live.' The common portayal of Enlightenment thinkers as cold, bloodless rationalists who wished to strip the universe of colour and passion is a grotesque caricature: the historian Peter Gay has pointed out that this generalisation would hold 'only if we disregarded the *philosophes*' defence of imagination, their pioneering analysis of passion, their bold creation of literary forms, and their almost unanimous infatuation with [Samuel] Richardson's sensibility'. Nevertheless, they did appreciate the danger of continually allowing the heart to rule the head. Just as the Romantic movement of the early nineteenth century reacted against their apparently chilly and soulless logic by asserting the primacy of fantasy and emotion, so the new Counter-Enlightenment is often characterised by intense sentimentality as well as metaphysical credulity – both at the expense of reasoned consideration. The presidency of Ronald Reagan has rightly been described as 'the era of good feelings'. His successor, George Bush, never understood how to exploit the public's emotional volatility, which may well explain his departure from the White House after only one term. Then came Bill Clinton, the master of empathy – a talent that won him huge popularity even after eight years of deception and dishonour.

Alas for the Democrats, Clinton's designated successor, Al Gore, had the misfortune to be a stiff and unemotional politician in an age when voters' hearts counted for more than their minds. He mocked his own woodenness, but every so often – every four years, to be precise, as an election loomed – he would try to jettison the reputation with a carefully rehearsed exercise in heart-tugging. In his vice-presidential acceptance speech at the 1992 Democratic national convention in New York, Gore described a car accident that nearly killed his son, Albert: 'Tipper [Mrs Gore] and I watched as he was thrown 30 feet in the air and scraped another 20 feet on the pavement after he hit the ground. I ran to his side and called his name, but he was limp and still, without breath or pulse. His eyes were open with the empty stare of death, and we prayed, the two of us, there in the gutter, with only my voice.' The experience 'changed me forever', he informed the moist-eyed delegates: 'When you've seen your six-year-old son fighting for his life, you realise that some things matter a lot more than winning. You lose patience with the lazy assumption of so many in politics that we can always just muddle through.' Had they been in a fit state for ratiocination, delegates might have wondered how the second sentence related to the first, and what any of it actually meant: happily, however, they were far too busy sobbing and sighing to demand anything as vulgar as coherence – which was, of course, Gore's very purpose in including this pointless parable. In the era of solipsism and subliminal marketing, rhetoric had been supplanted by mood music: how people 'felt' was far more important than how they thought.

Four years later, at the Democratic national convention in Chicago, Al Gore was preparing for a second outing as Clinton's running-mate but also looking ahead to the 2000 campaign – when, if all went according to plan, he would be the Democratic nominee in his own right. Hence the increasingly urgent need, as the *Washington Post* put it, 'both to move his audience and provide a more complex glimpse into his personality and life'. The tale of little Albert's brush with death might not be quite so effective at a second hearing, so this time Gore summoned up the ghost of his sister Nancy Gore Hunger, who had died of lung cancer in 1984 at the age of forty-six.

Not since Dickens re-enacted the death of Little Nell had an American audience witnessed anything quite like it. Nancy – whom Gore loved 'more than life itself' – started smoking at thirteen and had a lung removed thirty years later. 'Her husband, Frank, and all of us who loved her so much tried to get her to stop smoking. Of course she should have. But she couldn't.' Then the cancer returned and her family took turns to sit beside her hospital bed. 'By then her pain was nearly unbearable, and as a result they used very powerful painkillers. Eventually, it got so bad they had to use such heavy doses that she could barely retain consciousness . . . She looked up and from out of that haze, her eyes focused tensely right at me. She couldn't speak, but I felt clearly I knew she was forming a question: Do you bring me hope? But all I could do was to say back to her, with all the gentleness in my heart, "I love you". And then I knelt by her bed and held her hand. And in a very short time her breathing became laboured and then she breathed her last breath.' While tears dribbled down the cheeks of many delegates in the Chicago convention hall – and, no doubt, many more watching the speech live on network television – Gore came to the moral of his ghastly fable: 'Tomorrow morning, another thirteen-year-old girl will start smoking. I love her, too. Three thousand young people in America will start smoking tomorrow. One thousand of them will die a death not unlike my sister's, and that is why, until I draw my last breath, I will pour my heart and soul into the cause of protecting our children from the dangers of smoking.'

Applause for what the *Washington Post* called 'a powerful and personal story of pain and suffering' was almost unanimous (except for the right-wing wag who suggested that 'Tipper must be nervously eyeing the gorgeous go-go Gore girls and wondering on whose head the next quadrennial family tragedy will fall'), and no pundit was tasteless enough to question his sincerity. It was only several weeks later that one or two newspapers exposed the obvious flaws in Gore's epiphany. In 1988, four years *after* his sister's death, Gore had spoken to an audience of tobacco farmers while on the stump in North Carolina. 'Throughout most of my life, I raised tobacco,' he boasted. 'I want you to know that with my own hands, all of my life, I've put it in the plant beds and transferred it. I've hoed it. I've dug in it. I've sprayed it, I've chopped it, I've shredded it, spiked it, put it in the barn and stripped it and sold it.' No mention there of his heart-and-soul struggle against the evil weed. Another four years on, in 1992, Gore's doom-mongering book *Earth in the Balance* warned of the perils of addiction to drugs, alcohol, gambling, even overwork and TV-watching, but omitted any reference to the addictive leaf that was cultivated so profitably for decades on the Gore family farm in Tennessee. During that year's election campaign, both Bill Clinton and Al Gore accepted financial contributions from the tobacco lobby. How could he reconcile all that with his supposedly sacred duty to Nancy's memory, and to all those thirteen-year-old girls whom he loved dearly and wished to save? When a reporter eventually had the chance to ask him, Gore replied: 'I felt the numbness that prevented me from integrating into all aspects of my life the implications of what that tragedy really meant. We are in the midst of a profound shift in the way we approach issues. I really do believe that in our politics and in our personal lives, we are seeing an effort to integrate our emotional lives in a more balanced fashion.'

A skilled parodist would struggle to produce a more perfect specimen of the modern language of feeling. 'Nobody has mastered the feminisation of political discourse more thoroughly than Gore,' the conservative journalist Mark Steyn wrote. 'Even his habit of speaking. Very. Slowly. Seems to play well with the "soccer moms", reminding them of a concerned grade-school teacher taking the time to explain to little Johnny why eating too much candy is bad for you.'

Yet in this, as in all other contests, Gore would surely have to yield first place to Bill Clinton, the empathy-junkie who allegedly read John Gray's *Men Are from Mars, Women Are from*

Venus more than twenty times. As a sexually aggressive Alpha male, Clinton might seem an unlikely Venus-dweller; but by appropriating the old feminist phrase 'the personal is political' and turning it on its head, he managed to disguise self-indulgence as a progressive politics for the Oprah-watching generation. Mark Steyn pointed out that 'the new sentimentalised, feminised, Venusian media-digestible politics is . . . a drag-queen travesty of what the women's movement intended', but it seemed to work. President Clinton lied about his relationship with Monica Lewinsky ('that woman', in his contemptuous phrase), and sought to rescue his own reputation by traducing hers. Twenty or thirty years earlier, feminists would have known what to make of a man who behaved like this. Yet throughout the Lewinsky saga and beyond, Clinton enjoyed the support of Gloria Steinem, Betty Friedan and Erica Jong. No less remarkable was the willingness of so many men of God to accept Clinton's invitation to a televised 'prayer breakfast' at the White House immediately after his confession of mendacity – an event at which the disgraced chief executive sought once again to redeem himself by blubbing about his grief and hurt and regret, while showing no actual contrition whatever. Clinton – one must say it again – was the most powerful man on earth, a sexual predator and alleged rapist; a man of no discernible moral scruples who in 1992 interrupted his primary campaign and hastened back to Arkansas to execute a brain-damaged black man, Rickey Ray Rector, solely to forestall any suspicion that he was 'soft'. (A year later, the novelist Toni Morrison described Clinton as 'our first black president'.) In August 1998 he bombed a pharmaceutical factory in the Sudan to distract attention from Lewinsky's testimony to the Starr inquiry, which was due to begin that very day. Despite all this and more, he sought to portray himself as a victim. And many less exalted fellow-victims loved him for it: opinion polls found that if Clinton had been permitted to run for a third term, even after all the scandals and skulduggery, he'd have won with ease.

Here again, he proved himself a truly emblematic figure – representing an age in which even the most debauched and dissipated millionaire rock-stars were canonised after their inevitable deaths, and celebrities felt inadequate unless they had serious 'problems' that could be displayed to the public's empathetic gaze. In her 1991 autobiography, Ali MacGraw claimed to be a 'recovering alcoholic' and gave a lengthy account of her spell in the Betty Ford clinic.'The only flaw in this script', Lynn Barber noted in the *Independent on Sunday*, 'is that nobody who knows Ali MacGraw believes that she was ever an alcoholic. Her friends say they never saw her drinking; Bob Evans, her ex-husband and still a good friend, says the whole idea is absurd.' When Barber asked about her consumption, MacGraw said that she sometimes had two shots of tequila in an evening and once even drank a whole bottle and a half of red wine, but often went for months without a drink. 'So how could she be an alcoholic?' Barber wondered. 'Perhaps in California you can achieve a sort of Zen alcoholism without the consumption of alcohol. MacGraw keeps saying that she "behaved alcoholically" whether she was drinking or not.' MacGraw's friend Joan Juliet Buck suggested in *Vanity Fair* that the real purpose of her sojourn in the clinic was to reconcile herself to the fact that she was no longer a movie star. For actors who found their fame dwindling, the smart career move was to check into Betty Ford and then write a confessional autobiography about it.

In Britain, the undisputed champion of implausible self-pity was Lady Diana Spencer. At the time of her engagement to Prince Charles in 1981 she was just another dim, round-faced Sloaney girl of the kind you could see on almost every street in Pimlico, Kensington or Earl's Court, clad in the unprepossessing uniform that prompted some observers to liken her, cruelly but accurately, to a stewardess from Air Bulgaria. By the time of her funeral sixteen years later she was routinely if ludicrously described as one of the most beautiful women in the world, and the most saintly. ('Critical judgment musters no lustre beside the sheen of global celebrity, and royal celebrity at that,' the philosopher Glen Newey wrote. 'Imagine Diana's life as a comparably talentless prole – a single mother in Gateshead, say – and you get the picture.') More implausibly still, the simpering princess transformed herself into a feminist heroine with her 1995 appearance on the BBC's *Panorama*: staring nervously at the interviewer through smudgily kohl-rimmed eyes, she spoke of her betrayal by the man she adored, Major James Hewitt, and by the prince she married. Elaine Showalter hailed her as 'one of the great success stories of contemporary psychotherapy'.

Not everyone accepted the invitation to share her pain. 'That Diana's therapised victim-speak could turn her into a feminist role-model seems like a bad joke,' the literary critic Linda Holt complained. 'But it is the result of the way feminism – as a movement and ideology – has fragmented and become bound up in a cultural backlash against its original political project. Much of what has been called "victim feminism" has been absorbed into mainstream culture, shorn of its political context, no more than a licence for rampant subjectivity . . . In this "new feminism" even flamboyant consumerism, as exemplified by Diana's pursuit of fashion and beauty, can be celebrated as an emancipatory choice.' Plenty of Fleet Street commentators shared Holt's distaste, though for different reasons, and continued to deride her as a spoilt and manipulative little vixen until the very eve of her death.

All that changed with the car crash in a Parisian tunnel in the early hours of 31 August 1997 – so much so that the demise of Mother Teresa a few days later was all but eclipsed. Overnight, the 'simpering Bambi narcissist' became not only the loveliest woman of the century but also the Queen of Hearts, the Nabob of Sob. According to Elton John, singing his heart out in Westminster Abbey while mixing metaphors with glorious abandon, she was also England's rose, a candle that never faded with the sunset when the rain set in (as candles so often do) but strode off across England's greenest hills, its footprints preserved for eternity. The leader of the Conservative Party, William Hague, proposed that Heathrow be renamed Diana Airport without delay. The Chancellor of the Exchequer, Gordon Brown, wondered if the anniversary of her death should henceforth be a public holiday, Diana Day. But the prime minister effortlessly outdid them all with his instant oxymoronic soundbite about 'the People's Princess', and his hilariously hammy reading of a passage from Corinthians at her funeral service. Those commentators who praised Tony Blair for 'capturing the mood of the nation' had unintentionally stumbled on exactly the right verb: when he dubbed her the People's Princess, at 10.30 on the Sunday morning, most of the nation had scarcely taken in the news from Paris, still less transmuted its reaction into a 'mood'. (There was, to be sure, sadness and shock at a life cut short; but many viewers must also have wrestled uncomfortably with the knowledge that only a few days earlier, studying the pictures of Diana cavorting with a dodgy playboy on Mohamed Fayed's yacht, they had derided her as a hedonistic flibberti-gibbet.) Blair's pre-emptive tribute set the tone for the mourning, foreclosing any more measured assessment – and, as an American writer noticed, subliminally offered his own Christian decency and choirboy countenance as claim on the virtue represented by the deceased.

On that Sunday afternoon I was telephoned by a neighbour, a ferociously conservative columnist on the *Daily Mail*: 'I can't bear much more of this. Fancy a drink in the pub?' He had been given a week's holiday from the paper after informing the editor that he couldn't participate in the national ululation and genuflection; having watched several hours of hyperbolic homage on TV, he was beginning to fear that he might be the only sane person left in the country.

The obvious solution, to flee abroad for the next few months, would have offered no escape. In France, the publishers Descartes rushed out *Diana Crash*, a collection of essays by intellectuals such as Régis Debray and (inevitably) Jean Baudrillard. The princess's funeral was carried live on all American networks, after a week in which Diana had been the sole topic of conversation on all US chat-shows. For a front-page story on 13 September, the *New York Times* interviewed forty psychotherapists in New York and its suburbs, of whom only two said that their female patients hadn't talked about the princess. Tellingly, both were men. The *Times* reported that many women in therapy

> were stunned by the power of their reaction to her death, unable to talk of anything else, obsessed with reading every word and watching every newscast, and dismayed that the men in their life hadn't a clue what so moved them.
>
> 'She's a magnet for all their issues, a reflection of them writ large,' said Steven Tuber, a clinical psychologist and director of the doctoral program in psychology at City University of

New York. He was one of scores of therapists who called Diana – at once frail and beautiful, flawed and grand – a perfect transference symbol, a Rorschach test, a blank screen on which women could not resist projecting their fantasies and fears.

Even women who disdain the celebrity culture, who would never confess to reading *People* magazine or watching *Life Styles of the Rich and Famous*, devoted entire 50-minute hours and hundreds of hard-earned dollars to dissecting the parts of Diana's life that resonated for them. 'She spoke to their woundedness and to their battle to be heard and to be loved,' said Brenda Berger, a clinical psychologist in New York City and Larchmont, N.Y.

As several therapists pointed out, 'men didn't get it'. Dr Edgar A. Levenson of the William Alanson White Institute for psychoanalytic training said that while women considered her 'a member of the family', his male patients dismissed the event with a brusque 'It's too bad she got killed.' In the era of *Men Are from Mars, Women Are from Venus*, this was of course interpreted as further proof of male insensitivity, an inability to cope with intense emotion and self-revelation. But was 'it's too bad she got killed' really a less mature or reasonable reaction than that of New Yorkers who (in the words of Dr Levenson) 'grieved as if it was their own life'?

In Britain, supposedly the epicentre of grief, there were many women and men who declined to succumb to Diarrhoea: in the days after the crash, the BBC switchboard was inundated with calls from viewers demanding *less* coverage. But the few who managed to make their voices heard publicly found themselves treated as pariahs or worse. *Private Eye* magazine was banned from branches of W. H. Smith for daring to mock the humbug of people who, while deploring 'media intrusion' into the princess's life (and death), maintained a voracious appetite for every prurient word and titillating picture. Even the Queen incurred the wrath of the tabloid lynchmob for not emoting openly and extravagantly enough: 'Show Some Heart, Ma'am!', 'Your People Are Grieving', 'What About the Boys, Ma'am?' Among both the lowbrows and highbrows of the media – and the even higher brows of academe, which hosted dozens of jargon-strewn conferences and seminars on Diana – the hysteria was astonishingly contagious. The sober, serious *Independent*, thitherto famous for ignoring all royal stories, printed reams of drivel, including this effusion from its columnist Suzanne Moore the morning after the princess's death:

> Icons do not die. Diana's afterlife is only just starting. Forever frozen at the height of her beauty, Diana, like Marilyn, that other troubled goddess, will not age. She will continue to glow, forever young, forever vital, in the hearts of those she touched. For the pop princess, the people's princess, the media princess understood the power of touch, the language of intimacy, of a hug, a gesture that was always more eloquent than mere words.

Note the unexamined assumption that her status as a pop princess and media icon somehow confirmed her talent for intimacy, rather as if a facility for writing Hallmark-card verses might prove that one understood the secrets of the human heart. Two weeks after the event, under the headline 'New Britain', contributors to the *Observer* celebrated the Dianafication of Britain: the feminist psychotherapist Susie Orbach interpreted the Floral Revolution outside Kensington Palace as proof that we were 'growing up as a nation'; to the novelist

A. L. Kennedy it represented a new 'emotional maturity'; the paper's editor Will Hutton – radical social democrat and republican – claimed that the collective genuflection before a dead aristocrat showed that the British were 'freeing ourselves from the reins of the past'.

One man told the BBC that he had cried far more at Diana's funeral than at that of his own father eight years earlier. Was this, too, evidence of 'emotional maturity'? Or proof that the outpouring of emotion was not so much genuine love or grief as what Shelley called 'The desire of the moth for the star / Of the night for the morrow / The devotion to something afar / From the sphere of our sorrow'? For many months after the event, it was treasonous even to pose the question. In April 1998 Professor Anthony O'Hear of Bradford University suddenly achieved tabloid notoriety by writing a short article about the Diana phenomenon in a collection of essays published by the right-wing Social Affairs Unit. 'There is no doubt that she did quite a lot of good both for individuals and for the causes with which she was associated,' he acknowledged. 'There was something touching in her reaching out to the socially excluded . . .' Nor had the grieving crowds been hysterical or deranged: 'They were, in fact, quiet, orderly and in demeanour dignified.' All he ventured to suggest was that the reaction to Princess Diana lacked a sense of proportion – a point amply confirmed by the reaction to his own modest heresy. O'Hear was attacked by the *Daily Mirror* as a 'rat-faced little loser', described as a 'desiccated calculating machine' by Lord St John of Fawsley (a castle-creeping royal sycophant often nicknamed Lord Cringe-on-all-Foursly) and dismissed as an 'old-fashioned snob' by Tony Blair, who was visiting the Middle East at the time. Why would a British prime minister feel obliged to interrupt crucial diplomatic business to attack an eight-page essay written by an obscure academic for a little-known think-tank? The pillorying of O'Hear, like the rage of Caliban seeing his own face in the glass, appeared to confirm that he had discovered an intolerable truth.

A *Guardian* editorial argued that the Social Affairs Unit 'emerge as a slightly fogeyish bunch'. And yet, perversely, O'Hear was also criticised for not being fogeyish enough. 'The professor is right, of course, in his wider point that there is a powerful streak of sentimentality in the British character,' wrote Dominic Lawson, one of the princess's friends. 'But he is startlingly wrong in thinking that there is anything new in it. The British have been this way before, and at a time of greatness rather than of decadence.' Readers of Dickens will know that there was indeed plenty of mawkishness in nineteenth-century England: as the historian G. M. Young recorded in his classic *Portrait of an Age*, it was a period when ministers often wept at the dinner table and 'the sight of an infant school could reduce a civil servant to a passion of tears'. But these lachrymose performances were often little more than a pose: some Victorians deliberately smudged the ink on letters of condolence, sprinkling water over the page to simulate the tears they could not summon. Nevertheless, according to Lawson's interpretation, sentimentality was a grand old national tradition that should be cherished by true conservatives.

The 'language of feeling' first entered British discourse in the mid-eighteenth century through the novels of Laurence Sterne and Samuel Richardson, and the moral philosophy of David Hume. Sterne played it strictly for laughs, fearing that if he ever took anything seriously he would sink into a quicksand of melancholy. Richardson, who enjoyed a good blub, preferred to explore the 'feminine sensibility' of sighing and swooning. Hume's purpose was to examine the tension between passion and reason. In spite of their differences, however, all these authors regarded sentimentality as a cure for solitude – hence the title of John Mullan's excellent book on the subject, *Sentiment and Sociability*. 'The passions are so contagious', Hume wrote in his *Treatise of Human Nature*, 'that they pass with the greatest facility from one person to another, and produce correspondent movement in all human breasts.' This is precisely what happened in the late summer of 1997. Far from being signs of 'greatness' or emotional maturity, the periodic swellings of emotion in England over the past couple of centuries were the anguished pleas of a lonely and atom-ised populace, desperate for company. What fascinated many foreign visitors in London at the time of the princess's funeral was the obvious yearning for an excuse – any excuse – to talk to complete strangers without embarrassment. 'We have Independence Day and Thanksgiving,' one American said, 'but I suppose you don't have many occasions when you can get together as a nation.' In the last years of the twentieth century, absurdly and pathetically, Britons' only such oppor-tunity was the death of a pampered princess – whom they were then forced to beatify, in defiance of all reason, simply to justify their own rational desires.

'When they go on about fake sentimentality in relation to Princess Diana, people really felt that,' Tony Blair protested. 'Why is it fake?' But O'Hear never said it was. He emphasised that the emotion was spontaneous and genuine – 'misdirected maybe, as in the case of the man who said that Diana's death meant more to him than that of his parents, and, in that sense, irrational, but it was not insincere or superficial. Whatever it was people felt, they really felt it.' In his study of

eighteenth-century feelings, John Mullan argues that sentimental passion and sympathy offered 'a more inclusive
vocabulary of social coherence' than politics could provide.
This turned out to be equally true of the late twentieth
century. During the 1980s politics was dominated by somebody who insisted that 'there is no such thing as society,
only individual men and women and their families'; by 1997
Britain was governed by a Labour prime minister who
regarded comradeship and collective association as anachronisms that should be excluded from the political lexicon. Was
it any wonder that so many people clung to the memory of
'the Diana effect', just as an earlier generation tried to revive
the spirit of the Blitz or Dunkirk? If a large throng of demonstrators had stopped the traffic to express their solidarity with
a victimised trade unionist whom they had never met, Blair
would have been quick to condemn it as 'unlawful secondary
action'. To take to the streets on behalf of a victimised princess, however, was quite permissible, not least as a distraction
from the vacuous inadequacy of contemporary politics: far
better to have a mass emote than a mass debate. 'Grief is a
vital safety valve,' the Sun commented eight months after the
princess's funeral, accidentally giving the game away. It is
difficult if not impossible to weep and think at the same time.
And so, as the Sun cheerfully exhorted its readers: 'Keep
grieving.' The Observer columnist Euan Ferguson viewed this
orgy of narcissistic emoting as part of 'the Liverpudlianisation
of Britain . . . [which] turned us into a country that fills its
gutters with tears for girls we've never met and scrawls mawk-
ish thank-yous to the most privileged woman this land has
ever known'.

The arguments about the merits or dangers of unbridled
emotionalism produced some strange political bedfellows.

Several anti-monarchists hastened to defend the Queen against the belligerent indignation of those who wanted her to abandon the stiff upper lip and behave more like a guest on the Jerry Springer show. ('This was the expression of "feeling" at its worst,' one complained. 'There was something very unpleasant about the way in which the royal family was bullied and hounded for not displaying emotion in the way in which the tabloids approved; and I say that as a convinced republican.') Just as conservative pundits savaged the right-wing Professor O'Hear, so allegedly progressive feminist writers such as Linda Grant and Beatrix Campbell turned on liberals and socialists who declined to join the great Diana blubfest, scorning them as 'elitists' who couldn't cope with feeling. This provoked a spirited riposte from Professor Elizabeth Wilson in *New Left Review*.

In the case of Diana's death 'the Left' could be attacked also because socialism was a product of the Enlightenment that it is now fashionable to demonise as a terroristic project: there never was 'reason', there was only a different form of domination masquerading as rational. Thus grief for Diana privileges the values of feeling over reason and is therefore a good, whereas ideas associated with socialism, such as justice and equality, make a fatal claim to rationality and are therefore bad.

Into this political vacuum of thought step the twin figures of Tony Blair and Princess Diana. And, just as 'Candle in the Wind' reduces the whole complex story of Diana to one single, easy sob, so the myth of the 'People's Princess' condenses the whole complex political challenge of our times into one poignant moment of regret without real change.

In his reply to Professor O'Hear, Tony Blair said that 'Diana's power is born out of emotion, and there's nothing wrong with that – I'm an emotional person too.' Only a week or two later the British tabloids tracked down Mary Bell, who committed a notorious child-murder back in the 1960s. Although she had served her sentence and subsequently lived in apparently blameless anonymity with her daughter, the press chose this moment to hound her out of her house and into protective custody – with the blessing of the prime minister and his home secretary, whose backing for the campaign tipped several gallons of petrol on to a moral panic that was already dangerously ablaze. A few days later, on a TV chat-show hosted by the right-wing rabble-rouser Richard Littlejohn (England's answer to Rush Limbaugh), a man who dared to suggest that lynch-law was a bad idea found himself howled down and threatened by the studio audience. When a woman on the same programme revealed that she had shot dead two men whom she suspected of paedophilia, she was given a thunderous ovation.

All this was merely a curtain-raiser for the madness that swept the nation in the summer of 2000, when the *News of the World* announced that it would publish the whereabouts of every paedophile in Britain. 'There are 110,000 proven paedophiles in the UK,' it declared. 'Today we start by identifying the first of these offenders but we make a pledge that we will not stop until all 110,000 are named and shamed. Week in, week out, we will add to our record . . .' Although the newspaper did warn that 'our campaign will be counter-productive if it provokes any display of animosity to those we name', its editorial began with this ringing battle-cry: 'There must be no hiding place for the evil perverts who prey on our children . . . We are taking the first step to publish the names and addresses.' The consequences were all too predictable: within days, lynch-mobs were rampaging through dozens of British towns – smashing windows, setting cars alight and screaming threats through the letterboxes of anybody who had a vaguely similar name to someone once rumoured to be a child-molester. (A *Private Eye* cartoon showed a man running from one such mob, pleading 'But I'm a *paediatrician*!' As ever, reality caught up with satire: shortly afterwards a paediatrician in Wales fled her home after being menaced by illiterate *News of the World* readers.) Throughout all this mayhem, neither the emotional Tony Blair nor any of his colleagues was prepared to condemn the newspaper's incitement to ochlocracy: the Home Office minister Paul Boateng daringly opined that the *News of the World*'s behaviour was 'unhelpful' – but then praised the paper for making 'an important contribution to the debate'.

Many people remember Lord Macaulay's famous line: 'We know no spectacle so ridiculous as the British public in one of its periodical fits of morality.' Few, however, have read the essay in which it appears, a review of Thomas Moore's *Life of Byron* from 1831. In general, Macaulay wrote, scandals are discussed for a day and then forgotten. 'But once in every six or seven years our virtue becomes outrageous. We cannot suffer the laws of religion and decency to be violated. We must make a stand against vice . . . Accordingly some unfortunate man, in no respect more depraved than hundreds whose offences have been treated with lenity, is singled out as an expiatory sacrifice.' As Macaulay argued, it is right and desirable that public opinion should condemn vices. 'But it should be directed against them uniformly, steadily and temperately, not by sudden fits and starts. There should be one weight and one measure . . . It is good that a certain portion of disgrace should constantly attend on certain bad actions. But it is not good that the offenders should merely have to stand the risks of a lottery of infamy.' Or, conversely, a lottery of sanctity (as with the Princess of Wales), which can be just as oppressively authoritarian in its consequences for those who fail to cheer the winner.

These periodical fits of hysteria are easy enough to incite but far harder to subdue. 'Men, it has been well said, think in herds,' the Scottish journalist Charles Mackay wrote in *Extraordinary Popular Delusions and the Madness of Crowds*, published more than 150 years ago; 'it will be seen that they go mad in herds, while they only recover their senses slowly, and one by one.' The need to temper instinct with reason, and find a harmony between individual and social needs, has long preoccupied thinkers who (unlike Tony Blair) appreciate that governance by raw emotion is tantamount to tyranny. In the eighteenth century, Bishop Butler argued that human nature was 'not merely a system of impulses . . . but a system in which some springs of action are naturally governing and regulative, while others are naturally submissive to regulation'. The importance of balancing what Butler called Universal Reason and Egoistic Reason, or Conscience and Self-Love, is also emphasised in Pope's *Essay on Man*:

> Two principles in human nature reign;
> Self-love, to urge, and Reason, to restrain;
> Nor this a good, nor that a bad we call,
> Each works its end, to move or govern all.

The emotional populism of modern politicians – as manifested in Al Gore's lachrymose convention speeches, Bill Clinton's televised prayer breakfasts and Tony Blair's promotion of the

Diana cult – may seem to be a form of collective experience. In truth, however, by asserting the primacy of feeling over reason, of the personal over the political, it stands revealed as nothing more than a disguised version of self-love.

9

Right is the new left

We are all Keynesians now.

PRESIDENT RICHARD M. NIXON, 1971

No serious challenge on the Left exists to Third Way thinking anywhere in the world. This is hardly surprising as globalisation punishes hard any country that tries to run its economy by ignoring the realities of the market or prudent public finances. In this strictly narrow sense, and in the urgent need to remove rigidities and incorporate flexibility in capital, product and labour markets, we are all 'Thatcherite' now.

PETER MANDELSON MP, 2002

In Andrew Martin's novel *Bilton*, published in 1998, we are introduced to a British prime minister named Philip Lazenby. 'Lazenby', Martin writes, 'had begun as a humane, enterprising, but conventional enough manager of the free market, but a year after his second election victory he surprisingly announced that he had a "guiding light" after all. "And that guiding light," he fatally intoned, "is Social Dynamics."'

No one has a clue what Lazenby means. After a blizzard of 'Initiatives', however, the outline of Social Dynamics becomes vaguely discernible through the fog of jargon. Individuals or

businesses or voluntary organisations will be rewarded finan-
cially – 'through an incredibly complex network of tax breaks
or Community Payback Vouchers' – for any act deemed to
be socially useful and dynamic. To be eligible (as measured
on Interlocking Sliding Scales, devised for the government by
a helpful maths professor who specialises in squaring circles),
such an act must promote any three of the following: individual responsibility; a spirit of community; an increase in
'generative capacity'; a reduction in public spending.

> Why [Martin's narrator asks] was the policy so very irritating?
> Well, it was billed as being bold and radical, but if you exam-
> ined the small print, which no one could ever be bothered
> to do, it appeared hedged about with self-defeating contradic-
> tions, recondite in the extreme and ideologically ambiguous.
> Was it left-wing or right-wing? Lazenby himself proudly
> announced, with the alienating gleam of the pioneering
> zealot, that it was 'both, either or neither'.
>
> On the one hand, there was the word 'community',
> pietistically repeated at every turn, which seemed to imply
> egalitarian intent. Yet, on the other hand, the profit motive
> appeared to be at the heart of Social Dynamics. It was, you
> might say, like one of those trick drawings of a staircase which
> at first glance looks plausible enough, but which then takes
> on the appearance of something quite unclimbable.

Had a satirical novelist not invented it first, some modish
academic or think-tank would undoubtedly have come up
with Social Dynamics eventually, and would by now probably
be organising seminars at 10 Downing Street to explain the
triangulatory brilliance of the scheme to Tony Blair. It is
certainly no less persuasive than much of the theoretical

gibberish that he has willingly bought from snake-oil salesmen over the last decade or so.

I first met Blair soon after Margaret Thatcher's arrival in Downing Street when he started offering occasional articles to the *New Statesman*, for which I worked. As a young, left-wing barrister who often acted for trade unions he was particularly alarmed by the Thatcherites' apparent ambition to crush organised labour. In a spirited *New Statesman* article from February 1980, for instance, he denounced the plans by Jim Prior, the employment secretary, to limit the unions' legal immunity. 'These proposals are not moderate,' he warned. 'They are a concerted attempt to destroy the effectiveness of industrial action.' Another feature by 'barrister Anthony Blair', published in November 1981, attacked Thatcher's persecution of secondary pickets as 'a draconian limitation on effective industrial action which involves anyone other than the immediate parties'. When he entered parliament, at the 1983 general election, he boasted of his commitment to unilateral nuclear disarmament and withdrawal from the European Community. And he seldom missed an opportunity to taunt renegades such as Dr David Owen, who had resigned from Labour in protest at those very policies and founded a Social Democratic Party. Writing for the *London Review of Books* in October 1987, he noted with a sneer that the SDP was 'being relaunched as the political wing of Sainsbury's' – a reference to the retail tycoon David Sainsbury, who was financing Owen's party at the time. (Perhaps Sainsbury didn't notice this jibe: a few years later he donated £2 million to New Labour, and was rewarded with a ministerial post in the first Blair government.)

The essay in the *London Review of Books* was published soon after the Tories' third successive election victory, by which time even some Labour supporters had begun to re-examine some of their economic shibboleths. Not Blair, however. 'The "free" market does not distribute fairly or efficiently,' he wrote. 'There is a tremendous danger – to which Dr Owen has succumbed – in believing that "Thatcherism" is now somehow invincible and that all the rest of us can do is debate alternatives within its framework. The fundamental error of Dr Owen has been to surrender to Mrs Thatcher's philosophy and say that power can only be devolved through the market. The 1990s will not see the continuing triumph of the market, but its failure.'

Few ordinary members of the Labour Party realised quite what a revolution they were precipitating when they chose Tony Blair as their new leader in the summer of 1994, following the sudden death of John Smith. As the shadow home secretary for the previous two years, he had been an effective parliamentary performer who made all the right liberal noises about civil liberties. Even his supposedly daring catchphrase 'tough on crime, tough on the causes of crime' – causes such as poverty and social dislocation – could be interpreted primarily as a riposte to right-wingers who believed that punishment alone was the solution. But what did he think about education, or defence, or privatisation? Thanks to the rule that opposition frontbenchers confine themselves to the subjects for which they are spokesmen, he had avoided giving hostages to fortune; and there were none to be found in his leadership manifesto, a stew of banalities seasoned with alluring but meaningless abstract nouns – 'partnership', 'innovation', 'fairness'. As the Labour backbencher Brian Sedgemore commented at the time: 'I have been quite surprised at how he has dealt with questions and answers since he was standing. He is quite stoically bland. The sheer blandness of it is difficult to penetrate, if he can hold it and not be embarrassed.'

Blandness can easily be mistaken for indecision or pusillanimity; but this was belligerent blandness, vagueness with a vengeance. 'It is time we had a clear, up-to-date statement of the objects and objectives of our party,' he announced impatiently at the annual Labour conference that autumn. Out went the declaration of intent that had remained unchanged since 1918, with its aspiration 'to secure for the workers by hand or by brain the full fruits of their industry and the most equitable distribution thereof that may be possible upon the basis of the common ownership of the means of production, distribution and exchange'. The new version endorsed 'a dynamic economy . . . in which the enterprise of the market and the rigour of competition are joined with the forces of partnership and cooperation to produce the wealth the nation needs'.

Over the past decade, with BSE and foot-and-mouth disease, Britons have become accustomed to the grisly spectacle of whole herds of cattle being slaughtered. Tony Blair's massacre of sacred cows in the mid-1990s was just as ruthless. In 1986 he had signed an advertisement in *Sanity*, newspaper of the Campaign for Nuclear Disarmament, advocating the unilateral removal of all nuclear weapons from British territory; now he was committed to the nuclear deterrent – and, he said, 'prepared to use it'. The man who had described Margaret Thatcher's curtailment of union rights as 'a scandalous and undemocratic measure against the trade union movement' now announced that 'the basic elements of that legislation – ballots before strikes, for union elections [and] restrictions on mass picketing – are here to stay'. In 1988 Blair had demanded 'an active, interventionist industrial policy'; by

1996 he was reassuring the Nottingham Chamber of Commerce that 'New Labour does not believe it is the job of government to interfere in the running of business.' Having opposed all the Tory privatisations – of gas, water, rail, electricity, British Airways and much else – he now argued that with public utilities 'the presumption should be that economic activity is best left to the private sector, with market forces being fully encouraged to operate'. As a young shadow Treasury spokesman in 1987, Blair had told the House of Commons that 'income tax cuts are the worst thing that can be done for the economy and the least effective way to provide jobs'; now he promised to keep taxes down 'and, if possible, to lower them'. In the words of one traditionally Conservative newspaper, the London *Evening Standard*: 'We are now confronted by a Labour government which, on many of the issues about which the public care most, promises to pursue much the same policies as the Tories, but under the leadership of new and more effective ministers.' It was intended as a compliment.

Market solutions, privatisation, low taxation – these may all have seemed thrillingly 'modern' to Tony Blair, in the first flush of his born-again zeal, but they were also indistinguishable from the policies of Margaret Thatcher and John Major. As a *Guardian* headline asked: 'If Labour wins, how will we know?' Blair needed to find some way of persuading the electorate and his colleagues (and, perhaps, even himself) that the sum of these parts added up to something more than warmed-up neo-liberalism. In short, he needed a Big Idea – what George Bush, in a characteristically elegant formulation, had dubbed 'the vision thing'.

There was a precedent here. When the youthful and energetic Harold Wilson became leader of the Labour Party in

1963, after a similarly long period of Tory rule, he sought salvation in science – something which could simultaneously unite his fractious party (for, in those distant days, no one was *against* science) and bury its old-fashioned cloth-cap image. In his speech at the Labour conference in Scarborough he dazzled delegates with the wonders of modern technology, describing computers which 'do their calculations and take their decisions in a period of three-millionths of a second' as he evoked the prospect of a New Britain 'forged in the white heat of a technological revolution'. It was new, exciting and wonderfully uncontroversial: even right-wing newspapers could scarce forbear to cheer, while the Marxist *New Left Review* praised Wilson's desire 'to produce an economy that is progressively more efficient and uses its resources more rationally than the one we have been used to'.

Harold Wilson had unveiled his Big Idea before an audience of the party faithful in Scarborough. Tony Blair's chosen audience, by contrast, was a gathering of corporate executives in Singapore, a country where capitalism operates without the tiresome inconvenience of democratic institutions or public debate. Addressing the 'Singapore Business Community' in January 1996, he revealed the secret weapon which would enable Britain to become 'one of the really dynamic economies of the twenty-first century': 'We need to build a relationship of trust not just within a firm but within a society. By trust, I mean the recognition of a mutual purpose for which we work together and in which we all benefit. It is a stakeholder economy, in which opportunity is available to all, advancement is through merit, and from which no group or class is set apart or excluded.' The resemblance between this new socialist vision and old one-nation Toryism was cunningly disguised by his invocation of the 'stakeholder economy' – a phrase taken from Will Hutton's bestselling book *The State We're In.* Blair recited the S-word like a mantra: a stakeholder economy, a stakeholder society, a stakeholder welfare system, stakeholder universities. Three weeks after returning from Singapore he delivered a lengthy speech from the pulpit of Southwark Cathedral demanding nothing less than a Stake- holder Britain ('for the new millennium', he added fervently, thus working both the vogueish clichés of the moment into his text). Will Hutton basked in the appellation 'Blairite guru' – though not for long. When Blair belatedly noticed that the author of *The State We're In* was an unreconstructed Keynesian, stakeholding was dropped from the New Labour vocabulary.

Plenty of suitors were eager to replace Hutton, and Blair flirted with most of them. He was particularly attracted to strict disciplinarians such as the sociologist Amitai Etzioni, who had already seduced the US president with his 1993 bestseller *The Spirit of Community.* ('Thank you very much, Dr Etzioni,' Bill Clinton wrote in an ecstatic fan-letter. 'Thank you for the inspiration that your work has given to me and to so many others, and for your wonderful book.') In essence, Etzioni's 'communitarianism' was indistinguishable from Frank Buchman's sinister Moral Rearmament crusade of the 1930s: with too many freedoms and not enough responsi- bilities, decadent Westerners could no longer 'tell right from wrong' and were wallowing in 'rampant moral confusion and social anarchy'. He proposed that 'we should, for a period of, say, the next decade, put a tight lid on the manufac- turing of new rights'. The message was echoed by another member of Blair's intellectual harem, Geoff Mulgan, who argued in his book *Connexity* that 'the most pressing problems on the public agenda are not poverty or material shortage ... but rather the disorders of freedom: the troubles that result from having too many freedoms that are abused rather than constructively used'.

Many of these New Labour thinkers were sponsored and promoted by Demos, a policy-shop founded in 1993 by Geoff Mulgan and Martin Jacques 'to encourage radical and icono-clastic thinking about the long-term problems facing modern societies'. Mulgan and Jacques had a talent for clothing right-wing ideas in progressive language – or, if that failed, in cool-sounding jargon – as they had proved during the 1980s by writing awestruck tributes to Thatcherism in *Marxism Today*, the Communist Party's theoretical journal. The compliment was returned when their new think-tank won the backing of Margaret Thatcher's former advisers Sir Alfred Sherman and Sir Douglas Hague. Like Tony Blair, Demos claimed to have moved 'beyond left and right' by creating a 'big tent'. It was thrillingly modern – so much so that the research director, David Ashworth, challenged the tyranny of traditional nomen-clature by changing his name to 'Perri 6'.

When Demos spoke, Tony Blair listened. Whether he could understand what was being said is another matter. Its pamphlet *No Turning Back: Generations and the Genderquake*, pub-lished soon after he became Labour leader in 1994, was littered with diagrams provided by a company called Synergy Brand Values Ltd, in which words such as 'connected-ness', 'risk', 'sexuality', 'technophobia', 'balance', 'empathy', 'health', 'familism', 'accept' and 'rigidity' floated randomly across the page – thereby showing, apparently, that among people between the ages of eighteen and thirty-four there had been a swing away from 'sustenance-driven needs' to 'outer-directed values'. To win the support of these voters, it argued, Labour needed to 'develop a political language and agenda which resonates with [their] core values'.

As if that weren't enough for the new leader to chew on, Demos simultaneously published a 3,000-word 'open letter to Tony Blair' which purported to explain 'what sort of government Britain needs in the second half of the 1990s'. It was very radical and iconoclastic indeed: 'We should build on our strengths'; 'You could help people regain a sense of control over their locality by enabling them to forge new communities'; 'At all times your government should be on the side of the people against the elites.' Finally, Blair must 'bring in different expertises into policy formulation and implementation, and to test new ideas'. Such as, presumably, the 'ideas' pouring forth from Martin Jacques and Geoff Mulgan.

The grandiosity of Demos's ambitions was seldom reflected in its actual prescriptions: as public macro-policy was ceded to the Bank of England and powerful industrialists, it could only advocate small if eye-catching changes at the margin. One paper by Perri 6 declared that government must be about 'nothing less than changing the whole culture'. How could this be done? By 'prompt payment of government invoices'. Demos's project to 'rebrand Britain', led by twenty-three-year-old Mark Leonard, was endorsed by the new Labour prime minister soon after his election, but its achievements were not exactly the stuff of revolution: a new 'mission statement' for the Foreign Office, a new red box for the Chancellor to carry to the House of Commons on budget day (replacing one that had been used since the time of Gladstone) and a few cocktail parties for pop-singers at 10 Downing Street. Oh, and some temporary 'lifestyle pods' in Westminster. These provoked snorts of hilarity from the veteran American TV presenter Morley Safer when CBS's *60 Minutes* despatched him to London to report on Cool Britannia:

Safer (*voiceover*): The Blair government seems intent on celebrating those things that are available just about everywhere else. The old slogan 'Come to Britain' could be replaced by 'Why Bother?' A case in point: the magnificent stretch of gravel known as Horse Guards Parade, near 10 Downing Street, was the venue for Mr Blair to erect these giant pods, inflatable buildings to show off the best of Britain.

Tony Blair: What I hope you can see here is that some of what is happening in Britain today in design, in modern engineering, is immensely exciting and is something to offer the world. And we're very proud of it.

(*Footage of displays inside the lifestyle pod of coat hangers and luggage.*)

Safer (*voiceover*): Here in the lifestyle pod, Mr Blair displayed his wares: coat hangers for a new age; luggage, presumably for leaving Cool Britannia.

Tony Blair (*voiceover*): But when people come here, they see not just a great country with the pageantry and the ceremony and tradition, but also a country right at the cutting edge of modernity as well.

(*Footage of displays in the lifestyle pod; Robin Cook addressing an audience.*)

Safer (*voiceover*): How is this for cutting edge? At last, a trolley full of toasters.

Thus ended the 'rebranding' of Britain. But it did Demos no harm: Geoff Mulgan was hired by No. 10 as a policy adviser, and bright young wonks from his think-tank continued to address ministerial seminars on 'holistic government', 'flexible networks' – or, most irresistibly, 'the Third Way'.

What was the Third Way? No one ever knew, but it was somewhere between the Second Coming and the Fourth

Dimension. Although Demos pushed the idea strenuously it was actually the brainchild of Professor Anthony Giddens, another former left-winger who had lurched to the right but couldn't quite bring himself to admit it. His book *The Third Way*, which became a sacred text for Blairites, asserted that 'children should have responsibilities to their parents, not just the other way round. It is worth at least considering whether this should be legally binding.' A Tory who proposed such a scheme would be condemned as a patriarchal bully. Coming from a sociology professor and student of Max Weber, however, it could be disguised as thoroughly modern radicalism.

According to Giddens, the Third Way sought 'to go beyond those on the right who say "government is the enemy", and those on the left who say "government is the answer".' This grotesque caricature of all previous arguments about the role of the state had about as much intellectual rigour as *Bambi*, but it clearly appealed to insecure political leaders who hoped to be all things to all people. His admirers included not only Blair and Clinton but also Chancellor Schröder of Germany and President Cardozo of Brazil. 'In the past three months,' the *Guardian* reported in March 1999, 'he has given more than 90 interviews about his book *The Third Way*. When he arrived in Beijing five days after its publication last autumn, all the major mandarins had already read it. Stalin believed that socialism could be achieved in one country. Anthony Giddens is globalisation in one person.'

Since the Chinese were engaged in a bizarre project to reconcile Marxism with free-market capitalism, they probably recognised him as a natural ally. In *The Third Way and Its Critics*, the sequel to his *magnum opus*, he argued that 'companies should not be inhibited from expanding by the

existence of too many rules and restrictions'. The absurd
qualifier makes the sentence meaningless: even the most
unreconstructed old leftist wouldn't propose that we need
'too many' restrictions. But how many are sufficient? Very
few, to judge by his comments on page 75: 'Product, capital
and labour markets must all be flexible for an economy today
to be competitive . . . Flexibility does indeed entail deregulation.' By page 143, however, Giddens is citing Microsoft
as the sort of monopolistic corporation which 'left-of-centre
governments mustn't shirk confronting . . . Sometimes the
global economy is offered as a rationale for why regulations
on monopoly should be relaxed – on the grounds that very
large corporations have to compete with others of comparable size in the world marketplace. But the net effect is to
project monopoly onto a global scale.' So does the global
market require more deregulation or tighter regulation?
Both, apparently.

Tony Blair was so inspired by Giddens's circle-squaring that
he sat down to write a tract of his own. On 21 September
1998 the Fabian Society published his pamphlet, *The Third
Way: New Politics for the New Century.* Later that day he jetted
off to New York on Concorde – the only acceptable method
of transport for Tertiary Voyagers – to participate in a multi-
lateral wonkfest on this fashionable but enigmatic catchphrase. Hillary Clinton, who hosted the seminar, had been
coquetting with the idea for some time. In 1993 she told the
New York Times that she was seeking a 'unified field theory of
life', no less, which 'would marry conservatism and liberalism,
capitalism and statism, and tie together practically everything:
the way we are, the way we were, the faults of man and the
word of God, the end of communism and the beginning of
the third millennium, crime in the streets and on Wall Street,

teenage mothers and foul-mouthed children and frightening drunks in the parks, the cynicism of the press and the corrupting role of television, the breakdown of civility and the loss of community'. And she succeeded. As her husband announced proudly in his 1998 State of the Union address: 'My fellow Americans, we have found a Third Way.'

If the Holy Grail had indeed been located, why was Blair still searching for it? In his Fabian pamphlet he insisted that 'our work is at an early stage'. This might explain the lack of detail in some of his preliminary findings. 'The arts and the creative industries should be part of our common culture ... Education is not enough ... We support the efforts of peacemakers and peacekeepers abroad as an extension of our mission at home.' Who would have guessed it? Blair also revealed that the Third Way was 'vibrant' and 'passionate', rather like Bill Clinton's libido, but also 'flexible' and 'innovative', like Clinton's definition of sexual relations. It rejected 'selfishness' and 'inefficiency', preferring nice things to nasty things.

'There are even claims that it is unprincipled,' Blair admitted. 'But I believe that a critical dimension of the Third Way is that policies flow from values, not vice versa. With the right policies, market mechanisms are critical to meeting social objectives, entrepreneurial zeal can promote social justice.' Were entrepreneurs and corporate chieftains really so benign? Apparently so. 'Companies will devise ways to share with their staff the wealth their know-how creates,' he promised. In the very next paragraph, however, he argued that 'government intervention is necessary to protect the weak and ensure that all gain some of the benefits of economic progress. That is why we insist on minimum standards for pay and conditions at work.' If companies naturally share out the spoils fairly, why should government need to intervene at all? This was how the Third Way worked – reconciling contradictions by pretending that they didn't exist. 'Governments in the course of this century have proved themselves well equipped to cut or raise interest rates . . . That is why we have given operational independence in the setting of interest rate policy to the Bank of England.' Admittedly the first of those sentences appeared on page seven and the second on page eight, but they still made for a pretty weird dialectic.

Or try this. 'Dynamic markets and international competition are vital spurs to economic growth and innovation. That is one reason we have introduced in our first year one of Europe's toughest competition policy regimes.' And yet the prime minister's favourite tycoon, Rupert Murdoch, was one of the most determined monopolists in the world. Blair said that there must be no return to the old politics of 'tax and spend', but gave credit to previous Labour governments for producing 'a fairer sharing of taxation and growth, and great improvements in working conditions and in welfare, health and educational services'. How was this achieved if not through progressive taxation and spending? As Clinton's former colleague Robert Reich pointed out, 'the better-off have to pony up'.

Talking of ponies, one wonders if Blair knew of the fate of an earlier experiment in political innovation. Just over a century earlier, when the French proto-fascist General Georges Boulanger stood for election against a wet Radical, the socialist leader Jules Guesde urged disaffected electors to support a 'Third Way' candidate – Boulanger's horse. Though the nag won only a few hundred votes, it was still a more substantial alternative than the vapid, vacuous musings of Messrs Blair and Giddens, whose ceaseless appeals to 'duty' and 'prudence' are best answered by Roy Campbell's old verse on certain South African novelists:

> You praise the firm restraint with which they write –
> I'm with you there, of course:
> They use the snaffle and the curb all right,
> But where's the bloody horse?

10

Forward to the past

An argument that socialists ought to be prepared to meet, since it is brought up constantly both by Christian apologists and by neo-pessimists such as James Burnham, is the alleged immutability of 'human nature'. Socialists are accused – I think without justification – of assuming that Man is perfectible, and it is then pointed out that human history is in fact one long tale of greed, robbery and oppression. Man, it is said, will always try to get the better of his neighbour, he will always hog as much property as possible for himself and his family . . . The proper answer, it seems to me, is that this argument belongs to the Stone Age. It presupposes that material goods will always be desperately scarce. The power hunger of human beings does indeed present a serious problem, but there is no reason for thinking that the greed for mere wealth is a permanent human characteristic. We are selfish in economic matters because we all live in terror of poverty. But when a commodity is not scarce, no one tries to grab more than his fair share of it. No one tries to make a corner in air, for instance. The millionaire as well as the beggar is content with just so much air as he can breathe. Or, again, water. In this country we are not troubled by lack of water . . . Yet in dried-up countries like North Africa, what hatreds, what appalling crimes the lack of water can cause! So also with any other kind of goods. If they were made plentiful, as they so easily might be, there is no reason to think that the supposed

acquisitive instincts of the human being could not be bred out in a
couple of generations. And after all, if human nature never changes,
why is it that we not only don't practise cannibalism any longer, but
don't even want to?

GEORGE ORWELL, *Tribune*, 21 July 1944

In his book *Jihad vs. McWorld*, having identified the dominant forces in the modern world as tribalism and globalism, Benjamin Barber proceeded to treat those two impostors just the same: 'Neither needs democracy. Neither promotes democracy.' To market triumphalists, who liked to attribute high moral purpose to the often grubby business of money-making, this was nothing less than blasphemy, an updated version of the moral equivalence displayed during the Cold War by jaded *bien pensants* who professed hostility to both Washington and Moscow. Yet it was borne out by the record of one of their heroes, Rupert Murdoch.

Murdoch, a sworn enemy of regulation and Big Government, often described his global media empire as freedom's greatest messenger. In his commercial dealings with the autocrats of China, however, he shamelessly kowtowed to tyranny – or, as his defenders might prefer to say, applied the Realpolitik techniques of give and take to international business. Murdoch took BBC World Service TV off his Star network; the Chinese government gave him permission to start a cable TV station in Guangdong. Murdoch ditched *East and West*, a memoir by the former Hong Kong governor Chris Patten; President Jiang Zemin returned the favour by allowing the film *Titanic* into Chinese cinemas, to the delight of 20th Century-Fox (prop. R. Murdoch). On the fiftieth anniversary of the Universal Declaration of Human Rights in December

1998, Murdoch travelled to Beijing to express his 'admiration for China's tremendous achievements in every respect over the past two decades'; President Jiang repaid this compliment ten months later by granting an exclusive interview to *The Times* on the eve of his state visit to London.

For such an important assignment the newspaper naturally sent its best reporter, Lord Rees-Mogg. This could have been a serious diplomatic *faux pas*. Five years earlier, the Chinese ambassador to London had written to *The Times* protesting at Rees-Mogg's 'gross misjudgments', and as recently as April 1996 his lordship was still attacking China's 'insensitive and repressive' regime. Luckily, however, he was fully on-message for the interview in the Great Hall of the People. 'We are almost at the same age, but I'm two years older than you,' President Jiang chuckled. 'I was told you are a Lord. What's the difference between a Lord and a Sir?' They went on to chat about their families. 'He obviously has a very warm affection for his grandchildren,' Mogg wrote. 'Overall I found the president very relaxed, very friendly, very intelligent, a man at ease with himself . . . Among world statesmen he reminds me most of President Eisenhower, a natural conciliator.'

Eventually the banter had to stop. Mogg knew there was a question he must ask, but wasn't sure how to put it without causing offence. He phrased it thus: 'With globalism, the whole world is involved with issues of nationality and ethnic tension. In Britain we have our own controversies with our national relationship with Europe. You have the problem of the minorities. I have met the Dalai Lama on a number of occasions and regard him as a distinguished religious leader. Is there any prospect of reconciliation?' There was a moment's tense silence. Had the man from *The Times* been too fearless, too hard-hitting? 'I was not expecting to be asked that question,' Jiang replied at last, 'but you have asked it in a very friendly way, so I will answer it.' The president then revealed that his country's influence on Tibet had been entirely benign. Rees-Mogg was deeply impressed by this evidence of 'humanity' and 'respect for religious beliefs'.

Perhaps he hadn't read a 1,000-page report published by the US State Department the previous month, which highlighted the 'particularly severe' violations of religious freedom in China and six other countries. Political dissidents could also have told Lord Rees-Mogg a thing or two about their president's 'humanity': at the time of his visit, hundreds of people were still in jail for their part in the pro-democracy movement that was crushed in Tiananmen Square in the summer of 1989. (Liu Baiqiang, who was already serving a ten-year jail sentence in 1989, had allegedly written 'Long Live Freedom' on tiny scraps of paper in his cell; according to the official indictment, he then 'attached these to the legs of locusts and released the insects into the air'. He was given a further eight years for 'counter-revolutionary incitement and propaganda'.) Instead, Rees-Mogg filled a whole page of *The Times* with sycophantic drivel about Jiang Zemin's 'peace and goodwill' towards his people. 'Confucius made it the first of his five universal rules that "justice ought to be practised between an emperor and his subjects",' he drooled. 'This idea of a direct contract between ruler and people – one interpreted in a very different way from modern Western understanding – still stands at the heart of Chinese government.'

The example of Rupert Murdoch is merely one among many confirming Benjamin Barber's point. The former British prime minister Edward Heath and the former US secretary of state Henry Kissinger, both of whom had extensive business interests in China, regarded the country's pro-democracy campaigners as a pestilential nuisance. ('No government in the world would have tolerated having the main square of its capital occupied for eight weeks by tens of thousands of demonstrators,' Kissinger wrote after the Tiananmen Square massacre.) When President Jiang Zemin paid his state visit to Britain in October 1999, the London police were ordered to arrest any Chinese dissidents who exercised their freedom to demonstrate against Jiang – and this under a British government supposedly committed to an 'ethical dimension' in foreign policy. At the same time Margaret Thatcher and other 'friends of freedom' were battling vigorously to defend General Pinochet, a man who had demonstrated that a market economy can flourish under a brutal military dictatorship.

If capitalism required democracy, the economic record of Chile under Pinochet – as of Singapore and Hong Kong – would be wholly inexplicable. Nevertheless, Barber's reasonable observation was all but drowned out by the *fortissimo* hosannas of those who regarded the global market as a benign universal deity – immortal, invisible, omniscient, omnipotent. No mere metaphor, this: the hot gospellers of the new age saw themselves as disciples of a literally divine power which compelled their worship. Books such as *God Wants You to Be Rich* and *Jesus, CEO* became bestsellers; the management guru Tom Peters wrote an essay entitled 'The Market's Will Be Done'. (Dozens of other examples are collected in Thomas Frank's vigorous debunking of the religion, *One Market Under God*.) When the Harvard divinity professor Harvey Cox decided to start reading the business pages, he 'was surprised to discover that most of the concepts I ran across were quite familiar': myths of origin, legends of the fall and doctrines of sin and redemption, thinly disguised as chronicles about the creation of wealth, the seductive temptations of statism, captivity to faceless economic cycles, and ultimate salvation through the advent of free markets. Just as the prophets of Israel repaired to the desert and then returned to announce whether Yahweh was feeling benevolent or wrathful, so the market's fickle will – sometimes 'apprehensive', sometimes 'jubilant' – was clarified by daily bulletins. Here, Cox concluded, was that true and sure faith described by St Paul as the evidence of things unseen. But one element was missing from the analogy:

> One sometimes wonders, in this era of Market religion, where the sceptics and freethinkers have gone. What has happened to the Voltaires who once exposed bogus miracles, and the H. L. Menckens who blew shrill whistles on pious humbuggery? Such is the grip of current orthodoxy that to question the omniscience of The Market is to question the inscrutable wisdom of Providence. The metaphysical principle is obvious: If you *say* it's the real thing, then it must *be* the real thing. As the early Christian theologian Tertullian once remarked, '*Credo quia absurdum est.*' ('I believe because it is absurd.')

If the new faith had a single gospel, it was probably *The Lexus and the Olive Tree* (1999), by the *New York Times* columnist Thomas L. Friedman, which sold more than 150,000 copies in hardback alone and went straight to the top of President Clinton's reading list. Perhaps because the title sounded like an echo of *Jihad vs. McWorld*, Friedman was eager to reveal that it had in fact occurred to him as long ago as 1992. Returning from a visit to the Lexus factory in Japan – where one of the most luxurious cars in the world is assembled largely by robots – he noticed a story in the *Herald*

Tribune about yet another land dispute between Israelis and Palestinians. Eureka! In an instant, Friedman realised that this was the future division of humankind: between the modern masses of aspirant consumers who lusted after a Lexus, and a dwindling number of disgruntled dodos who were still (as he contemptuously summarised the Palestine question) bickering over who owned which olive tree.

Not that the dodos were all in the Middle East. A large flock of them could be found in Europe – in France, to be precise. To Friedman, as to so many American evangelists for globalisation, there was something uniquely irritating about the French – an apparently rich and civilised people who nevertheless seemed reluctant to join McWorld, clinging perversely to their own language, culture, institutions and economic habits. As he grumbled a few months after publication of *The Lexus and the Olive Tree*, 'The book is coming out in Arabic, Chinese, German, Japanese and Spanish. There is only one major country where my American publisher could not find a local publisher to print it: France.'

And no wonder. Readers of the *New York Times* had often been entertained by Friedman's tirades against Gallic stubbornness. Here, for instance, is a despatch he sent from Casablanca on 26 February 1997:

Although French culture and education has [*sic*] been imbedded in Morocco's major cities since the early 1900s, there are now four American schools here, and they are in such demand they have waiting lists for the waiting lists. In addition, English-language schools are mushrooming all over. Visa requests to study in America, particularly for MBAs, are skyrocketing. What gives? It's actually a fascinating cultural competition between America and France for the soul of the new generation in traditionally French-dominated North and West Africa. Now that the cold war is over, and the Western model has triumphed over Communism, all the competition now is between different Western models for succeeding in a free-market world. In this region, it's a competition America is increasingly winning . . .

You can't understand the tension between the US and France today over NATO if you don't appreciate this cultural competition. It's clearly making the French a little crazy. How else can one explain their recent attempt to prevent Georgia Tech's overseas campus in France from using English on its Internet Web site? That's insane! But it's the act of people who feel the world is changing and they want to stop it, not master it.

The French can try to beat America at its own game, which they are quite capable of doing if they get focused, or they can play footsy with the enemies of America, who are often the enemies of modernity – in which case France risks becoming increasingly marginal.

Presumably in a spirit of mischief, in the summer of 1999 the journal *Foreign Affairs* invited Friedman to debate globalisation with Ignacio Ramonet, editor of *Le Monde Diplomatique*. Once the opening civilities were over, the American quickly lost patience. 'Ramonet falls into a trap that often ensnares French intellectuals, and others, who rail against globalisation,' he complained. 'They assume that the rest of the world hates it as much as they do, and so they are always surprised in the end when the so-called little people are ready to stick with it . . . The fact is the wretched of the earth want to go to Disneyworld, not to the barricades. They want the Magic Kingdom, not *Les Misérables*. Just ask them.'

There are 1.3 billion human beings in the world who subsist on less than a dollar a day and have yet to make their first phone call, let alone send an email. Is their desire for food, clean water, education, shelter and employment really over-shadowed by the desperate yearning for a holiday in the Magic Kingdom or a Lexus car? Has Friedman himself ever asked them? During the ceaseless travels recorded in *The Lexus and the Olive Tree*, and in his newspaper columns, he seems to mix only with the international elite. The opening sentences of his 1997 report from Morocco are all too typical: 'The frigate USS Carr pulled into Casablanca harbour last week and the US Embassy held a reception on board, replete with Budweiser and chicken fingers, for local dignitaries. I dropped by and was soon conversing with a senior Moroccan official. Sporting a tailored suit and speaking elegant French, he explained why he was sending his two children to the American school . . .'

But wait: close study of Friedman's book discloses at least one occasion when he actually encountered one of those 'wretched of the earth'. While visiting Hanoi, he paid a dollar every morning to have himself weighed by a Vietnamese woman who had installed herself on the pavement with a set of bathroom scales. This, he explains, was 'my contribution to the globalisation of Vietnam. To me, her unspoken motto was: "Whatever you've got no matter how big or small – sell it, trade it, barter it, leverage it, rent it, but do something with it to turn a profit, improve your standard of living and get into the game."' It was another Eureka moment, convinc-ing him that 'globalisation emerges from below, from street level, from people's very souls and from their very deepest aspirations . . . It starts with a lady in Hanoi, crouched on the sidewalk, offering up a bathroom scale as her ticket to the Fast World.'

Only someone with limitless dogmatic fervour could interpret this poor woman's struggle for existence as proof that she had learned to love the god of the global market (and was, no doubt, already sending off for her Disney World brochure). But how could even the most blinkered zealot conclude also that 'globalisation emerges from below'? The institutions which seek to impose the new economic orthodoxy – the International Monetary Fund, the World Bank, the World Trade Organisation – have been created and directed, with minimal public scrutiny or accountability, by a small elite conclave of capitalist cardinals.

Evangelists such as Friedman assume that the global economy severely restricts the scope of nation states and governments to direct their own affairs (though this assumption may well be exaggerated, as Paul Hirst and Grahame Thompson show in their book *Globalisation in Question*). They deduce from this that it transfers power to the people, creating a vast and ever-swelling army of 'super-empowered individuals'. As soon as that Hanoi street-woman has a laptop and a few hundred dollars, she too can join the Electronic Herd (as Friedman calls it), roaming the world via cyberspace for luscious pastures on which to graze. Anyone can do it, from a Vietnamese beggar to a senior reporter on the *New York Times*. By way of example, Friedman quotes what he told the Thai prime minister when they met in 1998:

Mr Prime Minister, I have a confession to make. I helped oust your predecessor – and I didn't even know his name. You see, I was sitting home in my basement watching the Thai baht sink (and watching your predecessor completely mismanage your economy). So I called my broker and told him to get me out of East Asian emerging markets. I could have sold you out myself, via the Internet, but I decided to get my broker's advice instead. It's one dollar, one vote, Mr Prime Minister. How does it feel to have Tom Friedman as a constituent?

The temptation to reply with a smack in the face must have been hard to resist. One dollar, one vote: this crass formula accidentally confirms that fund managers and speculators with billions of dollars at their disposal – the big beasts of the Electronic Herd – have effectively disfranchised everyone else. They are free to trample over entire continents without a care for the social dislocation, economic insecurity and environmental devastation they leave behind. Who, then, will clear up the mess? During his exchanges with Ignacio Ramonet in *Foreign Affairs*, Friedman hotly denied ever suggesting that it would all somehow be magicked away:

> Ramonet says that I believe all the problems of globalisation will be solved by the 'invisible hand of the market'. I have no idea where these quotation marks came from, let alone the thought. It certainly is not from anything I have written. The whole last chapter of my book lays out in broad strokes what I believe governments – the American government in particular – must do to 'democratise' globalisation, both economically and politically.

Naturally, one turns to Friedman's final chapter in search of this democratising recipe – only to find an assertion that the American government must be willing to use military force on recalcitrant nations who resist the imperatives of globalisation: 'The hidden hand of the market [yes, he did use the phrase] will never work without a hidden fist. McDonald's cannot flourish without McDonnell Douglas, the designer of the US Air Force F-15. And the hidden fist that keeps the world safe for Silicon Valley's technologies to flourish is called the US Army, Air Force, Navy, and Marine Corps ... With all due respect to Silicon Valley, ideas and technology don't just win and spread on their own.' In short, the Pentagon must loose the fateful lightning of its terrible swift sword against all who have no appetite for Big Macs; and what these people ought to understand is that they are being pulverised *for their own good*, since the forcible imposition of American burger joints is the guarantor of their future peace and security. For, according to Friedman, no two countries that have a McDonald's ever fight a war against each other. This 'Golden Arches Theory of Conflict Prevention' (he has a real talent for glibly sonorous phraseology) was first propounded in his *New York Times* column on 8 December 1996, and recycled in *The Lexus and the Olive Tree*. Alas! By the time the book appeared the US Air Force was already bombing Belgrade, which had no fewer than seven branches of McDonald's. Friedman then devised a cunning explanation to show that the Golden Arches Theory had in fact been confirmed. Why did Milošević withdraw his forces from Kosovo after only seventy-eight days? Not, as everyone else in the world assumed, because of Nato's assault and the threat of more to come. The Serb leader was obliged to retreat because Belgrade was 'a modern European city, a majority of whose citizens wanted to be integrated with Europe and the globalisation system ... It turns out in the end the Serbs wanted to wait in line for burgers, not for Kosovo.' The Balkan war of 1999 was, therefore, 'only a temporary exception that proved my rule'.

Full marks for ingenuity, if nothing else. There is, of course, some truth in the general suggestion that countries which are assimilated into the world economy will be more reluctant to declare all-out war on one another than those which remain outside it. However, modern wars are usually fought not between states but within states. How does Big Mac diplomacy help there? 'Civil wars and skirmishes', Friedman replies hastily, 'don't count.' The dismissive style is characteristic of the globalisers' ruthless attitude to anything for which their simple prescriptions don't appear to work. 'Bosnia, Albania, Algeria, Serbia, Syria and many African states have been unable to make the transition,' he notes sternly in his book. 'But these states are weak enough and small enough that the system just builds a firewall around them.' Farewell, Africa; see you again in a century or so, if you're still alive.

For all their talk of 'empowering individuals', few masters of the modern world evince any human sympathy for those less potent than themselves. Like the machines of Kipling's poem, they can neither love nor pity nor forgive. Almost the only emotion of which they are capable is glee – both at their own gilded success and at the misfortunes of others. 'Think of participating in the global economy today like driving a Formula One race car, which gets faster and faster every year,' Friedman writes. 'Someone is always going to be running into the wall and crashing, especially when you have drivers who only a few years ago were riding a donkey.' Even those countries which willingly obey the order to enter this lethal Grand Prix are not allowed the passing tribute of a sigh when they crash and burn. 'I believe globalisation did us all a favor by melting down the economies of Thailand, Korea, Malaysia, Indonesia, Mexico, Russia and Brazil in the 1990s, because it laid bare a lot of rotten practices and institutions in countries that had prematurely globalised.'

If in doubt, blame the victims. For Friedman knows full well who encouraged these nations to globalise 'prematurely' and thus precipitated the meltdown. The Asian financial panic of 1997, a contagion that later spread as far as Russia and Brazil, was a direct consequence of American insistence that countries such as Thailand open their capital markets to foreign funds – even if the countries in question, with a tradition of high domestic savings, had no particular need of extra capital, and even though there was no evidence that unhampered capital inflows necessarily brought higher growth. Far from it: as the Asian economies learned in 1997, the foreign money that flows in so easily can rush out again with even more startling suddenness, as irrational exuberance gives way to equally irrational pessimism. Although the International Monetary Fund tells governments to accept the 'discipline' of capital markets, in practice these markets have routinely proved themselves to be undisciplined, reckless and downright fickle.

The exodus of dollars caused a problem which was soon transformed into a major crisis by the IMF's austerity measures. In Indonesia, at Washington's behest, interest rates reached 80 per cent and the government had to abandon its attempts to subsidise the cost of living of the poor through price controls on essential goods such as kerosene. The result of this externally imposed 'cure' was a 20 per cent fall in gross domestic product. Undaunted, the IMF quack-doctors were soon dispensing the same remedy elsewhere: Brazil was ordered to borrow $42 billion to prop up its overvalued currency, while Russia had to endure interest rates as high as 170 per cent for the same purpose – a pointless endeavour, since both currencies collapsed anyway. The IMF's justification for this crazy attempt to hold back the tide was that devaluation would lead to hyperinflation. Even more irrationally, however, its programme also demanded an end to price-controls – which, when applied in Russia, led to an inflation rate of 520 per cent within three months.

Although the IMF is depicted by its enemies, and some admirers, as a posse of itinerant missionaries for free-market fundamentalism, the practice is often strikingly different from the theory – rather as business tycoons who praise the beauty of competition will, in their own corporate backyard, work tirelessly for the establishment of a monopoly or (failing that) a cartel. One of the few critics to have noticed the distinction is Mark Weisbrot, director of the Centre for Economic and Policy Research in Washington DC, who points out that the free-market solution in those countries which sacrificed their economies to maintain a fixed exchange-rate – Russia, Brazil, Argentina – would have been to abandon the peg and let the currency find its own level. Instead, he writes, 'one of the few things that Washington actually did accomplish [in the Asian crisis] was to get the governments of the region to guarantee the privately held debt of foreign lenders, rather than letting the banks be subjected to the discipline of the market.' The IMF and other Washington institutions are not so much evangelists seeking to convert the world as enforcers trying to prevent developing and transitional countries from threatening the financial interests of the West. Weisbrot cites the example of intellectual-property rights:

Patent monopolies are the most costly, inefficient and – in the case of essential medicines – life-threatening form of protectionism that exists today. From an economic point of view, they create the same kinds of distortions as tariffs, only many times greater. Yet the attempt to extend US patent and copyright law to developing countries has become one of the primary objectives of America's foreign commercial policy.

The expansion of foreign intellectual-property claims not only drains scarce resources from developing countries but also makes it difficult for them to follow the more successful examples of late industrialisation, such as South Korea or Taiwan, where diffusion of foreign technology played an important role. This is part of a more general problem that is reflected in the economic failure of the last twenty years. There have historically been many paths to development, but none resembles the collection of policies that Washington foists on developing countries today.

Historically, economic development has been the essential precondition for trade liberalisation – and this economic development has often been made possible by a combination of import restrictions, tariffs, state subsidies and exchange-rate controls. Yet the Washington consensus now holds that poorer nations must somehow reverse the process, liberalising their trade policies long before they are ready or able to compete on the international market. In the words of the economist Ha-Joon Chang, the rich countries are 'kicking away the ladder'.

Many 'anti-globalisation protesters' miss this essential point: the problem is not globalisation *per se*, but the fact that the rules of the game have been set by the winning side – which, while enforcing them elsewhere, feels no obligation to apply them to its own conduct. Upholders of the 'Washington Consensus', which argues that governments should play a minimal role in economic management and regulation, maintain that they are merely applying principles which have created prosperity in the United States. For all its justified reputation as one of the least statist industrial democracies, however, America has accepted the need for official intervention and supervision ever since the great globalisation of the mid-nineteenth century. As the economist Joseph Stiglitz records:

> In the United States, government promoted the formation of the national economy, the building of the railroads, and the development of the telegraph – all of which reduced transportation and communications costs within the United States. As that process occurred, the democratically elected national government provided oversight: supervising and regulating, balancing interests, tempering crises, and limiting adverse consequences of this very large change in economic structure. So, for instance, in 1863 the US government established the first financial-banking regulatory authority – the Office of the Comptroller of Currency – because it was important to have strong national banks, and that requires strong regulation . . .
>
> Agriculture, the central industry of the United States in the mid-nineteenth century, was supported by the 1862 Morrill Act, which established research, extension and teaching programmes. That system worked extremely well and is widely credited with playing a central role in the enormous increases in agricultural productivity over the last century and a half. We established an industrial policy for other fledgling industries, including radio and civil aviation. The beginning of the telecommunications industry, with the first telegraph line between Baltimore and Washington DC, was funded by the federal government.

This tradition endures: the Internet, lest we forget, was created by the Pentagon. And American agriculture is still heavily subsidised and protected, as are the steel industry and many other sectors of the world's biggest 'free-market economy'. At times of economic slowdown, even under presidents who denigrate the role of government, the US will increase its deficit to finance expansionary fiscal and monetary policies. Yet when a developing country encounters the same problem, the IMF insists on stern contractionary measures that push it further into recession.

At home, the US has long accepted the necessity of creating rules and institutions to govern the market economy in the national interest. As Stiglitz points out, economic decisions within the government are largely taken by the National Economic Council, which includes the secretary of labour, the secretary of commerce, the chairman of the Council of Economic Advisers, the treasury secretary, the assistant attorney-general for anti-trust, and the US trade representatives. All these officials are part of an administration that must face Congress and the electorate. Internationally, by contrast, only the voices of the financial community are heard, since the IMF reports solely to ministers of finance and the governors of central banks, even though its decisions affect every aspect of life. Hence its apparent heedlessness to the human and environmental cost of its diktats.

By imposing world governance without world government America is essentially demanding rights without responsibilities, promoting a global market while refusing to accept the political consequences. It imposes the New World Order on rogue states, yet opts out of its own international obligations elsewhere – the land mines treaty, the international criminal court and the Kyoto protocol on global warming, all of which have been denounced in Washington as intolerable infringements of America's sovereign powers. When poorer nations try to assert their own national sovereignty, by contrast, they are punished for impeding free trade and the movement of capital.

The US is accused of two apparently contradictory crimes – imperialism and isolationism. Oddly enough, both charges have some validity. But the same criticism can be applied in reverse to America's detractors, who support Kyoto and other attempts at international regulation while objecting to the World Trade Organisation not merely because of its secrecy and remoteness but because it tries to enforce common international rules and standards. Left-wing critics of the New World Order disapprove of attempts by Western nations to act as 'world policemen' – except when it suits them, as with the arrest in London of General Pinochet. Nevertheless, although they campaigned for Pinochet to be sent for trial in Madrid, they opposed Slobodan Milošević's extradition to the Hague as outrageous interference in the internal affairs of Yugoslavia.

F. M. Cornford's famous Principle of the Wedge holds that 'you should not act justly now for fear of raising expectations that you will act still more justly in the future'. He meant it satirically – a point overlooked by figures such as Noam Chomsky and Harold Pinter, who argued that Nato's failure to protect people in Rwanda somehow disqualified it from trying to save the Kosovars. In the words of another Cornfordism, the Principle of the Dangerous Precedent: 'Nothing should ever be done for the first time.' For almost twenty-five years after the invasion of East Timor in 1975, the crusading journalist John Pilger continually (and rightly) criticised the Western powers for not halting Indonesia's illegal, genocidal occupation. So did Pilger rejoice when the United Nations finally despatched a peacekeeping force of British and Australian soldiers to confront the Indonesian militias after the bloody referendum of 1999, thus enabling the country to regain its independence from Jakarta? Especially since the foreign minister of the subsequent government was his old hero Jose Ramos-Horta, champion of the East Timorese resistance and winner of the 1996 Nobel peace prize? Of course not. To Pilger, Chomsky and countless others it is axiomatic that the West can never be right – damned if it doesn't intervene, damned if it does. He duly condemned the UN peacekeepers as villainous imperialists whose only purpose was to keep East Timor 'under the sway of Jakarta and western business interests'.

Much rhetoric from modern anti-capitalist pundits is equally contradictory or incoherent – apparently endorsing the imposition of certain universal standards while deploring most attempts to enforce them. 'Act locally, think globally' may be a fine-sounding slogan, but what does it actually mean? Do they want localisation, or world government? (Banners flourished by demonstrators at the WTO's 1999 meeting in Seattle included several from the Worldwide Campaign Against Globalisation.) And what is their attitude to modernity? Kirkpatrick Sale, a 'New Luddite' guru who symbolically smashes computers with a sledgehammer at public meetings, has argued that 'the computer, particularly the PC, will bring unmitigated disaster, simply because it enables the powers of this society to do faster and more efficiently the kinds of things it likes to do, with resulting social disintegration, economic polarization, and environmental devastation'. Where did he say this? In one of his many online conversations, of course. The murderous recluse Ted Kaczynski, better known as the Unabomber, now disseminates his technophobic ravings via prison-cell interviews that can be read on the oxymoronic website primitivism.com.

Improved technology can't be turned back or disinvented. In this sense Thomas Friedman and the IMF are half right:

there is no alternative. But when they use the phrase they mean to imply that there is no alternative to allowing them to shape the world according to their own design. They detest the heterogeneity and infinite variety that exist even among capitalist economies, from Sweden to Argentina, Japan to India. What they want, however, is not homogenised capitalism – which would imply blending elements from different systems – but hegemony. The selfsame people who argued that the 'command economy' of the Soviet Union was against nature now wish to create a rigid command economy of their own; after years of mocking the Communist faith in 'inevitability' they now promote another determinist fallacy. Have they learned nothing from history?

Globalisation did not begin in the 1980s. It has been an increasingly dominant force since the great voyages of discovery in the fifteenth and sixteenth centuries, when the European empires began their long ascendancy, and by the time of the Enlightenment it had become an everyday subject of discussion among political economists. In 1770 the Abbé Raynal described a 'revolution in commerce, in the power of nations, in the customs, the industry and the government of all peoples', whereby continents were linked as if by 'flying bridges of communication' as traders 'circulate unceasingly around the globe'. 'The proprietor of stock is properly a citizen of the world, and is not necessarily attached to any particular country,' Adam Smith wrote in 1776, the same year in which the Marquis de Condorcet characterised the owner of financial capital as someone 'who, by a banking operation, within an instant becomes English, Dutch or Russian'.

There has been much talk lately of the economic 'domino theory', particularly since the devaluation of the Thai baht in 1997 triggered a financial crisis through much of Asia:

even George Soros, the currency speculator who was accused by some Asian governments of precipitating the meltdown, warned soon afterwards that the power and capriciousness of the Electronic Herd now constituted a mortal threat to global stability. Similar comments were heard after the liquidity crisis of 1772, when the collapse of one small Anglo-Scottish bank in London led to the failure of Dutch banks, the bankruptcy of the chairman of the East India Company, and bankruptcies and suicides in Virginia. 'One link gave way,' a Hamburg linen merchant said. 'The charm was instantly dissolved, leaving behind it consternation in the place of confidence, and imaginary affluence changed to real want and distress.'

Driven as it was by huge joint-stock corporations such as the East India Company, the commercial revolution of the eighteenth century has much in common with the modern form of globalisation exemplified by Microsoft and McDonald's, and aroused many of the same anxieties and resentments. In 1997 the Institute for Policy Studies in Washington DC issued a report which claimed that fifty-one of the largest economies in the world were corporations and only forty-nine were countries: General Motors, with annual sales of $148 billion, was 'bigger' than Denmark or Thailand; the Ford Motor Co. was bigger than Turkey; Wal-Mart was bigger than Greece. Although the figures were misleading, since they compared a company's turnover with a nation's GDP (which measures value added rather than sales), the general point about the size and power of transnational businesses seemed undeniable, and prompted many alarmist headlines about this 'new' phenomenon. As the economic historian Emma Rothschild has reminded us, however, the East India Company collected more than £3.5 million in taxes at a time when the total expenditure of the British government was £7 million.

Indeed, the extraordinary omnipotence of the East India Company is beyond the dreams of even the most rapacious modern corporation: a series of royal charters in the seventeenth century had granted it the right to mint its own coins, raise armies, declare war, form international alliances and exercise direct jurisdiction over millions of subjects in India. The term 'civil servant', now taken to mean a government employee, was originally coined to describe the massed ranks of administrators trained and employed by the Company. 'In such a case,' Edmund Burke observed, 'to talk of the rights of [national] sovereignty is quite idle.'

It was the tea exported by the East India Company to Massachusetts that provoked the Boston Tea Party of 1773, which in turn sparked the War of Independence. The American revolutionary John Dickinson said his country might as well be 'devoured by rats' as succumb to the East India Company – whose Nabobs, having corrupted England and ravaged India, were now casting their eyes on America 'as a new theatre whereon to exercise their talents of rapine, oppression and cruelty'. The British prime minister Lord North was quite baffled, asking why anyone 'would resist at being able to drink their tea at ninepence in the pound cheaper'. Similar puzzlement is often heard from modern Americans who cannot understand why (for instance) the farmer José Bové became a French national hero in the summer of 1999, described by *Le Monde* as a new Vercingetorix, for driving a tractor into the McDonald's restaurant in his hometown of Millau. Who could possibly object to a company that provides cheap and convenient (if pappily bland) meals to the world? But Bové's protest was not a gastronomic criticism – or at least not solely – any more than the Boston eruption was prompted by a preference for chocolate over tea.

Just as the United States is now accused of seeking to dominate the world not only economically but also culturally and
politically, so in 1793 the French revolutionary Bertrand
Barère bemoaned the 'ridiculous Anglomania' that was
sweeping through Europe in the wake of British export success. The German economist Adam Müller – himself such
an Anglomaniac that he tried to pass himself off as a rich
Englishman in Göttingen – noticed that his compatriots who
bought English goods also began to revere 'English manners,
the English language, even the British constitution'. But the
process had barely begun. As the joint-stock adventurers gave
way to the more formal imperialist projects of the nineteenth
century, and the cost of transport and communications fell
rapidly, globalisation entered a new and astoundingly dynamic
phase.

The most concise account of how the world was shrunk
can be found in *The Communist Manifesto* of 1848, written by
Marx and Engels:

> The need of a constantly expanding market for its products
> chases the bourgeoisie over the whole surface of the globe. It
> must nestle everywhere, settle everywhere, establish connec-
> tions everywhere.
>
> The bourgeoisie has through its exploitation of the world
> market given a cosmopolitan character to production and
> consumption in every country. To the great chagrin of Reac-
> tionists, it has drawn from under the feet of industry the
> national ground on which it stood ... In place of the old
> wants, satisfied by the productions of the country, we find new
> wants, requiring for their satisfaction the products of distant
> lands and climes. In place of the old local and national
> seclusion and self-sufficiency, we have intercourse in every

direction, universal inter-dependence of nations. And as in material, so also in intellectual production. The intellectual creations of individual nations become common property . . .

The bourgeoisie, by the rapid improvement of all instruments of production, by the immensely facilitated means of communication, draws all, even the most barbarian, nations into civilisation. The cheap prices of its commodities are the heavy artillery with which it batters down all Chinese walls, with which it forces the barbarians' intensely obstinate hatred of foreigners to capitulate. It compels all nations, on pain of extinction, to adopt the bourgeois mode of production; it compels them to introduce what it calls civilisation into their midst, i.e. to become bourgeois themselves. In one word, it creates a world after its own image.

Although many evangelists for globalisation dismiss Karl Marx as a myopic ideologue who failed to understand capitalism, neither Marx nor Engels would have been at all surprised to see Microsoft and MTV bestriding the modern world. However, neophiliac hucksters for the 'new economy' of online shopping and global markets might well be surprised to read *The Economic Consequences of the Peace* by John Maynard Keynes. Writing immediately after the First World War, Keynes looked back at a lost world in which the internationalisation of social and economic life 'was almost complete':

What an extraordinary episode in the economic progress of man that age was which came to an end in August 1914! The inhabitant of London could order by telephone, sipping his morning tea in bed, the various products of the whole earth, in such quantity as he might see fit, and reasonably expect their early delivery on his doorstep; he could at the same moment and by the same means adventure his wealth in the natural resources and new enterprises of any quarter of the world, and share without exertion or even trouble, in their prospective fruits and advantages; or he could decide to couple the security of his fortunes with the good faith of the townspeople of any substantial municipality in any continent that fancy or information might recommend.

He could secure forthwith, if he wished it, cheap and comfortable means of transit to any country and climate without passport or other formality, could dispatch his servant to the neighbouring office of a bank for such supply of the precious metals as might seem convenient, and could then proceed abroad to foreign quarters, without knowledge of their religion, language, or customs, bearing coined wealth upon his person, and would consider himself greatly aggrieved and much surprised at the least interference. But, most important of all, he regarded this state of affairs as normal, certain and permanent, except in the direction of further improvement, and any deviation from it as aberrant, scandalous and avoidable.

What cars, aircraft, telephones and television were to the mid-twentieth century, the railways and steam ships and intercontinental telegraphs were to the mid-nineteenth. The laying of the first transatlantic cable in 1866, which allowed 'real-time information' to be exchanged between markets in New York and London, was at least as significant in the history of global finance as the creation of online share-trading.

This phase peaked in the period evoked so wistfully by Keynes, when one-fifth of the world's land mass belonged to the British Empire and King George V reigned over 410 million subjects. Then it relapsed, as a consequence of two world wars and the Great Depression, resuming again only in the 1950s. But it has never regained that early impetus. Between 1870 and 1913 capital outflow from Britain as a proportion of GDP averaged 4.6 per cent; no country in the world has reached this level since. Even in the 1990s, when the global movement of capital was supposedly gathering pace, British capital flows were 2.6 per cent of GDP, while the figure for the USA was just 1.2 per cent. In short, there is actually *less* capital mobility now than a century ago. David Henderson, head of the Organisation for Economic Co-operation and Development's economics and statistics department, reported in 1991 that the world economy 'is clearly further away from full integration than it was in July 1914', when there was more free trade, free capital movement, free migration and travel. Even the economic 'liberalisation' of Thatcher and Reagan had remarkably little effect: of OECD's twenty-four industrialised member states, only four – Australia, Japan, New Zealand and Turkey – had more liberal trade regimes at the end of the 1980s than at the beginning.

The governments of the world's richest countries demand the free movement of capital and goods (or at least of *their* capital and goods – perennial tariff disputes between the United States and the European Union confirm that this owes less to high principle than to simple self-interest). But their dislike of official barriers does not extend to the free movement of labour. This is perhaps the biggest difference from the globalisation of the late nineteenth century, when legal or bureaucratic obstacles to migration scarcely existed; and it is a fatal contradiction of the present order. In Britain, for example, ministers ceaselessly emphasise the distinction between 'genuine asylum-seekers' – who have to be accepted,

even if with thoroughly bad grace and no welcoming ceremony – and 'bogus' incomers who are mere 'economic
migrants' and must be deported forthwith. But then they
bewail the shortage of doctors, nurses and schoolteachers,
and hastily place advertisements all over the world begging
foreigners to come and rescue Britain's collapsing public services. (In 2000 the *Guardian* reported the case of a woman
from Mauritius who had worked as a nurse in Britain's
National Health Service for six years until being told by the
Home Office that she would be kicked out of the country as
an 'overstayer'. When she contacted her family back home
to say that she might be returning, she discovered that the
newspapers in Mauritius were full of adverts from the Department of Health in London – pleading for nurses to come
and work in Britain.)

Economic migration has been a motive force of human
history – and progress – since *homo erectus* first left Africa to
see if the grass was greener elsewhere. It is what made the
United States the wealthiest nation on earth. The market
determinists assure us that there is no alternative to the
Washington consensus (like sunrise, says Thomas Friedman),
even though the world survived for many centuries without
it. Yet when confronted with a rhythm that is as genuinely
unstoppable as a tidal flow, they declare that it can and
must cease.

During the nineteenth century about 60 million people
left Europe for the Americas, Oceania or Africa; 10 million
moved from Russia to Central Asia and Siberia; 12 million
Chinese and 6 million Japanese emigrated to East and South
Asia; 1.5 million left India for South-East Asia and Africa. No
country in the world today has an immigration rate anywhere
near this. The same politicians who demand the abolition of

all impediments to the mobility of goods and services have been busily erecting mighty barriers to rebuff an accompanying wave of human beings. In the words of the economist Martin Wolf, 'for all the changes that have occurred over the course of a century, neither the markets for goods and services nor those for factors of production are significantly more integrated than they were a century earlier ... and [they are] far less integrated for labour'. Those determinists who maintain that globalisation is the inevitable consequence (and cause) of technological progress – as heedless of political interference as the waves were of King Canute – have some explaining to do here. Wolf, himself a prominent advocate of global integration, admits that governments proved more powerful than market forces, and were indeed able to stem the tide: 'Globalisation is not predestined, but chosen.'

The zealots forget it happened before, a hundred years ago – and then had to be contained because it was too destructive and unstable. If anything, the new global market is less solid and substantial than that which crumbled with the start of the First World War. As Martin Wolf has to concede, we have lost 'the stability and predictability inherent in the move from the gold standard of the 1870–1914 era to the generalised floating of today ... Moreover, the vast scale of short-term finance [today] is probably both a consequence of exchange-rate instability and an important contributory cause.'

As the 1990s wore on, the dangers became apparent. The Asian meltdown of 1997 and the Russian collapse of 1998 were the beginning of the end for the triumphalism of the previous two decades, and for the IMF's 'one size fits all' solutions. The countries that were almost bankrupted in 1997 – Thailand, Indonesia, South Korea, Malaysia, the Philippines – were precisely those 'tiger economies' which had played by the new rules of the game, only to find themselves trashed overnight by a few foreign speculators who, quite literally, sold them short. Similarly, during the mid-1990s Boris Yeltsin obediently handed control of the Russian economy to Jeffrey Sachs and a handful of other professors from Harvard (acting as agents for the US government), who imposed deregulation, privatisation and all the other things they teach you at Harvard Business School. His reward? George Soros wrote a letter to the *Financial Times* suggesting that the rouble was overvalued and the currency collapsed at once, thus reducing millions of Russians to near-destitution.

These severe jolts – along with corporate scandals in the West, and the pricking of the dotcom bubble – ought to puncture the complacency of Panglossian pundits such as Thomas Friedman. Even George Soros, who was blamed for both the Asian and the Russian débâcles, now sounds more like a banner-waving protester dodging tear-gas in Genoa: he warns that market fundamentalism is 'a new global imperialism', and that the herd instinct of the new moguls must be controlled before they trample us all underfoot. Bill Gates, too, has had a miraculous conversion. In the 1990s he often declared that the spirit exemplified by Microsoft could solve all the world's problems. In October 2000, however, he astonished an audience of computer moguls and financiers at a conference in Seattle called 'Creating Digital Dividends', whose thesis was that technology can make entrepreneurs and consumers out of even the poorest people in the developing world. 'Let's be serious,' he snapped. 'Do people have any concept of what it means to live on less than $1 a day? There's no electricity. Do they have PCs that don't use electricity? There are things those people need at that level other than technology. You're buying food, you're trying to stay alive . . .' The much discussed 'digital divide', he said, was far less important than the health-care divide, the human-rights divide, the education divide. In short, the richest man on earth no longer believed that unfettered capitalism would be the salvation of the 1.3 billion people whose daily income is a dollar or less – almost a quarter of the world's population.

There is no historical evidence for the contention that simple *laissez-faire* is the prerequisite for trade and prosperity. The IMF may say so, but its own figures tell a different story. Its report on 'The World Economy in the Twentieth Century', published in May 2000, includes a graph – printed very small, perhaps in the hope that no one would notice – which shows that the period between 1950 and 1973 was by far the most successful of the twentieth century. This was an era character-ised by capital controls, fixed exchange rates, strong trade unions, a large public sector and a general acceptance of government's role in demand management. The average annual growth in 'per capita real GDP' throughout the world was 2.9 per cent – precisely twice as high as the average rate since then.

The myth that two decades of liberalisation have been accompanied by swift economic progress, particularly in the developing world, is hard to dislodge. 'Few economists and almost no journalists have seen fit to make an issue out of what history will undoubtedly record as the most remarkable economic failure of the twentieth century aside from the Great Depression,' writes Mark Weisbrot. Yet the data from the IMF and the World Bank are unambiguous. In Latin America and the Caribbean, GDP grew by 75 per cent per person from 1960 to 1980; in the next twenty years it rose by just 7 per cent. In sub-Saharan Africa there was an increase of about 34 per cent in the 1960s and 1970s; between 1980 and 2000 per-capita income actually *fell* by 15 per cent. Even if one includes the fast-growing economies of South and East Asia, average per-capita growth in 1980–2000 was less than half its average for the previous two decades. And, predictably enough, there has been a slackening in 'social indicators' such as life expectancy, literacy, child mortality and education.

Growth isn't everything, of course, but as Weisbrot points out, 'it's all that the authorities who have directed policy for most of the developing world – the International Monetary Fund, the World Bank, the US Treasury department – have promised to deliver'. The prescriptions imposed by these authorities have created problems and then exacerbated them. Relative disparities in incomes are far wider than twenty years ago, and even in absolute terms there is little evidence of the 'trickle-down' effect in which Ronald Reagan and Margaret Thatcher believed so devoutly. The poorest 10 per cent of the world's population – 400 million people – lived on 72 cents a day in 1980. Ten years later the figure was 79 cents, and by 1999 – after two decades of rampant liberalisation – it had slipped back to 78 cents. In seventy countries, people were on average poorer than they were in 1980. The income of the wretched of the earth hadn't even kept pace with inflation.

11

Voodoo revisited

In reading the history of nations, we find that, like individuals, they have their whims and their peculiarities; their seasons of excitement and recklessness, when they care not what they do. We find that whole communities suddenly fix their minds upon one object, and go mad in its pursuit; that millions of people become simultaneously impressed with one delusion, and run after it, till their attention is caught by some new folly more captivating than the first. We see one nation suddenly seized, from its highest to its lowest members, with a fierce desire of military glory; another as suddenly becoming crazed upon a religious scruple, and neither of them recovering its senses until it has shed rivers of blood and sowed a harvest of groans and tears, to be reaped by its posterity . . . Money, again, has often been a cause of the delusion of multitudes. Sober nations have all at once become desperate gamblers, and risked almost their existence upon the turn of a piece of paper . . . Men, it has been well said, think in herds; it will be seen that they go mad in herds, while they only recover their senses slowly, and one by one.

CHARLES MACKAY, *Extraordinary Popular Delusions and the Madness of Crowds* (1841)

The economic experiment that Margaret Thatcher initiated in Britain a quarter-century ago was later imposed on much of the world by her drooling epigones, and copied even by liberal and social democratic politicians. Yet the new orthodoxy has lamentably failed to match the achievements of its much despised predecessor – and, for all its apparently elegant logic, has proved to be a fundamentally irrational system. Echoing Adam Smith's *Wealth of Nations* ('What is prudent in the conduct of every private family can scarcely be folly in that of a great kingdom'), Thatcher often said that her principles represented nothing more than common sense, the application of normal rules of domestic economy and good housekeeping on a grand scale. If true, this suggests that Thatcherites inhabit very chaotic households indeed, where one is continually kept awake by the noise of *Torschluss-panik* – that marvellously expressive German word (literally 'door-shut panic') describing the frenzy as people fight to rush through a door before it is slammed in their face.

One legacy of her revolution was the liberalisation of financial services, which were supposed to replace old-fashioned manufacturing as the engine of economic progress. This led to *Torschlusspanik* galore, as Thatcher herself witnessed when she ventured into the least regulated sector of the financial industry, 'hedge funds', which acted only for big banks or immensely wealthy individuals and were therefore assumed to require no official oversight. In May 1998 she joined the advisory board of Tiger Management, a firm created eighteen years earlier with an initial investment of $8 million by Julian Robertson, 'the Wizard of Wall Street'. By the time of her recruitment Tiger had assets of more than $18 billion and was the second biggest hedge fund in the world – outdone only by George Soros's fund, which in 1992 had effectively destroyed John Major's government (and collected a $1 billion jackpot) by forcing the pound out of the

European exchange rate mechanism. In return for a salary of $1 million from Tiger Management, Thatcher was expected to attend five board meetings a year and hold regular telephone discussions with Robertson about world markets, 'using her political insight and experience to help inform investment decisions'. The benefits of the great stateswoman's wisdom were apparent almost immediately: five months later Tiger dropped $2 billion in a single day after betting on a fall in the Japanese yen. With further hits from rash investments in the Royal Bank of Scotland and NatWest, its losses for October 1998 alone were $3.4 billion.

A few weeks earlier the Federal Reserve and a consortium of banks had been obliged to rescue a rival hedge fund, Long-Term Capital Management, when it lost $3.2 billion by gambling on interest-rate movements. But Tiger's high-rolling investors still seemed to be in a celebratory mood. After hearing the bad news at their annual meeting in New York on 2 November, they adjourned to the Metropolitan Museum of Art for a gala dinner-dance hosted by Robertson and Thatcher. *The Times* reported the next day that Tiger Management was 'in no danger of collapsing' since it 'still has assets worth $17 billion'. Just over a year later, after yet more ill-judged speculative flutters, that had plummeted to $6 billion and Robertson's dinner-guests were demanding their money back. Fittingly enough, Tiger finally shut up shop on April Fool's Day, 2000. In a bad-tempered resignation statement, the chairman blamed his downfall on 'an irrational market'.

This, of course, was the same market that had made him rich in the first place: for how did one become a Wizard of Wall Street if not by profiting from irrationally valued stocks or currencies? No less a figure than Alan Greenspan, the normally taciturn chairman of the Federal Reserve, said in December 1996 that 'irrational exuberance has unduly escalated asset values, which then become subject to unexpected and prolonged contractions'. According to the *Financial Times*, his remarks 'hit global markets like a thunderbolt': they produced the biggest one-day fall in the FTSE 100 index since June 1994 and similar selling sprees in Paris, Frankfurt, Tokyo and New York. Which, it seemed, was precisely what the Fed chairman had intended. According to one Paris dealer, 'Greenspan sent a clear message to the markets: "Gentlemen, you are overdoing it. Restrain yourselves."' He was not going to risk the Wall Street bubble becoming so dangerously over-inflated that it burst, and unless investors restrained their exuberance he would do it for them by raising interest rates.

Greenspan's reference to 'unduly escalated asset values' was a sharp reminder that a company's share price ought to have some rough correlation with its earnings. But the warning was soon forgotten: over the next few years markets exhibited a madness not seen since the Dutch tulip craze of the 1630s and the South Sea Bubble of 1720, as they succumbed to dotcom mania. Price-earnings ratios had undoubtedly been dangerously high at the time of Greenspan's rebuke in 1996, but at least most of these stocks represented corporations that actually made some money, even if not enough to justify their valuation. Between 1998 and 2000, however, investors scrambled and jostled to buy shares in companies which, as often as not, had *no earnings at all*, nor any prospect of ever turning a profit. To justify this apparently insane agiotage they maintained that such a revolutionary business as the Internet required a revolutionary business model, in which balance sheets were irrelevant. 'We have one general response to the word "valuation" these days: "Bull market'',' wrote Mary Meeker, a stock analyst at Morgan Stanley. 'It [the Internet] has all introduced a brave new world for valuation methodologies and it is a time of especially high risk/reward, in our view. When you overlay the high valuation of many "start-ups" with the relatively high valuation of the general market, well, we are where we are, just trying to do our jobs and find some early-stage great companies. If they execute, the valuations will take care of themselves. Again, it's about monster markets, great management teams and good products.'

This implies that stock-buyers diligently sorted the wheat from the chaff, carefully selecting only those few propositions with some semblance of solidity. But the record shows a wholly indiscriminate enthusiasm for pressing hundred-dollar bills on any scruffy mendicant with a half-formed idea on the back of an envelope. To take a notorious but all too typical example: how long did J. P. Morgan, Goldman Sachs, Benetton and other investors brood or ponder before hurling their money at boo.com, an online retailer of designer clothes? A moment's thought should have aroused misgivings, since for most women who enjoy fashion shopping the visit to the store – especially if accompanied by a friend – is part of the pleasure. On the other hand, boo.com did have certain useful assets for an Internet venture: photogenic young founders (two twentysomething Swedes, Kajsa Leander and Ernst Malmsten) who gadded about the world on executive jets and had fresh fruit delivered to their staff every day. Only when Leander and Malmsten finally went online in November 1999, a year late, did the backers realise that this might not be enough. The creaky boo.com website took eight minutes to load, had about 400 technical bugs in its software – and couldn't be accessed at all by anyone with an Apple Mac. By the following April, total sales were barely over $1 million. The company filed for bankruptcy a few weeks later, having burned its way through $185 million in just eighteen months.

Two months before boo.com's collapse, Leander and Malmsten were featured in a photographic exhibition celebrating '21 Leaders for the twenty-first century' at the National Portrait Gallery in London. 'Although some of them are still in their twenties, these people have already made their mark on British business,' said Rufus Olins, editor-in-chief of *Management Today*, the magazine which sponsored the exhibition and chose the pin-ups. 'They are a new breed of leaders whose management style will dominate the new economy.' And, he believed, there was substance as well as style. Two of the entrepreneurs, Martha Lane Fox and Brent Hoberman, were the founders of lastminute.com, a retailer of eleventh-hour holidays and gifts, which was floated on the stock exchange a week after the exhibition opened. At the end of the first day's trading lastminute.com was valued at £733 million – not bad for a company whose turnover in the previous quarter had been just £490,000. Within three days the share-price had halved from its original high of 555p to 270p. 'During the madness of the bullish period it was about "pass the parcel",' confessed Michael Whitaker, chief executive of the 'Internet incubator' NewMedia Spark. 'It wasn't about whether it had a good business model, but whether you could pass it on to a greater fool by floating it. Venture capitalists got caught in the madness of the gold rush and lost sight of reality.'

The insanity spread far beyond venture capitalists. In 1998, the year when Yahoo!'s share price rose by 584 per cent and Amazon.com's by 970 per cent despite the fact that neither company had yet made a penny of profit, *Money* magazine asked the two questions uppermost in many minds: 'One, is Internet mania based on nothing more than hype? And, two, is it too late to get in on the action?' The answers were most reassuring: 'First, the Internet boom is for real . . . Second, you are not too late.' There was no need to worry about the disparity between valuations and earnings. 'Yahoo! . . . trades at more than 40 times sales; by comparison, even premium-priced Microsoft goes for less than 15 times sales. But the Internet's potential is so great that even today's rich prices will likely be justified for many companies in the long run.' The rest of the media thought so too. The business TV network CNBC featured a continuous parade of bullish experts, having discovered that its viewers found doom-sayers a turn-off. *Time* magazine had the Yahoo! founder Jerry Yang on its cover in July 1998 ('we hope you've bought some Yahoo! stock', the accompanying puff-piece told readers), and in December 1999 named Amazon.com's boss Jeff Bezos as its Person of the Year. 'It was unbelievable how traditional media fell over themselves to praise and cover Internet companies,' the founder of SonicNet, an online music site, recalled. 'Every day we all got streams of visitors from traditional media trying to write positive things about Web companies because their readers were demanding it. It sold magazines and made them look hip.' It also brought in advertisements from the cool new Internet entrepreneurs: even the staid *New York Times* added an extra weekly section ('Circuits') to accommodate them all.

Wall Street, too, had a strong incentive to resist scepticism and sobriety. Until the 1980s there had been rigid 'Chinese walls' between the brokers who advised investors and the merchant bankers who managed share-issues for corporations. With the liberalisation of the financial industry, however, the distinction became increasingly blurred as brokers and banks merged into 'all-purpose financial supermarkets' such as Morgan Stanley Dean Witter and J. P. Morgan Chase. A former chairman of the Federal Reserve, Paul Volcker, described these conglomerates as 'bundles of conflicts of interests', an assessment borne out by their performance during the dotcom hysteria.

The millions of Americans who entrusted their money to the stock market in the 1990s were lured in partly by the exhortations of supposedly independent analysts such as Henry Blodget, Merrill Lynch's Internet guru, whose buoyant optimism guaranteed him regular appearances on CNBC. 'Unlike with other famous bubbles,' he wrote in January 1999, 'the Internet bubble is riding on rock-solid fundamentals, perhaps stronger than any the market has seen before. Underlying the crazy price increases are the foundations of what could become the early 21st century's leading growth companies . . . Just because the Internet stock phenomenon looks like a bubble, it isn't a given that the bubble will burst.' Even when particular shares were plummeting, Blodget promised that they would soon surge back. What he omitted to mention was that the dud companies he recommended tended to be those which had paid Merrill Lynch to promote their lucrative initial public offerings (IPOs). The truth emerged only in 2003, when New York's attorney-general, Elliot Spitzer, took up the cudgels on behalf of small investors who had been ruined by heeding the experts' advice. The investigation discovered that while Blodget had been publicly urging Merrill clients to risk their life savings on firms such as GoTo.com and Excite@Home, his private emails to colleagues described the same stocks as 'junk', 'a dog' and 'a piece of shit'. In April 2003 he was fined $6.5 million and barred from ever working in the financial industry again. His counterpart at Citibank, Jack Grubman, incurred a penalty of $24.4 million for producing 'fraudulent and misleading' research reports on Internet stocks. Meanwhile, ten of the most powerful finance houses on Wall Street agreed to pay $2.26 billion in compensation – including $130 million for 'investor education' – and to restore the old Chinese walls by separating their banking and research departments.

Mere dishonesty, however, is not a sufficient explanation for the hysteria of the late 1990s. Many cynics adopted the principle of 'devil take the hindmost', a slogan which first came into popular usage at the time of the South Sea Bubble: of course they knew that dotcom shares were ludicrously overvalued, but wouldn't it be madder still to shun the market while thousands of greater fools remained eager and willing to buy? Getting out too soon, according to this theory, is just as foolish as getting out too late. *Fortune* magazine learned the lesson after running a cover story in April 1996 – 'How Crazy is This Market?' – on the inevitability of a 'confidence-shattering crash'. A year later, with the Dow-Jones 2,000 points higher, readers who had heeded the warning and sold their shares might well have felt cheated. 'Not surprisingly,' the financial journalist John Cassidy wrote, '*Fortune*'s coverage of the stock market became notably less questioning as time went on.'

Other preachers of the dotcom gospel were genuine believers. Although Elliot Spitzer's sleuths found plenty of incriminating evidence against Henry Blodget and Jack Grubman, the internal emails from Mary Meeker of Morgan Stanley showed no discrepancy between her private thoughts and public pronouncements. She really did think that Internet technology had repealed the traditional laws of financial gravity: it was 'a new paradigm'.

This fashionable phrase was pillaged from Thomas Kuhn's book *The Structure of Scientific Revolutions*, which proposed that scientific advance came not in gradual incremental stages but in occasional giant leaps by a Galileo or an Einstein, who instantly rendered all previous theories obsolete. 'These', he wrote, 'are the men who, being little committed by prior practice to the traditional rules of normal science, are particularly likely to see that those rules no longer define a playable game and to conceive another set that can replace them.' Since economics was a science (if a dismal one), why not extend Kuhn's concept to financial innovation? Thus the claim by hedge funds that they could ensure high absolute returns even in a falling equity market was termed 'a new paradigm in asset management'. By the end of the twentieth century, almost any unorthodox business method could be justified as a paradigm shift, even if it seemed uncannily similar to an ancient scam that had been perpetrated at regular intervals for several centuries. 'When you see reference to a new paradigm,' John Kenneth Galbraith said in 1998, 'you should always, under all circumstances, take cover . . . There was never a paradigm so new and so wonderful as the one that covered John Law and the South Sea Bubble – until the day of disaster.' *Living on Thin Air*, the title of Charles Leadbeater's starry-eyed guide to the 'weightless economy', certainly sounded like a fraudulent prospectus from the last days of the South Sea Bubble, or maybe one of the harebrained schemes satirised by Jonathan Swift in *Gulliver's Travels* ('he had been Eight Years upon a Project for extracting Sun-Beams out of Cucumbers, which were to be put in Vials hermetically sealed, and let out to warm the Air in raw inclement Summers'). In a chapter headed 'Dianomics' Leadbeater argued that there was 'no better exemplar' of

thin-air business than Princess Diana, who had become a
'global brand' even though she had few formal qualifications
and worked from home: 'Diana was the upstart challenger,
an entrepreneur who used new technology to outmanoeuvre
the established but tired incumbent.' For the Royal Family,
read IBM; for Diana, read Yahoo! It was a more accurate
analogy than he intended, since the princess charged no
fees and made no great profit but would undoubtedly have
been a darling of Nasdaq had she ever floated herself on the
stock market.

Although Leadbeater's book was compulsory reading for
New Labour ministers when it appeared in 1999, after the
dotcom débâcle they turned against their guru. The industry
secretary Patricia Hewitt said in May 2002 that 'industrial
policy in [Labour's] first term of office was mistaken, placing
too much emphasis on the dotcom economy at the expense of
Britain's manufacturing base', and blamed it on Leadbeater's
weightless theorising: 'The idea of *Living on Thin Air* was so
much hot air.' Would she have dared say as much before the
bubble burst, especially since Leadbeater's treatise arrived
with tributes from her colleagues Tony Blair and Peter
Mandelson on its dust-jacket?

Everyone can be wise after the event, but anybody who
raises a quizzical eyebrow while the emperor is still parading
in his new birthday suit can expect no gratitude. In the 1980s,
the Yale economics professor Robert Shiller published a
paper in the *American Economic Review* arguing that the validity
of 'efficient markets theory' was undermined by the volatility
of share prices, which bore no relation to actual dividends.
This earned him a magisterial rebuke from the financial
theorist Robert Merton, who insisted that speculative markets
were 'not too volatile'. Merton later won the 1997 Nobel

prize 'for a new method to determine the value of derivatives', but suffered massive losses to both his reputation and his bank balance soon afterwards as one of the principals in the Long-Term Capital Management hedge fund, which was brought close to ruin by the speculative instability whose existence he denied. Understandably enough, Shiller couldn't resist gloating over this 'irony' in his book *Irrational Exuberance*, published in 2000. Yet even then many reviewers were unpersuaded by his warning that the market had gone mad. 'It just may be', William Wolman wrote in *Business Week*, 'that the Information Revolution is so profoundly different from what has gone before that it will continue to produce super gains.' In the *Financial Times*, Gerard Baker argued that although most protestations that 'this time it really is different' prove illusory, 'rebutting them ultimately requires something more than an appeal to the immutability of popular credulity'. The extra evidence he required was delivered at once. In mid-March 2000, when *Irrational Exuberance* appeared, the new-economy Nasdaq index reached a peak of 5,048.62; by 14 April the index had plunged to 3,321.29, losing a third of its value in a month. As Shiller noticed at his bookshop talks, however, the collapse did little to break the willing suspension of disbelief that has been a common feature of all bubbles since the seventeenth century: the investing public was still reluctant to abandon its daydream of a new economic landscape that could yield almost unlimited returns. True, some of those online petfood retailers may have been slightly flaky, but there were other exciting new business models that inspired real confidence. What about the energy giant Enron, which was named by *Fortune* magazine as America's 'most innovative company' for five consecutive years after 1996 and collected two awards from the *Financial*

Times in 2000 – 'Energy Company of the Year' and 'Boldest Successful Investment Decision'?

The paradigms of the 1990s managed to fool so many people for so long largely because they fed on the delusions fostered by Thatcher and Reagan in the previous decade, and Enron provides an exquisitely emblematic case history. Privatisation made its rapid expansion possible, as it set out to gobble up utility firms all over the world. Deregulation permitted its daylight robbery. (One of its own executives boasted that the company operated in a 'regulatory black hole'.) Meanwhile, a soaring stock-price encouraged thousands of small investors to entrust their money to Enron shares – thus reinforcing another popular fantasy, that the market wouldn't let you down. It also appeared to justify the business gurus' doctrine that modern industry needed few hard assets. 'The future belonged to companies with no visible means of support,' the economist Paul Krugman wrote in the *New York Times*. 'Flexibility and vision were what counted, not bricks, mortar and tubular steel. And Enron ... prided itself on being an "asset light" company. OK, it owned some pipelines, but what it really offered was the vision thing: it would create markets in everything, and make money by trading in those markets. And if you couldn't understand why Enron's trading operation was as profitable as it seemed to be, that was because you just didn't get it.' (Krugman got it: in 1999 he collected $50,000 for delivering a lecture to Enron's advisory board on the significance of the Asian financial crisis.)

It was the new Elvis, the new Beatles, and the fans' swooning adulation matched that of any screaming teenybopper. Here's the opening paragraph of a *Fortune* article from April 2000:

Imagine a country-club dinner dance, with a bunch of old fogies and their wives shuffling around half-heartedly to the not-so-stirring sounds of Guy Lombardo and his All-Tuxedo Orchestra. Suddenly young Elvis comes crashing through the skylight, complete with gold-lamé suit, shiny guitar and gyrating hips. Half the waltzers faint, most of the others get angry or pouty. And a very few decide they like what they hear, tap their feet ... start grabbing new partners, and suddenly are rocking to a very different tune. In the staid world of regulated utilities and energy companies, Enron Corp. *is* that gate-crashing Elvis.

A telling analogy. The masters of the New Economy had learned from the example of those 1960s rock stars who continued to present themselves as daringly rebellious nonconformists even after acquiring country estates, Rolls-Royces, offshore tax-havens and the other trappings of traditional plutocrats: in the 1990s, capitalism was the new counterculture. As Thomas Frank wrote in his brilliant anatomy of corporate cool, *One Market Under God*, young executives:

were flooding into bohemian neighbourhoods like San Francisco's Mission District, chatting with guys in the band, and working on their poetry in Starbucks; they were going it alone with their millions and their out-of-wedlock child; they were abjuring stodgy ties and suits for 24/7 casual; they were leaping on their trampolines, typing out a few last lines on the laptop before paragliding, riding their bicycles to work, listening to Steppenwolf while they traded, drinking beer in the office, moshing at the Motley Crue show, startling the board members with their streetwise remarks, roaring down the freeway in their Lamborghinis, snowboarding in Crested, racing their jetskis by the platform at Cannes and splashing all the uptight French people.

A company's visible identity became ever more divorced from the reality of its particular enterprise. Benetton was a profitable clothing business, but from its advertisements you might take it to be a radical third-world pressure group or an Aids charity. The front-offices of once-fusty merchant banks began to resemble those of advertising agencies – while advertising agencies, not to be outdone, redesigned their foyers to look more like cafés or nightclubs. Kenneth Lay, the chairman of Enron, boasted of running 'the world's coolest company' and seriously considered wrapping a gigantic pair of sunglasses around the headquarters in Houston, Texas. Its London offices won awards for being the best workplace in England – equipped with art-nouveau sculptures, a twenty-four-hour gym offering stress-management classes and non-stop MTV videos, and an Italian restaurant to keep the chino-wearing employees supplied with skinny lattes and custom-made ciabatta sandwiches. There was also an in-house pharmacy, a dry cleaner and a post office. 'The company's motto, "Learn the power of why", forced everyone to question what they were doing and why they were doing it,' an Enron computer-whiz recalled. 'Innovation was king. It was only a partial joke among the staff in London that the motto displayed on the huge multiscreen video in reception should instead be "Resistance is futile".'

The mantra chanted ceaselessly in Enron's corporate literature – 'Why? Why? Why?' – was said to be 'the chosen word of the non-conformist'. (The company even set up a website, askwhy.com, to celebrate heretical thinkers down the ages.) One of its TV commercials showed fuddy-duddy politicians who refused to deregulate public utilities being confronted by a hip young gunslinger with the killer question; another likened Enron's crusade for 'freedom' to the struggles of Abraham Lincoln and Martin Luther King. 'Spend long enough around top Enron people,' the *Economist* reported, 'and you feel you are in the midst of some sort of evangelical cult. In a sense, you are. Mr Lay, with his "passion for markets", is the cult's guru. His disciples are Enron's managers, an intelligent, aggressive group of youngish professionals, all of whom "get it". The "it" is the rise of market forces in the long-staid energy business.' Lay applied to this staid business the techniques of Wall Street, trading in 'put options', 'call options' and 'swaps'; merely buying and selling gas would have been far too humdrum.

'This sort of circular logic – if you don't believe, that's because there's something wrong with you – is typical of extreme religious and political sects,' Paul Krugman wrote. But then, as the *Economist* noticed, Enron was indeed more like a religion than a business. Its worshippers in the press spoke of 'mission', 'vision', 'destiny' and 'faith'. Kenneth Lay, the son of a Baptist minister, was himself an active member of First United Methodist Church in Houston who summarised his credo thus: 'I believe in God and I believe in free markets.' Jeffrey Skilling, Enron's chief executive, wowed Wall Street analysts and investors at gatherings which one participant likened to 'revival meetings'. Both Skilling and Lay were invariably described as 'charismatic', a concept derived from the New Testament, where St Paul lists various χαρισμα (gifts) of the Holy Spirit. 'Today's extraordinary trust in the power of the charismatic CEO resembles less a mature faith than a belief in magic,' wrote Professor Rakesh Khurana of the Harvard Business School, author of *Searching for a Corporate*

Saviour: The Irrational Quest for Charismatic CEOs. A chief executive was now expected to offer 'a vision of a radically different future and to attract and motivate followers for a journey to the new promised land. In keeping with the religious conception of the CEO's role, the charismatic leader was also supposed to have the "gift of tongues", with which he could inspire employees to work harder and gain the confidence of investors, analysts and the ever-sceptical business press. Finally, in all too many cases, the charismatic leader was supposed to have the power to perform miracles.'

Kenneth Lay was once asked by the religious affairs correspondent of the *San Diego Union-Tribune* what Jesus Christ would do if he were chief executive of a company that bought and sold an essential energy resource. 'Jesus attempted to take care of the people around him, attempted to make their lives better,' he replied. 'He also was a freedom lover. He wanted people to have the freedom to make choices.' Deregulation, according to this reading of the Gospel, was nothing less than a spiritual imperative.

At the time of Enron's creation in the mid-1980s, from the merger of two medium-sized firms operating natural-gas pipelines, its business was closely supervised by government. By lobbying aggressively for liberalisation and exploiting every tiny loophole in the law, Lay swiftly achieved an overwhelming dominance in the gas and electricity markets: Enron's sales raced from $4.6 billion in 1989 to $40.1 billion a decade later. (Having expanded the company's market capitalisation ninefold, Lay was asked how he could possibly top that. 'We'll do it again this coming decade,' he bragged.) Yet for all its apparent hatred of Washington, and its celebration of unconventional methods, in practice Enron had the same relations with officialdom as most big corporations down the ages: it bribed politicians of any and every party who might get into power. And, as its adverts might have asked, why not? At a time when even the British Labour Party had come to believe that 'market solutions' were always to be preferred in the public sector, there could be no shame in applying the principle to political funding.

On 5 December 2000, even before Al Gore had conceded defeat in the interminable presidential vote-count, a press release from the Bush–Cheney team included this delightfully candid announcement: 'Applicants interested in serving in the administration will be able to apply online via a secure server. Contributions are limited to $5,000 and can be donated online or via mail to the Bush-Cheney transition effort.' Quite a bargain, you might think; but the 'limit' of $5,000 was little more than a gratuity, since the actual bill had already been paid. Kenneth Lay, known to George W. Bush as 'Kenny-boy', donated $310,500 to the Republican Party between 1998 and 2000, and raised about another $1 million from his firm – more than any other corporation. Lo and behold, Kenny-boy was promptly appointed to the Bush transition team as 'an adviser to the energy department'. He was also one of the lucky thirty-two business leaders invited to 'give their ideas' to the new president, and since Enron's income depended on further deregulation of gas and electricity it requires little imagination to guess what Lay recommended.

In Britain, where the Blairites had an insatiable thirst for transatlantic fads and fashions, Lay's company became a great favourite of New Labour. To the untrained eye this might seem rather strange. In 1995 Enron was named by Multinational Monitor as one of 'the world's ten worst corporations', and two years later it became the only company (rather than government) to be the subject of a special investigation by Amnesty International, following violent attacks by Enron's private police against poor Indian villagers who objected to a power station in Maharashtra which was polluting fisheries and depleting the local water supply. The World Bank also condemned the plant, which obliged Maharashtra to pay three times as much for its electricity as other Indian states. Worse still, until the 1997 general election Labour frontbenchers were loudly committed to saving the coal industry and opposing the Tories' 'dash for gas' – bad news indeed for Enron, which hoped to sprint into the British utilities market without delay. The firm hired Karl Milner, a former aide to Gordon Brown who had found more lucrative employment with the political lobbyists GJW. It also made three payments to the Labour Party totalling £27,500.

Seldom has a small investment paid bigger dividends. Three weeks after the 1998 Labour Party conference, at which Enron spent £15,000 sponsoring a 'gala dinner', the government decided not to refer its £1.5 billion takeover of Wessex Water to the monopolies commission – thus giving the American company a monopoly of water supplies in much of south-west England. After being renamed Azurix, Wessex Water was floated on the New York stock exchange, to the great enrichment of its Enron-appointed directors, while the hapless customers endured price increases of up to 34 per cent. The new chief executive, Rebecca Mark, who had a pay-and-incentives package worth £33 million, promised that the company would soon control water supplies around the globe. (The results failed to match her world-conquering ambition: Mark resigned in the summer of 2000, and Enron had to repurchase its stock at less than half the flotation price.)

The best was yet to come. When the *Observer* investigated

Westminster's political lobbyists in the summer of 1998, Milner bragged to the paper's undercover reporter that he would get Enron exempted from the government's moratorium on the building of private gas plants. 'The way you go about it is that you play on the existing prejudices within the cabinet for coal, you play on the existing prejudices within the cabinet for competition, and you play the forces off against each other. It's intimate knowledge of what's going on that produces results in the end.' In the summer of 1999 the government duly relaxed its ban to allow Enron Europe Ltd to build a gas-fired power station at Teesside, and on 16 November 2000 the energy minister Stephen Byers sounded the death knell of the coal industry by lifting the moratorium altogether and giving his consent to another Enron gas plant, on the Isle of Grain in Kent. The New Year honours list six weeks later included a CBE for Ralph Hodge, the chairman of Enron Europe – 'for services to the power generation and gas industries'. (True, he didn't get a peerage, but for a measly £27,500 you can't expect everything.) By the following December, in a perfect finale to this modern morality play, Enron was the biggest bankruptcy in American corporate history. Thousands of shareholders learned too late that its image of success had been created with smoke and mirrors: investment capital appeared in the books as pure profit, while real losses were transferred to shell companies known as 'special partnerships' and thus excised from the balance-sheet. The fictional earnings figures kept the share-price high, which in turn enabled Enron to raise yet more investment money that could then be added to the next quarter's 'profits'.

During its heyday, even Enron fans would sometimes admit that, if the company had a fault, it was arrogance. 'And how does Mr Lay respond to this charge?' asked the *Economist*, one of the few business magazines not to fall for his sales patter, in a remarkably prescient article published in June 2000.

> To illustrate that it is baseless, he points to what he considers another great firm unfairly maligned by its critics as arrogant: Drexel Burnham Lambert, a freewheeling investment bank that shot from nowhere to market prominence in the junk-bond boom of the 1980s. Mr Lay speaks glowingly of the heyday of Drexel and of its star trader, Michael Milken, whom he counts as a friend: they were accused of arrogance, he grouses, but they were just being 'very innovative and very aggressive'. The comparison is not especially well chosen, for it is worth recalling what then happened: Mr Milken ended up in jail for pushing the law too far, and the arrogant Drexel collapsed in a heap of bad debts and ignominy. For all of its arrogance, Enron is hardly likely to share that fate: but hubris can lead to nemesis, even so.

The *Economist* added wryly that Enron had its origins in Texas, 'birthplace of many wacky cults'. Like any other sect, it required blind, unquestioning worship from the faithful, but the acolytes included many pundits who were themselves known as 'gurus' – such as Gary Hamel, author of *Leading the Revolution* (2000), who said that Enron had 'institutionalised a capacity for perpetual innovation ... where thousands of people see themselves as potential revolutionaries', thus proving the point made by Peter Drucker, one of the saner management theorists, that people use the word 'guru' only because 'charlatan' is too long. 'It was one of the great fantasies of American business,' the *Wall Street Journal* reported after the cult's implosion. 'A deregulated market that would send cheaper and more reliable supplies of electricity coursing into homes and offices across the nation.' However, the same newspaper had itself argued strongly for energy deregulation in the early 1990s, and rejoiced when it occurred. A feature in September 1999 contrasted the 'boringly predictable' regulated utilities of old (sneeringly dismissed as 'safe havens for widows and orphans') with 'bright, energetic newcomers' such as Enron, which were 'trying all sorts of ways to compete in their new unregulated, anything-goes world' and 'hold the promise of skyrocketing returns'.

Serious business journals profiled Enron's bosses in a style more commonly associated with *People* magazine. Jeffrey Skilling, the chief executive, was a ruthless thug who had once been asked by a teacher at Harvard Business School what he would do if he discovered that one of his products had fatal side-effects. 'I'd keep making and selling the product,' he replied. 'My job as a businessman is to be a profit centre and to maximise return to shareholders.' To readers of *Fortune* magazine, however, he was presented as an all-American family man – 'a lively, impish character who disdains the huge, serene, high walled office he occupies atop the Enron building, forty stories above downtown Houston. "Too quiet. Too removed," he complains. His kids often play Koosh ball in it and store their racquets in a corner.' Rebecca Mark, who led Enron's quest for world domination, had *Forbes* magazine salivating: 'With her honey-blonde hair, big brown eyes and dazzling white teeth that offset a toast tan, Rebecca Mark could be taken for a movie star.' Of Lou Pai, the Chinese *émigré* who launched Enron Energy Services and several other subsidiaries, *Forbes* wrote: 'Pai is bursting with competitive energy. Skilling calls him "my ICBM".' A more accurate analogy than Skilling intended, since Pai was indeed a destructive high-flyer. None of the Enron enterprises he ran ever made money, a fact concealed by financial jiggery-pokery: Enron Energy Services, for instance, was able to show a profit only by transferring $500 million in losses to another branch of the company. Unlike a ballistic missile, however, he survived the moment of impact unscathed, having pocketed a flabbergasting $270 million from the sale of his stock-options in the year before the crash.

In December 2001, when the company filed for bankruptcy protection, an editorial in *Business Week* chastised Wall Street, mutual funds and credit-rating agencies for having 'each, in its own way, celebrated what is now revealed to be an arrogant, duplicitous company managed in a dangerous manner'. Then it turned the scourge on itself: 'The business press, including *Business Week,* did no better . . . The press blithely accepted Enron as the epitome of a new, post-deregulation corporate model when it should have been much more aggressive in probing the company's opaque partnerships, off balance sheet manoeuvres, and soaring leverage.' Quite so. Although Enron's accounts may have been deliberately byzantine they were not wholly impenetrable; but the only reporter who took the trouble to scrutinise the small-print was Jonathan Weil of the *Texas Journal,* a four-page weekly supplement to Texan editions of the *Wall Street Journal.* The more closely he studied the complexities of the balance-sheet, the more puzzled he became. In September 2000, after two months of research, Weil set out his misgivings in an article headlined 'Energy Traders Cite Gains, But Some Math is Missing', which explained for the first time why Enron's amazing profits might be an illusion conjured up by exotic accounting techniques. 'Investors counting on these gains could be in for a jolt down the road,' he warned. Luckily for Enron, no reporter followed up Weil's story: even the *Wall Street Journal* declined to run it in the national edition. But it was noticed by a hedge-fund manager named James Chanos, who then undertook his own close analysis of the company's documents, filling the margins with exclamation marks and marking particularly dubious transactions with yellow Post-It notes. In February 2001 Chanos tipped off Bethany McLean, a reporter at *Fortune*, who wrote an article the following month asking 'Is Enron Overpriced?'

Après ça, le déluge. The Enron affair was swiftly followed by similar scandals at WorldCom, Tyco, Global Crossing and other large corporations. (The history of Global Crossing, a telecoms firm trading in Internet bandwidth, can be told in one sentence: it was formed in 1997, went public in 1998 amid wild excitement, achieved a market capitalisation of almost $50 billion in February 2000 – more than that of General Motors – and filed for bankruptcy in January 2002.) Worse still, the collapse of these mighty institutions coincided with the destruction of the World Trade Centre by Islamic terrorists. How could the dazed and battered American economy avoid a catastrophic recession? In the mid-twentieth century, 'pump priming' and demand management would have been the obvious answer, but hadn't these remedies been discredited long since?

Perhaps not. President Bush's immediate announcement of a $15 billion 'aid package' for airlines was the first clue. 'A year ago we would have been a little surprised [by] a several-billion-dollar bailout for the airlines,' John Kenneth Galbraith observed. 'Now it goes through without debate.' The allocation of further billions to infrastructure projects and assistance for the unemployed seemed to confirm that

adversity had suddenly rendered many old Thatcherite prejudices obsolete. 'The US may have rediscovered Keynesianism,'
the *Financial Times* reported on 6 October 2001. 'This week,
with little ceremony, President George W. Bush quietly
brought to a close more than a decade of US economic policy
orthodoxy. By signalling his support for lower taxes and
higher public spending in the next year that could reach as
high as $130 billion, he threw the US administration's weight
behind the proposition that a temporary deficiency in aggre-
gate demand should be met by a shift in government finances
from surplus to deficit.' This argument, a simplified version of
Keynes's theory, had long been heresy in most industrialised
nations, who placed their faith in the monetary policy of
central banks rather than fiscal stimulus from central government. But with the world's three largest economies – America,
Germany and Japan – all on the edge of recession, the conventional wisdom no longer seemed quite so wise. As President
Bush explained to a meeting of business leaders, 'We've got
to do what it takes to make sure this economy gets growing
so people can work.'

His words must have come as quite a shock to diehard
Thatcherites – and to the former British prime minister Jim
Callaghan, who had informed his party members in 1976 that
although 'we used to think that you could spend your way
out of a recession and increase employment by cutting taxes
and boosting government spending . . . I tell you in all can-
dour that that option no longer exists'. Exactly twenty-five
years after a British Labour leader buried John Maynard
Keynes, a right-wing Republican president exhumed him. For
the political historian Professor Charles O. Jones, this was
'the most dramatic agenda replacement . . . certainly since
Pearl Harbour'. But he added that it wasn't only conservatives

who would need to question their traditional assumptions after 11 September: 'Ideologies are based on long-standing understandings, and that's not the case here. There is no precedent for what has happened, so everyone is cut loose from their moorings.'

As TV crews interviewed bystanders amid the dust and rubble of Manhattan in September 2001, one question was heard again and again from baffled New Yorkers: 'Why? Why do they hate us?' For liberals and leftists, the hardest challenge was to accept that rational materialism alone might not provide the answer. 'A tough materialist analysis would be fine,' the philosopher Michael Walzer wrote,

> so long as it is sophisticated enough to acknowledge that material interests don't exhaust the possibilities of human motivation. The spectacle of European Leftists straining to find some economic reason for the Kosovo War (oil in the Balkans? a possible pipeline? was NATO reaching for control of the Black Sea?) was entertaining at the time, but it doesn't bear repeating. For the moment we can make do with a little humility, an openness to heterodox ideas, a sharp eye for the real world, and a readiness to attend to moral as well as materialist arguments. This last point is especially important. The encounter with Islamic radicalism, and with other versions of politicised religion, should help us understand that high among our interests are our values: secular enlightenment, human rights, and democratic government. Left politics starts with the defence of these three.

It certainly should start there – but does it? Since the Ayatollah Khomeini's return to Tehran, the left had mostly preferred to apply the my-enemy's-enemy principle. The weakness of contemporary Islam, according to Khomeini, was its reluctance to apply religious principles to politics, and during his French exile he had embellished conservative theology with anti-imperialist rhetoric borrowed from Frantz Fanon and Jean-Paul Sartre. (Another Iranian expatriate, Dr Ali Shari'ati, translated Fanon's *The Wretched of the Earth* and Che Guevara's *Guerrilla Warfare* into Persian in the hope of arousing the Shi'ites from their habitual quietism.) These radical adornments convinced Parisian leftists – as well as the poor gullible leaders of the Iranian Communist Party – that Khomeini was a liberation theologian, a Muslim version of the rebel Catholic priests in El Salvador and Nicaragua. As late as 2000, in their bestselling book *Empire*, the Marxist intellectuals Antonio Negri and Michael Hardt were still as intoxicated by his potent cocktail as Michel Foucault had been more than twenty years earlier. The Iranian upheaval was 'the first post-modernist revolution', they raved; since Islamic fundamentalism rejected Western hegemony, it 'should not be understood as a return to past social forms and values' but rather as 'a new invention . . . a powerful refusal of the contemporary historical passage in course'. The violence associated with Islamism merely enhanced its allure. Negri, who had himself been jailed for his connections with the Italian Red Brigades during the 1970s, denied that there was any such thing as terrorism – 'a crude conception and terminological reduction that is rooted in a police mentality'. He and Hardt also praised the Soviet Union as 'a society criss-crossed by extremely strong instances of creativity and freedom' and paid tribute to the 'military and civil valour' of the German Nazis. (Say what you like about post-modernists, they certainly have strong stomachs.)

The spread of Islamism after 1979, and its several spectacular coups – the kidnapping of fifty-two American diplomatic personnel in Iran, Hezbollah's suicide-bombings at American offices and barracks in Beirut – seemed to prove that this new force must be essentially progressive, since it was giving the United States a bloody nose. For, like good progressives the world over, the Islamists knew that Washington was the ultimate source of all evil: although the US government had no involvement whatever in the seizure of Mecca's Grand Mosque by 250 heavily armed Sunni militants in November 1979, or the ensuing gun-battle with Saudi troops, Pakistani fundamentalists nevertheless vented their wrath at the desecration of Islam's holiest shrine by sacking the American embassy in Islamabad.

There was one exception to the left's generally benign attitude towards the holy warriors. In Afghanistan, the mujahedin not only enjoyed the support of Reagan and Thatcher but threatened to bring down a Soviet-backed government – so they were excoriated as murderous reactionaries. After the Russian withdrawal, however, and the eventual installation of an Islamic regime which was indeed viciously murderous and reactionary – but had meanwhile turned against the West – these objections melted away. Valiant feminists who protested at the compulsory wearing of the burka or the abolition of girls' schools were accused of 'racist arrogance': how dare they, living in the West, presume to pass judgment on poorer and weaker nations? Besides, the rulers of Kabul had demonstrated their anti-imperialist commitment by sponsoring al-Qaeda, the defenders of the downtrodden. To publicise or criticise the Taliban's barbarity was therefore 'objectively' imperialist – the left's most lethal adverb.

The philosopher Gilbert Ryle invented the term 'category

mistake' to describe the yoking together of two incompatible concepts, as in 'love is a rectangle' or 'Thursdays are purple', and the depiction of Islamism today as an essentially *political* movement is a classic of the genre. Its bloodline does include some political antecedents, though not necessarily of the kind that appeasers would wish to acknowledge: the founder of the Muslim Brotherhood in Egypt had 'considerable admiration for the Nazi brownshirts' and called his organisational units *falanges* as a tribute to General Franco. But fascism itself is incomprehensible to conventional political scientists unless they also have some understanding of the psychopathology that yearns for submission, terror and martyrdom. Islamic terrorists don't bother to call themselves freedom fighters, unlike their secular predecessors. Their only ambition is to exterminate infidels and establish the dominance of shariah law. If they die in the struggle, so much the better – since they will be welcomed into paradise by seventy-two virgins, ready to satisfy every sensual need. (This titillating inducement may not be all it seems. A scholarly new Koranic study by Christoph Luxenberg suggests that the legend of the virgins is based on a misinterpretation of the word *hur*, which translates from Arabic as 'houris' but in the Syriac language meant 'white raisins'. Imagine the disappointment of a suicide-bomber who arrives in heaven expecting a bevy of gorgeous maidens, 'chaste as hidden pearls', only to be offered a bowl of dried grapes instead.)

Even some devout Muslims were surprised by the readiness of European sophisticates to condone eschatological fanaticism. 'While humane representations of Islam ease our conscience, they do little to address the problems within Islam itself,' Ziauddin Sardar wrote, in a courageously honest essay for the *New Statesman*.

The problem with all varieties of Islam as it is practised today, not as it is envisaged by liberals, is that it has lost its humanity. Our religion has become a monster that devours all that is most humane and open-minded. Instead of retreating to an imagined liberal utopia, we Muslims need to ask some tough questions about our faith. What, for example, makes so many pious Muslims such nasty and intolerant individuals? Why is it that every time a country enforces the shariah – the so-called Islamic law – it retreats into medieval barbarity? Why do Muslims still insist on treating women as though they were an inferior race, sent to earth only to deprave and spread corruption?

Sardar thought that Muslims had 'fetishised the Prophet' to the point where all his human qualities evaporated, and devoted themselves to imitating him in every antique detail. 'The quest for this status . . . becomes a pathological end in itself. And all forms of violence and oppression are justified to achieve the end in the name of the Prophet.'

Yet Mohammed himself sanctioned few of their supposedly sacred beliefs. The source of the shariah, for example, is not the Koran but the opinions of jurists in the eighth and ninth centuries, when Islam was in one of its imperialist phases. It was they who divided the world into 'the abode of Islam' and 'the abode of war', equating apostasy with treason despite the Prophet's unequivocal assertion that 'there is no compulsion in religion'. The famous 'two-for-one formula' in the shariah legal code, whereby a woman's testimony is worth half that of a man, has no Koranic authority; nor does the stoning to death of adulterers and rape victims. 'What this means in reality', Sardar wrote, 'is that when Muslim countries apply or impose the shariah – the demand of Muslims from Algeria through Pakistan to Nigeria – the contradictions that were inherent in the formulation and evolution of this jurisprudence come to the fore. The shariah's obsession with extreme punishment generates extreme societies. That is why, wherever the shariah is imposed, Muslim societies acquire a medieval feel. We can see that in Saudi Arabia, the Sudan and the Taliban-ruled Afghanistan. But this is what even the moderate elements of the Islamic movement want.'

As a Muslim himself, Sardar felt entitled to make such a bold generalisation; but woe betide anyone else who drew attention to extremism within 'the Islamic movement'. Only a few months before writing his *New Statesman* article, he published a book called *Why Do People Hate America?* which castigated the Western media for spreading 'misinformation' about the shariah. 'All Islamic schools of law', he insisted, 'are grounded in, refer to, and are justified by reasoning based on the practice of the Prophet Mohammed.' He was equally severe on those who attributed a religious motive to Islamist terrorism, which actually represented nothing more than a violent expression of legitimate grievances against America's foreign and economic policies. 'This', he warned in the introduction, 'is not a book about the positive sides of the United States: those looking for a straightforward counterblast to the hatred expressed for America should stop reading now.' There then followed a long catalogue of crimes, from the massacre of Lakota Indians at Wounded Knee in 1890 to the creation of the Big Mac ('the hamburger is a particular source of hatred of America'). Fair enough: one can find much to criticise in the record of any US administration or corporation. But does it really help us understand the ecstatic nihilism of an al-Qaeda volunteer bent on martyrdom?

In his *New Statesman* essay Ziauddin Sardar referred to 'the self-delusion that we Muslims have turned into a fine art', and anyone wanting to study his own artistic talent need look no further than *Why Do People Hate America?* However, self-delusion is also the congenital deformation of secular liberals who talk like children of the Enlightenment but think like militant flat-earthers, refusing to contemplate any possibility outside their own *idées fixes*. As Michael Walzer wrote after the al-Qaeda attacks on New York and Washington:

Ideologically primed Leftists were likely to think that they already understood whatever needed to be understood. Any group that attacks the imperial power must be a representative of the oppressed, and its agenda must be the agenda of the Left. It isn't necessary to listen to its spokesmen. What else can they want except the redistribution of resources across the globe, the withdrawal of American soldiers from wherever they are, the closing down of aid programs for repressive governments, the end of the blockade of Iraq, and the establishment of a Palestinian state alongside Israel? I don't doubt that there is some overlap between this program and the dreams of al-Qaeda leaders – though al-Qaeda is not an egalitarian movement, and the idea that it supports a two-state solution to the Israeli-Palestinian conflict is crazy. The overlap is circumstantial and convenient, nothing more. A holy war against infidels is not, even unintentionally, unconsciously, or 'objectively', a Left politics. But how many Leftists can even imagine a holy war against infidels?

In *The Eighteenth Brumaire of Louis Bonaparte*, Karl Marx remarks that just as someone learning a new language always retranslates it into his or her mother-tongue, so people who witness an unfamiliar political phenomenon 'anxiously summon up the spirits of the past to their aid, borrowing from them names, rallying-cries, costumes, in order to stage the new world-historical drama in this time-honoured disguise and borrowed speech'. Sure enough, after 11 September 2001 the chorus of grief in the United States was answered by traditional rallying-cries from across the Atlantic.

'It has become painfully clear that most Americans simply don't get it,' an exasperated Seumas Milne wrote in the *Guardian*, less than forty-eight hours later. 'Perhaps it is too much to hope that, as rescue workers struggle to pull firefighters from the rubble, any but a small minority might make the connection between what has been visited upon them and what their government has visited upon large parts of the world. But make that connection they must . . .' According to Milne, it was the US's 'unabashed national egotism and arrogance' that 'drives anti-Americanism among swaths of the world's population'. With the al-Qaeda attack on the Twin Towers, 'the Americans are once again reaping a dragon's teeth harvest they themselves sowed'.

So it was all their own fault – even if many of the victims were in fact not American citizens. The *New Statesman*'s editorial that week was more specific about their culpability. 'American bond traders, you may say, are as innocent and as undeserving of terror as Vietnamese or Iraqi peasants. Well, yes and no . . . No, because Americans, unlike Iraqis and many others in poor countries, at least have the privileges of democracy and freedom that allow them to vote and speak in favour of a different order. If the United States often seems a greedy and overweening power, that is partly because its people have willed it. They preferred George Bush to Al Gore and both to Ralph Nader. These are harsh judgments, but we live in harsh times.' There was plenty more in the same vein: even while bodies were being retrieved from the ruins, the left's instinctive reaction was one of coolly supercilious relativism. The *New Statesman*'s two-page editorial included only one brief expression of sympathy. 'Such large-scale carnage is beyond justification,' it conceded, 'because it can never distinguish between the innocent and the guilty.'

The point was taken up immediately by the left-wing American film-maker Michael Moore. 'If someone did this to get back at Bush,' he complained, 'then they did so by killing thousands of people who DID NOT VOTE for him! Boston, New York, DC and the planes' destination of California – these were the places that voted AGAINST Bush!' As John O'Sullivan commented in the *National Review*, 'It's good to know that if the terrorists ever hijack a Cruise missile and send it in America's direction, Mr Moore will be on hand to divert it from Berkeley or the Upper West Side of Manhattan to less deserving voters such as the coal miners of West Virginia.' Or, one might add, to the residents of Michael Moore's own home town of Flint, Michigan.

While expressing obligatory if perfunctory regret at Osama Bin Laden's methods, many self-styled 'progressives' seemed to find his motives wholly explicable, and even reasonable. Although the left had no difficulty in seeing small crackpot cults – such as those led by the Rev. Jim Jones or David Koresh – for what they were, the idea that thousands or millions of people might go out of their minds and join a pathological sect was literally inconceivable. But hadn't Nazi Germany shown that it can and does happen? In his book *Terror and Liberalism*, the American socialist Paul Berman suggests that his old comrades' sense of history was befogged by their unyielding faith in human rationality.

Let us suppose that, in some remote tropical backwater or untracked desert, a social or political movement does appear to be showing, in fact, indisputable signs of a pathological attachment to murder and suicide. In that case, there has got to be – there *must* be – a rational explanation. Perhaps some unspeakable social condition has provoked the murderous impulse. Perhaps small groups of explorers or imperialists, through their terrible deeds, have driven thousands or even millions of people out of their minds. Perhaps a population has been humiliated beyond human endurance. Unbearable social conditions might well breed irrational reactions – though, in such a case, the irrational reactions ought not to be seen as irrational. For the human race does not generally act in irrational ways.

How many times those sceptical doubts and alternative explanations have appeared and reappeared in the course of these [last] eighty years, in how many strange and mutant versions! Everyone remembers the several arguments that, once upon a time, used to convince liberal-minded people of the virtue and progressive nature of Stalinism and the Communist movement, even in its worst days. The claim that Stalin was deliberately starving to death millions of Ukrainian farmers, or that Stalin had reintroduced slave labour, or that Stalin was whimsically liquidating his own followers and comrades – those claims seemed so extraordinary, so unlikely, so impossibly at odds with the known goals and civilised ideals of the Marxist movement. It was much easier to suppose that, as the Communists argued, Stalin had been slandered by bourgeois propagandists, by right-wing manipulators, and by Trotskyite wreckers. And everyone remembers how those same arguments in Communism's defence were updated and reapplied to other circumstances in later decades – to China during the heyday of Mao Zedong, and to Cambodia during the time of Pol Pot, and to other places and despots.

Not only Communist despots, either: some high-minded liberal democrats gave friendly nods to Mussolini and even Hitler – including a majority of Socialist members in the French national assembly, who 'gazed across the Rhine and simply refused to believe that millions of upstanding Germans had enlisted in a political movement whose animating principles were paranoid conspiracy theories, bloodcurdling hatreds, medieval superstitions and the lure of murder'.

As Berman says, it may be that we remember all this too well for our own good. With hindsight, everyone derides useful idiots such as Beatrice and Sidney Webb, authors of *Soviet Communism: A New Civilisation*, or the British lawyer Dudley Collard QC, who returned from the Moscow show-trials of the 1930s convinced that the defendants' confessions were all genuine. (To say that they were extracted under torture or duress would imply that Comrade Stalin was 'not a gentleman', a possibility which Collard refused to entertain.) 'We can't imagine, we modern sophisticates, how anyone could have made such mistakes in the past,' Berman writes. And so the mistakes are repeated.

Long after the character of Soviet tyranny was fully apparent to anyone who bothered to read or listen, liberal fellow-travellers persevered with a political version of double-entry book-keeping – offsetting the Gulag against, say, Moscow's backing for anti-colonial movements in Africa or its distaste for the profit motive. As late as 1982, when defending Solidarnosc in Poland, Susan Sontag shocked many of her fellow-liberals by saying that repression was the rule rather than the exception in the Soviet Union and its satellite states:

Imagine if you will, someone who read only the *Reader's Digest* between 1950 and 1970, and someone in the same period who read only *The Nation* or *The New Statesman*. Which reader would have been better informed about the realities of communism? The answer, I think, should give us pause ... We had identified the enemy as fascism. We heard the demonic language of fascism. We believed in, or at least applied a double standard to, the angelic language of communism ... The émigrés from communist countries we didn't listen to, who found it far easier to get published in the *Reader's Digest* than in *The Nation* or the *New Statesman,* were telling the truth. Now we hear them. Why didn't we hear them before?

She ended by spelling out the truth which many ('and I include myself') had been unable or unwilling to accept: that Soviet Communism was 'fascism with a human face'.

There was little obvious humanity in the terrorists who conducted the massacres of 11 September, you might think; but nor had there been in the Soviet Union's psychiatric prisons, and that never inhibited its apologists from accentuating the positive. Once again the progressive account-ants reached for their ledgers, and after a few minutes' calculation they had prepared a damning balance-sheet. The only entry in the credit column – condolences for the dead and bereaved – was vastly outweighed by a long list of mitigat-ing and extenuating factors. On closer scrutiny many of these were as flimsy as Enron's profits, but they proved just as allur-ing to true believers who didn't wish to have their precon-ceptions dislodged. No independent audit was needed: the United States had been declared morally bankrupt. Its sup-port for Israel, its intervention in Kosovo, its non-intervention in East Timor, its enforcement of 'no-fly zones in Iraq', perhaps even its refusal to ratify the Kyoto treaty – these and innumerable other crimes were cited as possible reasons for al-Qaeda's assault on the United States, though Osama Bin Laden had never shown much interest in the Palestinian cause, still less the problem of global warming. (The mention of East Timor was particularly rich in irony since Bin Laden in fact supported the Indonesian occupation, on the ground that the Christians of East Timor had no right to independence from their Muslim masters. 'We warned Australia before . . . against its despicable effort to separate East Timor,' al-Qaeda announced in October 2002, after killing 200 revellers at a Bali nightclub that was popular with young Australian tourists. 'It ignored the warning until it woke up to the sounds of explosions in Bali.')

Like generals who fight the last war instead of the present one, socialists and squishy progressives were so accustomed to regarding American imperialism as the only source of evil in the world that they couldn't imagine any other enemy. 'The responses to 11 September by parts of the Left – Noam Chomsky, Edward Said, Alexander Cockburn, the "critical" minds who are always predictable – threaten to dissociate the word "left" from morally intelligent politics,' Professor Mitchell Cohen wrote in an editorial for *Dissent*, the only left-wing magazine which dared to think the unthinkable instead of reaching for time-honoured disguise and borrowed speech. 'One almost expects them to explain that Bin Laden's crew attacked the World Trade Center because Thomas Jefferson owned slaves.'

The most extreme manifestation of this fallacy was *L'Effroyable Imposture* ('The Dreadful Fraud'), a book by the socialist Thierry Meyssan which sold 200,000 copies in France and has since been translated into sixteen languages. Meyssan claimed that what hit the Pentagon on 11 September was not an aeroplane but a cruise missile fired on the orders of right-wingers in the US government itself, and that the same plotters 'teleguided' two empty jets to crash into the Twin Towers in New York. Their motive? To persuade George W. Bush to increase defence spending – as if he needed any persuasion.

Meyssan may fairly be dismissed as a mad conspiracy theorist, even if the fact that his book topped the French bestseller list for several weeks shows that he wasn't exactly a lone nutter. So let us turn instead to a far more eminent and representative figure of dissent, Professor Noam Chomsky of the Massachusetts Institute of Technology, whose instant pamphlet on 9/11 sold 160,000 copies within a few weeks, and has been translated into as many languages as *L'Effroyable Imposture*. Chomsky is undeniably an influential thinker – the most frequently quoted living intellectual, according to the Arts and Humanities Citation Index. (Even among the dead he has already overtaken Cicero and is gaining on Freud.) 'Certainly,' the *Washington Post* reported in 2002, 'he's the only silver-haired MIT professor to appear on stage and on disc with bands Chumbawamba and Rage Against the Machine.'

Chomsky is a master of double-entry maths. After 11 September 2001 he decided that al-Qaeda's murder of 3,000 people was less appalling than President Clinton's missile strike three years earlier on a pharmaceutical plant in the Sudan (wrongly identified as a chemical weapons factory), which had claimed the life of a lone security guard. 'The Americans didn't even think about the outcome of the bombing,' he explained, 'because the Sudanese were so far below contempt as to be not worth thinking about.' Suppose, for example, that he were to step on an ant, without a second thought, while strolling down the street. 'That would mean that I regard the ant as beneath contempt. And that's morally worse than if I purposely killed that ant. So, if we're not moral hypocrites, we'd agree that Sudan was the morally worse crime than the World Trade Centre.' (Since Chomsky claims to be an admirer of George Orwell, one wonders if he has ever read Orwell's essay from 1945 on how the hatred of English left-wing intellectuals for the ruling class forbade them to admit that Britain's war strategy could succeed: 'There is no limit to the follies that can be swallowed if one is under the influence of feelings of this kind ... One has to belong to the intelligentsia to believe things like that: no ordinary man could be such a fool.')

The professor has an inexhaustible hoard of analogies and precedents that allow him to avoid the immediate issue. Asked in the 1990s why he opposed efforts by the international community to stop ethnic cleansing in Bosnia and Kosovo, he would reply that genocide in the Balkans was no worse than genocide in East Timor – and then segue into his well-rehearsed speech about Western support for Indonesia, nimbly sidestepping any discussion of Slobodan Milošević's thuggery. As the *Dissent* editorial noted:

A rhetorical tactic is at play: always change the subject. Censure terror? Well, let's talk about 'the real issue', globalisation. Ask about a crisis within Islam? No, that's bigoted, let's discuss the 'real' issue, Orientalism. Hasn't the Left been through something like this before – and been discredited by it? Confront Stalinist atrocities? Ummm ... let's address 'the real issues', czarism, capitalism, and imperialism. Changing the subject signifies evasion. Sometimes it's evasion of what means imply for ends and sometimes of the fact that the world doesn't always present to us comforting choices.

In extremis, wishful thinkers will abandon reality and morality altogether rather than forgo their comforting choices. During the late 1970s Chomsky consistently ridiculed the idea that Pol Pot might be a mass-murderer, despite the testimony of many Cambodians who had fled across the border. 'Refugees are frightened and defenceless, at the mercy of alien forces,' he told readers of the *Nation* in June 1977. 'They naturally tend to report what they believe their interlocutors wish to hear ... Specifically, refugees questioned by Westerners or Thais have a vested interest in reporting atrocities on the part of Cambodian revolutionaries, an obvious fact that no serious reporter will fail to take into account.' Two years later, after the overthrow of Pol Pot, the huge piles of skulls in his death camps confirmed that it wasn't the refugees who had deluded themselves. The most authoritiative estimate is that between April 1975 and January 1979 the Khmer Rouge killed 1.67 million Cambodians, or 20 per cent of the population – proportionally the greatest carnage ever inflicted by a government on its subjects. Yet even in 1980, when he published *After the Cataclysm: Postwar Indochina and the Reconstruction of Imperial Ideology*, Chomsky reproached those who applied the word 'genocide' to this Holocaust. 'The deaths in Cambodia were not the result of systematic slaughter and starvation organised by the state but rather attributable in large measure to peasant revenge, undisciplined military units out of government control, starvation and disease that are direct consequence of the US war, or other such factors.' Anyway, why keep harping on about those corpses? 'The positive side of [the Khmer Rouge] picture has been virtually edited out,' he grumbled. 'The negative side has been presented to a mass audience in a barrage with few historical parallels, apart from wartime propaganda.'

Noam Chomsky has always given the benefit of the doubt to 'anti-American' regimes such as those of Pol Pot or Slobodan Milošević, strenuously downplaying the scale of their terror and doubting even the most carefully verified evidence. With the United States, by contrast, no proof is required. In October 2001 he stated as a fact that Pentagon strategists were planning 'the slaughter and silent genocide' of three or four million Afghans during their military campaign against the Taliban. What was Chomsky's source for this shocking information? Answer came there none: by the time the Taliban fell – with no genocide, silent or otherwise – he and his army of disciples had already changed the subject again.

If they weren't in such a hurry, they might sometimes have to pursue the logic of their own argument – which isn't really an argument at all, merely an unending buffet of savoury propagandist canapés with no main course to follow. During the war against the Taliban they continually reminded us, with a triumphant smirk, that previous American governments had funded and trained the fundamentalists in Afghanistan. Perfectly true, of course, and well worth mentioning. But mightn't this historical guilt actually strengthen the moral obligation to undo the harm caused? As Christopher Hitchens asked:

> May we now agree to cancel this crime by removing from the Taliban the power of enslavement that it exerts over Afghans, and which it hopes to extend? Dead silence from progressives. Couldn't we talk about the ozone layer instead? In other

words, all the learned and conscientious objections, as well as all the silly or sinister ones, boil down to this: Nothing will make us fight against an evil if that fight forces us to go to the same corner as our own government. (The words 'our own' should of course be appropriately ironised, with the necessary quotation marks.) To do so would be a betrayal of the Cherokees.

America's previous indifference to the Taliban, like its collusion with states such as Saudi Arabia, might also appear to refute the allegation that it was engaged in a 'war against Islam', especially since every Western intervention in the previous decade or so had been undertaken in defence of Muslim populations – in Kuwait, Iraqi Kurdistan, Bosnia, Somalia, Kosovo, Afghanistan and then Iraq again. (Ah yes, the Chomskyites retort, but the Gulf Wars of 1991 and 2003 were really 'about oil'. Despite their best efforts, however, no million-barrel gushers have yet been discovered in Kosovo or Somalia.)

The vision of the West and the Islamic world as two monolithic, irreconcilable civilisations was conjured up again and again. 'The leaders of the western nations are now coming out to make a point that this is not a war against Islam, stating that their real war is against the fanatics, the extremists and fundamentalists,' the Muslim journalist Abu Musab wrote in September 2001. 'However, by examining their statements we can see that this is a war [between] two separate beliefs.' Tony Blair had given the game away by pledging to defend reason, democracy and tolerance – which, according to Abu Musab, were anathema to all followers of the Prophet, not merely the fundamentalists. 'Islam does not believe in democracy, freedom, tolerance or reason. It is well known that sovereignty belongs to Allah (Subhana Wa Ta'ala). There is no freedom from Allah's rule, or tolerance against Allah's rule or reasoning of Allah's rule. Allah (Subhana Wa Ta'ala) commands: "*The Rule is for none but Allah.*"' Paradoxically, many anti-American Muslims thus endorsed the thesis of Professor Samuel Huntington, who wrote in *The Clash of Civilizations?* that 'Western ideas of individualism, liberalism, constitutionalism, human rights, equality, liberty, the rule of law, democracy, free markets, the separation of church and state often have little resonance in Islamic, Confucian, Japanese, Hindu, Buddhist or Orthodox cultures.'

Haven't we heard this before? It sounds eerily like the specious inductive reasoning that was once deployed to explain why the suffrage could not be extended to females, or the population of India, or black South Africans. As Paul Berman writes, there is nothing new (or even post-modernist) in the theory of unbridgeable fault-lines between civilisations, peddled by both Samuel Huntington and Osama Bin Laden:

> In the late nineteenth century it was argued that liberal democracy descended from ancient Anglo-Saxon customs and, for racial reasons, would never spread beyond the Anglo-Saxon world. Sometimes it was argued, a little more expansively, that liberal democracy was a racial product of the forest-roaming peoples of Northern Europe as a whole, and could not be transferred to people from warmer climes. Then again, it was argued that liberalism and democracy descended from the Protestant Reformation, and Protestants would therefore enjoy the benefits of liberty – but Catholic countries could never follow suit.

Even in the mid-twentieth century, many pipe-sucking pundits ridiculed the idea that a southern and Catholic nation such as Spain would ever embrace democracy. When this prejudice was confounded the fault-line shifted eastwards, with 'Slavs' and 'Orthodox Christians' being substituted for the Spaniards. ('Nothing', Berman notes, 'is more ephemeral than a theory about changeless cultures.') Or perhaps it was only Christian societies that cherished liberal institutions? The resilience of democracy in India shattered that illusion. But no Asian countries outside the British empire have followed this example, have they? Well, only if you choose to ignore the democratic advances in South Korea, the Philippines and Taiwan since the early 1990s.

'The Asiatic countries have an entirely different view of political democracy from what we have in the West,' the former British prime minister Edward Heath said in 1997 during a televised debate with Hong Kong's veteran pro-democracy campaigner Martin Lee, who had demanded that China respect human rights. 'What they are working on is not one man one vote as we have it but a system of consultation and argument and settlement and so on.' When Lee, who is himself Chinese, pointed out that other large Asiatic nations such as India and Japan did in fact allow their citizens to vote, Heath accused him of being 'corrupt' and 'hypocritical'. 'The plain fact', he spluttered, 'is that the Chinese have different religious beliefs than what we have in the West' – as if this proved beyond doubt that they were unfit for democracy.

One expects nothing else from grizzled conservative 'realists' such as Heath and Huntington, or from medievalist zealots pursuing an eternal jihad: it is what they truly believe. The defenders of apartheid argued with equal conviction that the 'kaffirs' were genetically unsuited to freedom, and King Fahd of Saudi Arabia was probably quite sincere when he declared that 'the democratic system that is predominant in the world is not a suitable system for the peoples of our region . . . The system of free elections is not suitable to our country.' Now, however, this fatalistic nonsense is also recited by secular idealists who wear their anti-racist campaign medals with pride and of course *abhor* Orientalist stereotyping – but who hope to save themselves from the mortal sin of liberal arrogance by preaching a gospel of reactionary determinism, invoking the myth of hermetic civilisations and immutable ethnic characteristics.

There are no 'pure' or changeless civilisations. They evolve through the continual absorption of new and often foreign habits which soon acquire the status of ancient national traditions. The 'quintessentially British' meal of fish and chips owed its existence to Sir Walter Raleigh, who brought potatoes back from Virginia in the 1580s; it has in turn yielded place to the nation's new favourite, chicken tikka massala, an Anglo-Indian hybrid. Meanwhile, India may have become the world's largest producer, consumer and exporter of chillis, but the plant itself is native to Mexico: it was introduced to Europe by the Spanish in 1514 and thence to Asia by Portuguese seafarers a century later. How many Indians today regard the chilli as a symbol of Euro-American hegemony?

Cross-pollination is as fruitful, and inescapable, in culture as in culinary tastes. 'We ought not to be ashamed of applauding the truth, nor appropriating the truth from whatever source it may come, even if it be from remote races and nations alien to us,' the great ninth-century Arab philosopher al-Kindi wrote. 'There is nothing that beseems the seeker after truth better than truth itself.' Some Muslims who point with justifiable pride to the influence of Arab mathematicians and astronomers on the transformation of European science – forgetting that this scientific revolution created the modern civilisation which they supposedly despise – are not always so ready to admit that the exchange of ideas was mutual. Look at one of the earliest and most famous Islamic monuments, the Dome of the Rock in Jerusalem: the architecture of its minaret was inspired by Christian church-towers in Syria, while the style of its internal decoration derived from Byzantine art. Or, from the sublime to the banal, look at the Western military uniforms (and weapons) which are standard-issue for even the sternest Islamic regimes. Changeless cultures, eh?

Europeans and Americans can justly be accused of failing to recognise what they owe to older civilisations. One catalyst for the Renaissance, for example, was the rediscovery of Greek philosophy by medieval Muslim rationalists seeking a 'world of reason' to replace the 'world of muftis'. Because of these enlightened Arabs, the historian Leslie Lipson writes, 'Aristotle crept back into Europe by the side door ... The main source of Europe's inspiration shifted from Christianity back to Greece, from Jerusalem to Athens.' But, although an acknowledgment of the debt would teach Occidental triumphalists a salutary lesson, how much comfort or satisfaction does it offer Muslims? Recollection of past philosophical or scientific glories can only remind them that the ideas transplanted to Europe disappeared in the 'abode of Islam' itself as enlightened rationalism fell victim to sacred jurisprudence.

According to Abu al-A'la al-Mawdudi, the foremost ideologue of modern Islamism, 'there can be no reconciliation between Islam and democracy, not even in minor issues, because they contradict each other in all particulars' – and anyone who says otherwise is an apostate. This menacing injunction has been repeated by other fundamentalist intellectuals, such as Sayyid Qutb and Yusuf al-Qaradawi. But on what authority? If they were as devout and learned as they professed to be, they ought to have realised that it is itself a form of blasphemy. As one Muslim writer objects, 'these fundamentalist thinkers expound their *quite human* views, accord them a divine status, and dismiss their critics as ... heretics'. Thus they insist upon *hakimiyyat Allah* – 'God's rule' – as the correct alternative to democracy, even though it can be found nowhere in the Koran or the *hadith* (the Prophet's sayings), the only two authoritative texts. Certainly one can construct a historical and doctrinal case for the incompatibility of Islam and democracy, but the Iranian scholar Hamid Enayat has shown that by diligent exegesis from respected Islamic sources it is 'neither ... inordinately difficult nor illegitimate to derive a list of democratic rights and liberties'.

Even so, an unavoidable obstacle remains: there can be no political rights or liberties without religious pluralism and toleration. As Thomas Jefferson wrote in 1782:

> Subject opinion to coercion: whom will you make your inquisitors? Fallible men; men governed by bad passions, by private as well as public reasons. And why subject it to coercion? To produce uniformity ... Millions of innocent men, women, and children, since the introduction of Christianity, have been burnt, tortured, fined, imprisoned; yet we have not advanced one inch towards uniformity. What has been the effect of coercion? To make one half the world fools and the other half hypocrites. To support roguery and error all over the earth.

Which brings us back to the Enlightenment – and to its most flourishing offshoot, the country damned by Islamists as the great Satan but exalted by Tom Paine as 'the cause of all mankind'. The genius of America's founding fathers was to guarantee freedom of religion and freedom from religion simultaneously. In the words of the First Amendment: 'Congress shall make no law respecting an establishment of religion, or prohibiting the free exercise thereof.' Muslims who assume that any such Bill of Rights must be fatal to piety should note that America has in fact preserved the religious imagination it imported from Europe, whereas Europe itself – much of which still resists disestablishment – is now the most godless continent on earth.

The erection of what Thomas Jefferson called 'a wall of separation between church and state' may be unimaginable to many people in the Islamic world, even eighty years after Kemal Atatürk abolished the Caliphate in Turkey and created a secular constitution; but it would have been no less inconceivable to medieval Christians. John Locke himself might have been startled by the indiscriminate tolerance decreed in Jefferson's Bill to establish religious freedom in Virginia (drafted in 1779, enacted in 1786), which declared that 'truth is great and will prevail if left to herself; that she is the proper and sufficient antagonist to error, and has nothing to fear from the conflict unless by human interposition disarmed of her natural weapons, free argument and debate; errors ceasing to be dangerous when it is permitted freely to contradict them'. Jefferson recalled in his memoirs that a member of the Virginia general assembly who proposed inserting the words 'Jesus Christ' into the preamble 'was rejected by a great majority, in proof that they meant to comprehend, within the mantle of its protection, the Jew and the Gentile, the Christian and Mohammedan, the Hindoo and Infidel of every denomination'.

To judge by his self-penned epitaph ('Author of the Declaration of American Independence, of the Statute of Virginia for Religious Freedom, and Father of the University of Virginia'), Jefferson took greater pride in this accomplishment than in having been the third president of the United States – as well he might, since his statute was the first of its kind anywhere in the world. 'The Virginia act for religious freedom has been received with infinite approbation in Europe, and propagated with enthusiasm,' he wrote to James Madison while visiting Paris in December 1786.

> It is inserted in the new *Encyclopédie*, and is appearing in most of the publications respecting America. In fact, it is comfortable to see the standard of reason at length erected, after so many ages, during which the human mind has been held in vassalage by kings, priests, and nobles; and it is honourable for us, to have produced the first legislature who had the courage to declare, that the reason of man may be trusted with the formation of his own opinions.

Truth is great and will prevail. Or, to quote the tougher formulation of the Spanish-American philosopher George Santayana, 'The truth is cruel, but it can be loved, and it makes free those who have loved it.' Visitors to the US Archives building in Washington DC can read another of Santayana's epigrams chiselled over the main entrance: 'Those who cannot remember the past are condemned to repeat it.' He described this as the condition of 'children and barbarians, in which instinct has learned nothing from experience'. But those who refuse to learn from experience, and strive instead to discredit the rationalism that makes such enlightenment possible – whether they be holy warriors, anti-scientific relativists, economic fundamentalists, radical post-modernists, New Age mystics or latter-day Chicken Lickens – are not only condemning themselves to repeat the past. They wish to consign us all to a life in darkness.

Notes

PROLOGUE: TWO MESSIAHS

vii **Three army tanks are sent** See 'Army Tanks Close Tehran Airport in Apparent Effort to Stop Khomeini' by Jonathan C. Randal, *Washington Post*, 24 January 1979.

viii **In Tehran, troops open fire** See 'Iran, in Apparent Shift, Hints Khomeini May Return' by Jonathan C. Randal, *Washington Post*, 30 January 1979.

ix **Accompanied by a retinue** 'Millions Welcome Khomeini to Iran' by William Claiborne, Jonathan C. Randal and William Branigin, *Washington Post*, 1 February 1979; 'Veil of Fears' by John Simpson, *Guardian*, 1 February 1994. See also 'With God Not on Our Side' by David Hirst, *Guardian*, 4 February 1989; obituary of Shahpour Bakhtiar, *Daily Telegraph*, 9 August 1991; 'Iran: The Impossible Revolution' by Fouad Ajami, *Foreign Affairs*, Winter 1988/89.

INTRODUCTION: DARE TO KNOW

2 **'Enlightenment is man's emergence'** 'Answer to the Question: What is Enlightenment? [*Beantwortung der Frage: Was ist Aufklärung?*]' by Immanuel Kant, *Berlinischer Monatsschrift*, September 1784. Reprinted in *Was ist Aufklärung? Thesen und Definitionen* edited by Eberhard Bahr (Reclam, Stuttgart, 1986).

3 **'I do not know whether we will ever reach mature adulthood'** 'What is Enlightenment?' by Michel Foucault, in *The Foucault Reader*, edited by Paul Rabinow (Pantheon Books, New York, 1984).

4 **'the chief challenger of the fundamentals'** *Radical Enlightenment:*

Philosophy and the Making of Modernity 1650–1750 by Jonathan Israel
(Oxford University Press, 2001).

4 **'By separating theology from natural philosophy'** *The Party of Humanity: Studies in the French Enlightenment* by Peter Gay (Weidenfeld &
Nicolson, London, 1964).

5 **'lies not so much in what was preached'** *The Enlightenment* by Jack
Lively (Longmans, London, 1966).

6 **'The Enlightenment made explicit'** 'Whatever Happened to Reason?'
by Roger Scruton, *City Journal* (New York), Vol. 9, No. 2, Spring
1999.

CHAPTER ONE: THE VOODOO REVOLUTION

12 **'I'm going to borrow some of her elegant phraseology'** See 'Jeane
Kirkpatrick: The Ambassador from *Commentary* Magazine' by James
Conaway, *Washington Post*, 1 November 1981.

13 **As Professor Stanley Hoffman pointed out** *New York Times*,
31 December 1980.

15 **'it is doing no good to the cause of party morale'** 'Tories: Thatcher-
Bashed', *Economist*, 1 March 1980.

15 **'The importance of Margaret Thatcher'** 'The British Election of
1979 and Its Aftermath' by Kenneth Watkins, *Policy Review*, Summer
1979.

16 **'The regime is dedicated'** 'Maggie Might Make Lots of Magic' by
Herbert Stein, *Fortune*, 10 September 1979.

16 **'What happens in Britain is of great importance'** 'Hooray for
Margaret Thatcher' by Milton Friedman, *Newsweek*, 9 July 1979.

17 **'I admire her greatly'** 'Wave of the Past? Or Wave of the Future?'
by Lawrence Minard, *Forbes*, 1 October 1979.

17 **'What happens here in Britain'** 'Britons Deflate US Economist' by
Leonard Downie Jr, *Washington Post*, 3 March 1980.

19 **'It's kind of hard to sell "trickle down"'** 'The Education of David
Stockman' by William Greider, *Atlantic Monthly*, December 1981.

20 **'no parallel upsurge of riches'** *The Politics of Rich and Poor* by Kevin
Phillips (Random House, New York, 1990).

22 **In 1988 a report** See *Sweatshops in the US* (US General Accounting
Office, Washington DC, August 1988).

22 **'Oh exactly. Very much so'** *Weekend World*, London Weekend Television, 16 January 1983.

24 'given every financial and other encouragement' *One of Us* by Hugo Young (Macmillan, London, 1989).

26 'The ideas and programmes' *One World, Ready or Not: The Manic Logic of Global Capitalism* by William Greider (Simon & Schuster, New York, 1997).

27 'I believe in "Judaeo-Christian" values' *The Downing Street Years* by Margaret Thatcher (HarperCollins, London, 1993). An interesting account of Thatcher's entrepreneurial theology can be found in 'Religion as an Environmental Influence on Enterprise Culture – The Case of Britain in the 1980s' by Alistair R. Anderson, Sarah L. Drakopoulou-Dodd and Michael G. Scott, *International Journal of Entrepreneurial Behaviour & Research*, Vol. VI, No.1 (2000).

27 'the future of the world depended on the few men and women' *Dartford Chronicle*, 8 June 1951.

27 'Are we to move towards moral decline' Transcript of speech by Sir Keith Joseph MP, Edgbaston, 19 October 1974.

27 'we must not focus our attention exclusively on the material' Transcript of speech by Margaret Thatcher, Zurich, 14 March 1977.

29 'If a man will not work' Transcript of speech by Margaret Thatcher to the general assembly of the Church of Scotland, The Mound, Edinburgh, 21 May 1988. (Her critics promptly dubbed this speech 'the Sermon on the Mound'.)

29 Alas for the theory Internal Revenue Service data on charitable deductions, cited in 'Look Who's Being Tightfisted', *Business Week*, 5 November 1990. See also the Gallup survey reported in 'US Charities See Increase in Gifts', *Boston Globe*, 16 December 1990.

31 'This debt is essentially the cost' 'When the Lending Stops' by Lester C. Thurow, *New Perspectives Quarterly*, Vol. 4, No. 3, Autumn 1987.

32 'In the months and years prior to the 1929 crash' 'The 1929 Parallel: Modern Stock Market Speculation' by John Kenneth Galbraith, *Atlantic Monthly*, January 1987. See also *A Short History of Financial Euphoria* by John Kenneth Galbraith (Viking Penguin, New York, 1993).

33 'In these latter days' 'The Royal Road to Bankrutpcy, By One Who Took the Ride', *Atlantic Monthly*, January 1933.

34 'I can calculate the motions' Quoted in 'The Speculation Mania' by Richard Lambert, *Financial Times*, 22 March 1986.

35 **'Why is the market so high'** 'The Bull Tops 2000' by George Russell, *Time*, 19 January 1987.

CHAPTER TWO: OLD SNAKE-OIL, NEW BOTTLES

41 **As the *Economist* noted** 'Tom Peters, Performance Artist', *Economist*, 24 September 1994.

42 **One man who certainly understood how to profit** See 'Let a Thousand Gurus Bloom', *Washington Post*, 12 February 1995.

43 **In the words of Mike Fuller** 'Gurumania' by Carol Howes, *Calgary Herald*, 1 October 1994.

46 **One corporate client, Atlantic Richfield** 'Soul Searching' by Kenneth L. Woodward, *Newsweek*, 8 July 1996.

48 **The comic writers Christopher Buckley and John Tierney** *God is My Broker: A Monk Tycoon Reveals the 7½ Laws of Spiritual and Financial Growth* by Brother Ty with Christopher Buckley and John Tierney (Nicholas Brealey Publishing, Santa Rosa and London, 1998).

49 **No coach class for him** For more on Chopra, see: 'A Touch of Oprah's Wand for a Guru of Self-Healing' by Paul D. Colford, *Newsday*, 15 July 1993; 'The End of History and the Last Guru' by Matt Labash, *Weekly Standard*, 1 July 1996; 'The New Age Gurus: Do They Need Therapy?' by Andrew Billen, *Observer*, 1 September 1996; 'How to Know Deepak' by Bill Amundson, *Denver Rocky Mountain News*, 12 March 2000; 'A Mystic Spinning Words into Gold' by Jim Remsen, *Philadelphia Inquirer*, 28 February 2001; 'The Multi-Millionaire Mystic' by Christopher Goodwin, *Evening Standard* (London), 10 May 2001.

53 **'Of course this benchmarking is only a rough guide'** Quoted in 'Gurus of Gobbledegook' by John Micklethwait and Adrian Wooldridge, *Sunday Telegraph*, 27 October 1996.

54 **Bill Clinton, who invited both Covey and Anthony Robbins to spend the weekend** *The Choice* by Bob Woodward (Simon & Schuster, New York, 1996).

55 **Ten days after the Camp David** 'Let a Thousand Gurus Bloom', *Washington Post*, 12 February 1995.

56 **As *Newsweek* pointed out** 'Self-Help USA' by Daniel McGinn, *Newsweek*, 10 January 2000.

57 **Government spending on private consultants rose** 'The Annual League Tables' by Philip Abbott, *Management Consultancy*, 1 August 2001.

57 **In the summer of 1996 he despatched** 'Andersen Androids Invade New Labour' by Richard Woods and Andrew Grice, *Sunday Times*, 24 November 1996.

CHAPTER THREE: IT'S THE END OF THE WORLD AS WE KNOW IT

64 **James Atlas of the *New York Times* posed the obvious question** 'What is Fukuyama Saying? And to Whom Is He Saying It?' by James Atlas, *New York Times* magazine, 22 October 1989.

66 **'When a serious work of history'** 'Against "Declinism" – American Power After the Cold War' by Joseph S. Nye Jr, *New Republic*, 15 October 1990.

67 **'How is it that some people become famous'** See Professor Philip Green's review of *Trust* by Francis Fukuyama, *Nation*, 25 September 1995.

67 **By the time he had expanded his essay into a book** *The End of History and the Last Man* by Francis Fukuyama (The Free Press, New York, 1992).

68 **'How far shall we trust a "Universal History"'** 'Francis Fukuyama and the end of history' by Roger Kimball, *New Criterion*, February 1992.

71 **'I am a child of Niehbur'** 'Looking the World in the Eye' by Robert D. Kaplan, *Atlantic Monthly*, December 2001.

74 **As Edward Said pointed out** 'We All Swim Together' by Edward Said, *New Statesman*, 15 October 2001.

75 **The only difference, as critics pointed out** 'Challenging Huntington' by Richard E. Rubenstein and Jarle Crocker, *Foreign Policy*, No. 96, Fall 1994, pp.113–28.

75 **The Nobel laureate Amartya Sen** 'Amartya Sen Rejects "Clash of Civilisations" Concept', *The Hindu*, 13 November 2001.

75 **'These are the two touchstones of any debate'** 'The Clash' by Joel Achenbach, *Washington Post*, 16 December 2001.

CHAPTER FOUR: THE DEMOLITION MERCHANTS OF REALITY

79 **Dons who normally confine their disputes** 'Unquiet Flow the Dons' by Dennis A. Williams and Anthony Collings, *Newsweek*, 16 February 1981.

79 **he did admit that it was the 'enormous explosion of work . . .'** See Colin MacCabe's letter in *Guardian Weekly*, 15 February 1981.

80 **As a young lecturer observed** 'Highbrows go witch hunting' by Andy Martin, *The Times*, 13 May 1992.

81 **'Students taking courses in literature'** 'Farewell to a Fad' by Barbara Ehrenreich, *The Progressive*, March 1999.

82 **'England is sick'** Quoted in *Literary Theory: An Introduction* by Terry Eagleton (Basil Blackwell, Oxford, 1983).

84 **They don't have the same regime of truth** 'Iran: The Spirit of a World Without Spirit', from *Politics, Philosophy, Culture: Interviews and Other Writings 1977–84* by Michel Foucault (Routledge, New York and London, 1988).

86 **'In pulling the rug out'** 'Where Do Post-Modernists Come From?' by Terry Eagleton, *Monthly Review*, July 1995.

86 **For the purposes of his experiment he needed a genre** See 'On the Simulation of Post-Modernism and Mental Debility Using Recursive Transition Networks' by A. C. Bulhak, Technical Report 96/264 (1996), Department of Computer Science, Monash University. For the Post-Modernism Generator, visit *www.elsewhere.org/cgi-bin/postmodern/*.

87 **'A writer on structuralism in the *Times Literary Supplement*'** From the lecture 'Science and Literature' (1968), reprinted in *Pluto's Republic* by Peter Medawar (Oxford University Press, 1982).

87 **'In the first place, singularities-events'** Quoted in 'Post-Modernism Disrobed' by Richard Dawkins, *Nature*, 9 July 1998.

89 **'For some years I've been troubled'** 'A Physicist Experiments with Cultural Studies' by Alan D. Sokal, *Lingua Franca*, May–June 1996.

90 **'that there exists an external world'** 'Transgressing the Boundaries: Toward a Transformative Hermeneutics of Quantum Gravity' by Alan D. Sokal, *Social Text* Nos 46/47 (Spring/Summer 1996).

94 **'He got it wrong'** 'Postmodern Gravity Deconstructed, Slyly' by Janny Scott, *New York Times*, 18 May 1996.

96 **'It is always possible to face up to any experience'** Quoted in *In Defence of History* by Richard J. Evans (Granta Books, London, 1997 and 2000).

97 **'There is in fact a massive, carefully empirical literature'** *In Defence of History, op. cit.*

98 **'Although historians often frame their criticisms'** 'Theorising the Writing of History' by Ellen Somekawa and Elizabeth A. Smith, *Journal of Social History*, Vol. 22 (1988).

99 **'The most usual ideological abuse of history'** 'Outside and Inside

History', lecture delivered at the Central European University, Budapest, 1993; reprinted in *On History* by Eric Hobsbawm (Weidenfeld & Nicolson, London, 1997).

100 **'What one generally calls a fact is an interpretation'** Quoted in *Intellectual Impostures* by Alan Sokal and Jean Bricmont (Profile Books, London, 1998).

102 **'While the parents of a six-year-old child can decide'** *Against Method* by Paul Feyerabend (New Left Books, London, 1975).

104 **'Science is about fact'** 'Problem is Politics', *Topeka Capital Journal*, 16 May 1999. See also letters page of same newspaper, 7 September 1999.

105 **'I suspect that politics is what keeps them silent'** 'Malone the Victor, Even Though Court Sides With Opponents, Says Mencken' by H. L. Mencken, *Baltimore Evening Sun*, 17 July 1925.

106 **The American presidential election of 1800** *The Enlightenment in America* by Henry May (Oxford University Press, New York, 1976), p. 278.

107 **to the Marquis de Condorcet** Quoted in *The Portable Enlightenment Reader* edited by Isaac Kramnick (Penguin, Harmondsworth, 1995).

109 **'Thank heaven I sat at the feet of Darwin and Huxley'** Quoted in 'Which Civilisation?' by Michael Lind, *Prospect*, 25 October 2001.

109 **'to show the people what fundamentalism is'** 'Darrow vs. Bryan', Associated Press, 20 July 1925.

111 **'The inferior man's reasons for hating knowledge'** 'Homo Neanderthalensis' by H. L. Mencken, *Baltimore Sun*, 29 June 1925.

112 **'This is a terrible, tragic, embarrassing solution'** Quoted in 'Candidates Are Evolving Backward' by David Sarasohn, *The Oregonian*, 1 September 1999.

113 **In March 2002 the *Guardian* revealed** 'Top School's Creationists Preach Value of Biblical Story Over Evolution' by Tania Branigan, *Guardian*, 9 March 2002.

115 **Even extra-terrestrial conspiracy theories were granted some academic respectability** *Aliens in America: Conspiracy Cultures from Outerspace to Cyberspace* by Jodi Dean (Cornell University Press, Ithaca, 1998). See also reviews of the book by John Leonard in *The Nation*, 15 June 1998, and by Mark Goldblatt in *Reason*, 1 March 1999.

CHAPTER FIVE: THE CATASTROPHISTS

118 'What is going to happen?' *Griffith Observer*, May 1962; quoted in 'The Millennium is Coming!' by John Mosley (program supervisor of the Griffith Observatory), *Skeptic*, Vol. 4, No. 4, 1996, pp. 46–54.

119 By 1980 even Gribbin himself *New Scientist*, 17 July 1980.

120 'Why this one-track emphasis' *Griffith Observer*, January 1975; quoted in 'The Millennium is Coming!' by John Mosley, *op. cit.*

122 'Travel agents, moving company workers, bottled-water suppliers' 'Quaking with Anticipation' by Beth Ann Krier and David Larsen, *Los Angeles Times*, 6 May 1988.

123 Returning home on 7 May 'First Lady's Astrologer Says Earthquakes Won't Come This Month', Associated Press, 11 May 1988.

124 'The image of two women, one of them peering into a crystal ball' 'The Stars Were Their Alibi' by Alexander Cockburn, *Nation*, 21 May 1988.

125 A study of Wall Street stockholders 'How They Sign Deals in Scorpio City – Washington High Fliers and their Astrologer Mentors' by Diana McLellan, *The Times*, 15 May 1988.

127 But why stop at professional astrologers? 'The Stars Are Out' by Francis Wheen, *Guardian*, 3 January 1996; 'Chance a Fun Thing' by Francis Wheen, *Guardian*, 10 January 1996.

130 'if you live in a Christian country' Interview with the Dalai Lama by Alice Thomson, *Daily Telegraph*, 7 May 1999.

130 'The ceremony took place at dusk' 'New Age Cherie Stops Blair Being Stick in the Mud' by Tom Baldwin, *The Times*, 15 December 2001.

132 'The inclusion of Indian ayurvedic medicine' 'Ministers Call for Herbal Cures on the NHS' by Jonathon Carr-Brown, *Sunday Times*, 30 December 2001.

132 According to a 1998 survey See *Journal of the American Medical Association*, 11 November 1998.

132 'Have you tried squid's cartilage?' *Snake Oil and Other Preoccupations* by John Diamond (Vintage, London, 2001).

134 An even more fantastic ratio See 'Homeopathy: The Ultimate Fake' by Stephen Barrett MD, on the excellent Quackwatch website.

136 'tap into the power of alternative therapy' 'Charles Helps to Build "New Age" Hospital' by Zoe Brennan and Nicholas Hellen, *Sunday Times*, 26 August 2001.

136 **The founder-editor of** *Flying Saucer Review*, **the Earl of Clancarty**
See obituary of the Earl of Clancarty, *Daily Telegraph*, 22 May 1995.

137 **How could one disprove it?** See 'Francis Wheen's Diary', *Independent on Sunday*, 12 May 1991.

138 **There was no respite in the commercial breaks** 'UFORIA' by Ed
Vulliamy, *Guardian*, 5 August 1997.

138 **'The thing you have to remember about** *The X-Files*' 'Adventures
in Alien Territory' by Jim White and Rebecca Fowler, *Mail on Sunday*,
21 September 1997.

139 **A teacher in Ontario** 'X-Files Mark the Spot' by Paul Benedetti,
Calgary Herald, 13 September 1997.

140 **'Soap operas, cop series and the like'** 'Science, Delusion and the
Appetite for Wonder', Richard Dimbleby Lecture by Professor
Richard Dawkins, transmitted on BBC television 12 November 1996.

140 **in** *Communion* **he finally confessed** *Communion* by Whitley Strieber
(Beech Tree Books, New York, 1987).

141 **'During the two-hour show'** 'That's Entertainment! TV's UFO
Cover-Up' by Philip J. Klass, *Skeptical Inquirer*, November/December
1996.

144 **The irony was redoubled** See 'Flash! Fox News Reports that Aliens
May Have Built the Pyramids of Egypt!' by Richard C. Carrier, *Skeptical Inquirer*, September/October 1999.

145 **'This film is the first hard evidence to emerge'** 'Space Oddity' by
Martin Walker, *Guardian*, 25 July 1995.

145 **The autopsy was shot in southern England** 'How We Faked Alien
Autopsy' by Nick Fielding, *Mail on Sunday*, 17 January 1999.

147 **'If you open your mind too much'** 'What a Load of Rubbish' by
Edward Fox, *Daily Telegraph*, 28 August 1995.

147 **As Elaine Showalter pointed out** *Hystories: Hysterical Epidemics and
Modern Culture* by Elaine Showalter (Columbia University Press, New
York, and Picador, London, 1997)

152 **'We had a UFO series recently'** See 'The Loopiest Tabloid of
Them All' by Francis Wheen, *Guardian*, 4 June 1997.

CHAPTER SIX: WITH GOD ON OUR SIDE

158 **'America discovered how useful the invocation'** *Who Paid the Piper?
The CIA and the Cultural Cold War* by Frances Stonor Saunders
(Granta Books, London, 1999).

159 **'Honestly, openly, and with firm conviction'** See 'Nationalist Republicans and the Cold War' by John Kenneth White, *The Public Perspective*, Vol. 8, No. 9, November 1997.

160 **'Jimmy Carter was more devout'** *Reagan's America: Innocents at Home* by Garry Wills (William Heinemann, London, 1988).

160 **'Let us pray for those'** 'Reagan Slams Godless Communism', *Guardian Weekly*, 20 March 1983.

162 **'there is no way to read that sentence'** 'Buchanan on the Firing Line; Buckley Calls on Candidate to Recant Antisemitic Statements' by Charles Trueheart, *Washington Post*, 12 December 1991. See also 'Buchanan Inconsistent with All Republican Traditions' by Alan J. Steinberg, *New Jersey Jewish News*, 21 October 1999; 'It's "Respectable" Buchanan Who Tars the Republicans' by Menachem Z. Rosensaft, *Los Angeles Times*, 1 January 1992.

165 **In his last will and testament** 'US Agents Discover Will of Hijackers' Leader' by Kate Connolly, *Observer*, 30 September 2001.

165 **'It is only the civilised who would be ashamed'** 'Damn Them All' by Nick Cohen, *Observer*, 7 October 2001.

CHAPTER SEVEN: US AND THEM

167 **'When I was coming up'** 'Bush Follows in the Mis-Steps of His Father' by Frank Bruni, *New York Times*, 23 January 2000.

167 **'There is no "us"'** See 'Why We All Love to Hate: Political psychologists bring hostile national groups together to explore the need for enemies' by David Gelman, *Newsweek*, 28 August 1989; 'Without Communism, America Looks for New Adversaries' by Jim Abrams, Associated Press, 5 May 1992.

168 **A Gallup poll** 'US Survey Rates Japan Greater Threat than USSR' by John N. Maclean, *Chicago Tribune*, 5 March 1991.

169 **'You and I may be friends'** 'Pat's Answers' by Tom Bethell, *American Spectator*, February 1992.

170 **'I'm from Louisiana'** 'Duke to Challenge Bush in GOP Primaries' by Steve Daley, *Chicago Tribune*, 5 December 1991.

170 **Meanwhile, in California** 'Official Draws Fire for Attack on Japanese' by Sonni Efron, *Los Angeles Times*, 6 December 1991.

171 **'a national epidemic of indifference'** 'US Interest in Japan at Rock Bottom' by Jim Mann, *Los Angeles Times*, 21 June 2000.

172 **'We must not relax our efforts'** Transcript of President Reagan's State of the Union message, 6 February 1985.

172 **'This conjunction of an immense military establishment'** 'Eisenhower's Warning' by William D. Hartung, *World Policy Journal*, 22 March 2001. See also 'How We Lost the Peace Dividend' by Ann Markusen, *The American Prospect*, Vol. 8, No. 33, 1 July 1997, and *Forging the Military-Industrial Complex: World War II's Battle of the Potomac* by Gregory Hooks (University of Illinois Press, 1991).

173 **'not fitting ... for a President to criticise Congress'** 'Military–Industrial Man' by Lars Erik-Nelson, *New York Review of Books*, 21 December 2000.

174 **Since Boeing had cunningly spread work** 'Cut the Budget Deficit? You Must be Joking' by Martin Walker, *Guardian*, 10 July 1989.

175 **'this money can be followed and frozen'** 'Costs a Bundle and Can't Fly; Dubious Weapons Systems Reap a Bush Budget Bonanza' by Jason Vest, *The American Prospect*, Vol. 13, No. 5, 11 March 2002.

175 **President George W. Bush appeared at the Elgin air force base** 'Sky High: The Military Busts the 2003 Federal Budget' by Frida Berrigan, *In These Times*, 18 March 2002; see also 'The Defence Chiefs Prepare to Go over the Top' by Peter Riddell, *The Times*, 4 March 2002.

179 **'The very concept of a war on drugs'** *In the Time of the Tyrants: Panama 1968–89* by R. M. Koster and Guillermo Sanchez Bourbon (Secker & Warburg, 1990); see also Christopher Hitchens's review in the *London Review of Books*, December 1990.

180 **'The blowback theory is dead wrong'** 'Back to Front' by Peter Beinart, *New Republic*, 8 October 2001.

181 **'it was an irony indeed'** 'The World in the 1980s: notes on the new political culture' by Fred Halliday, *Nation*, 4 September 1989.

182 **'There is something in human history like retribution'** *New York Daily Tribune*, 16 September 1857.

CHAPTER EIGHT: CANDLES IN THE WIND

185 **'stunning new study of ethics'** 'A Way Out of Moral Disarray' by Jim Miller, *Newsweek*, 14 September 1981.

186 **'What matters at this stage'** *After Virtue: A Study in Moral Theory* by Alasdair MacIntyre (University of Notre Dame Press, 1981).

188 **'One of the strange features'** 'Gray's Progress' by Jeremy Shearmur (Ms from Department of Political Science, Australian National University, 1997). See also 'The Ways of John Gray: A Libertarian Commentary' by Daniel B. Klein, *The Independent Review*, Vol. IV, No. 1, Summer 1999.

188 **'What ever happened to John Gray?'** See 'What's Wrong with Global Capitalism?' by Robert Skidelsky, *Times Literary Supplement*, 27 March 1998.

189 **Those who routinely deplore** Enlightenment anti-imperialism is a strangely neglected subject. For a pioneering study, see 'Enlightenment Anti-Imperialism' by Sankar Muthu, *Social Research*, Vol. 66, No. 4 (1999).

190 **'the Spaniard, the first to be thrown up'** *Political Writings* by Denis Diderot, edited by John Hope Mason and Robert Wokler (Cambridge University Press, 1992).

190 **'Byron and Kipling, Delacroix and Ingres'** 'George Washington's False Teeth' by Robert Darnton, *New York Review of Books*, Vol. XLIV, No. 5, 27 March 1997.

195 **Hence the increasingly urgent need ...** 'Again, Al Gore Gets Personal; Large Part of Speech Recounts Sister's Death from Lung Cancer' by Edward Walsh, *Washington Post*, 29 August 1996. See also 'The Forgotten Chapters: Al Gore's Uncomfortable Past Alliance with the Tobacco Industry' by Joan Beck, *Chicago Tribune*, 1 September 1996.

197 **'Nobody has mastered the feminisation of political discourse'** 'All Venusians Now' by Mark Steyn in *Faking It: The Sentimentalisation of Modern Society*, edited by Digby Anderson and Peter Mullen (Social Affairs Unit, London, 1998).

200 **'That Diana's therapised victim-speak'** 'Diana and the Backlash' by Linda Holt, in *After Diana: Irreverent Elegies* edited by Mandy Merck (Verso, London and New York, 1998).

202 **The *Times* reported that many women in therapy** 'Diana's Death Resonates with Women in Therapy' by Jane Gross, *New York Times*, 13 September 1997.

204 **'Icons do not die'** *Independent*, 1 September 1997. Quoted in Glen Newey's excellent essay 'Diarrhoea', in *After Diana: Irreverent Elegies*, *op. cit.*

208 **'the Liverpudlianisation of Britain'** 'Lennon Sucks, But Am I Just a Jealous Guy?' by Euan Ferguson, *Observer*, 20 October 2002.

209 **'In the case of Diana's death'** 'The Unbearable Lightness of Diana' by Elizabeth Wilson, *New Left Review*, November–December 1997.

CHAPTER NINE: RIGHT IS THE NEW LEFT

214 **'No serious challenge on the Left exists'** 'There's Plenty of Life in the "new" Third Way Yet' by Peter Mandelson, *The Times*, 10 June 2002.

214 **In Andrew Martin's novel** *Bilton* *Bilton* by Andrew Martin (Faber & Faber, London, 1998).

220 **'We need to build a relationship of trust'** Speech by Tony Blair to the Singapore Business Community, 8 January 1996.

221 **'Thank you very much, Dr Etzioni'** Quoted in 'Should We Live This Way?' by Joan Smith, *Independent on Sunday*, 22 June 1997, an excellent skewering of communitarianism's progressive pretensions.

222 **When Demos spoke, Tony Blair listened** See 'The Unspeakable in Pursuit of the Unthinkable' by Francis Wheen, *Observer*, 9 October 1994.

223 **'These provoked snorts of hilarity'** 'Waiving the Rules' by Morley Safer, *60 Minutes* programme broadcast on 15 November 1998.

225 **'In the past three months'** 'A Talent to Annoy' by Anne Karpf, *Guardian*, 11 March 1999.

CHAPTER TEN: FORWARD TO THE PAST

235 **'One sometimes wonders, in this era'** 'The Market as God: Living in the New Dispensation' by Harvey Cox, *Atlantic Monthly*, March 1999.

244 **'Patent monopolies are the most costly'** 'The Mirage of Progress' by Mark Weisbrot, *The American Prospect*, Vol. 13, No. 1, 1 January 2002.

246 **'In the United States, government promoted'** 'Globalism's Discontents' by Joseph E. Stiglitz, *The American Prospect*, Vol. 13, No. 1, 1 January 2002.

248 **F. M. Cornford's famous Principle of the Wedge** See *Microcosmographia Academica* by F. M. Cornford (Metcalfe & Co., Cambridge, 1908).

249 **'under the sway of Jakarta and western business interests'** 'Under the Influence: The Real Reason for the United Nations' Peace-keeping Role in East Timor is to Maintain Indonesia's Control' by John Pilger, *Guardian*, 21 September 1999.

250 **In 1770 the Abbé Raynal described** Quoted in 'The Politics of Globalisation Circa 1773', by Emma Rothschild, *OECD Observer*, 1 September 2001.

251 **'One link gave way'** Quoted in 'The Politics of Globalisation Circa 1773', *op. cit.*

253 **'The need of a constantly expanding market'** *The Communist Manifesto* by Karl Marx and Friedrich Engels (Penguin edition, London, 1967).

254 **'What an extraordinary episode'** *The Economic Consequences of the Peace* by John Maynard Keynes (Macmillan, London, 1919).

257 **In 2000 the *Guardian* reported** See 'Babs' Split Personality' by Francis Wheen, *Guardian*, 6 September 2000.

260 **'Few economists and almost no journalists'** See 'The Mirage of Progress' by Mark Weisbrot, *The American Prospect*, Vol. 13, No. 1, 1 January 2002.

CHAPTER ELEVEN: VOODOO REVISITED

265 **'Greenspan sent a clear message'** 'The Man Who Shakes the World' by Frank Kane and Garth Alexander, *Sunday Times*, 8 December 1996.

265 **'We have one general response'** Quoted in *Dot.Con* by John Cassidy (HarperCollins, New York, 2002), the most entertaining and instructive account of dotcom madness.

267 **'During the madness of the bullish period'** 'The Trail to the Dotcom Graveyard' by Thorold Barker, *Financial Times*, 28 December 2000.

268 **'One, is Internet mania based on nothing more than hype?'** 'It's Not Too Late to Grab Some Net' by Duff McDonald, *Money*, July 1998.

268 **'It was unbelievable how traditional media'** Quoted in *Digital Hustlers: Living Large and Falling Hard in Silicon Valley* by Casey Kait and Stephen Weiss (ReganBooks, New York, 2001).

271 **'a new paradigm in asset management'** 'Hedge Funds: Bubble or New Paradigm?' by Alexander M. Ineichen, *Journal of Global Financial Markets*, Vol. 2, No. 4, Winter 2001.

271 **'When you see reference to a new paradigm'** 'Galbraith on Crashes, Japan and Walking Sticks' by Ben Laurance and William Keegan, *Observer*, 21 June 1998.

272 **'Diana was the upstart challenger'** *Living on Thin Air* by Charles Leadbeater (Viking, London, 1999).

272 **'The idea of *Living on Thin Air'*** 'Hewitt Admits Labour's Industry Errors' by David Gow and Patrick Wintour, *Guardian*, 16 May 2002.

272 **speculative markets were 'not too volatile'** See *Irrational Exuberance* by Robert J. Shiller (Princeton University Press, 2000).

274 **'The future belonged to companies with no visible means'** 'Death by Guru' by Paul Krugman, *New York Times*, 18 December 2001.

275 **'Imagine a country-club dinner dance'** 'The Power Market: Once a dull-as-methane utility, Enron has grown rich making markets where markets were never made before' by Brian O'Reilly, *Fortune*, 17 April 2000.

275 **As Thomas Frank wrote** *One Market Under God: Extreme Capitalism, Market Populism and the End of Economic Democracy* by Thomas Frank (Doubleday, New York, 2000).

276 **'The company's motto, "Learn the power of why"'** See 'In the Belly of the Enron Beast' by Peter Wright, *salon.com*, 25 January 2002.

277 **'Spend long enough around top Enron people'** 'The Energetic Messiah', *Economist*, 3 June 2000.

277 **'I believe in God'** 'Prophet or Profit? Energy Chief, Religious Leaders Dispute God's Role in Utility Price Spiral' by Sandi Dolbee, *San Diego Union-Tribune*, 2 February 2001.

277 **'Today's extraordinary trust in the power'** 'The Curse of the Superstar CEO' by Rakesh Khurana, *Harvard Business Review*, September 2002.

281 **'And how does Mr Lay respond to this charge?'** 'The Energetic Messiah', *Economist*, 3 June 2000.

282 **'It was one of the great fantasies'** 'Shock Waves: Enron's Swoon Leaves a Grand Experiment in a State of Disarray' by Rebecca Smith, *Wall Street Journal*, 30 November 2001.

283 **A feature in September 1999** Special report on energy by Gaston F. Ceron, *Wall Street Journal*, 13 September 1999.

283 **Serious business journals profiled Enron's bosses** The examples in this paragraph are quoted in 'Enron: Uncovering the Uncovered Story' by Scott Sherman, *Columbia Journalism Review*, March/April 2002 – an excellent study of the press's role in promulgating hype and fantasy.

284 'The business press, including *Business Week*' 'Let Us Count the Culprits', *Business Week*, 17 December 2001.

284 'Investors counting on these gains' 'Energy Traders Cite Gains, But Some Math is Missing' by Jonathan Weil, *Texas Journal*, 20 September 2000.

286 'The US may have rediscovered Keynesianism' 'Keynes Revisited' by Gerard Baker and Ed Crooks, *Financial Times*, 6 October 2001.

286 'the most dramatic agenda replacement' 'For Bush, New Emergencies Ushered in a New Agenda' by John F. Harris and Dana Milbank, *Washington Post*, 22 September 2001.

287 'A tough materialist analysis would be fine' 'Can there be a Decent Left?' by Michael Walzer, *Dissent*, Vol. 49, No. 2, Spring 2002.

289 'racist arrogance' See 'Sectarian Propagandism: Bob Pitt argues that it is perfectly principled for socialists to defend the Taliban against imperialism', *Weekly Worker*, 18 October 2001.

290 'While humane representations of Islam' 'The Agony of a 21st-Century Muslim' by Ziauddin Sardar, *New Statesman*, 17 February 2003.

292 'All Islamic schools of law' *Why Do People Hate America?* by Ziauddin Sardar and Merryl Wyn Davies (Icon Books, Cambridge, 2002).

294 'It has become painfully clear' 'They Can't See Why They Are Hated' by Seumas Milne, *Guardian*, 13 September 2001.

294 'American bond traders, you may say' 'In Buildings Thought Indestructible', *New Statesman*, 17 September 2001.

296 'Let us suppose' *Terror and Liberalism* by Paul Berman (W. W. Norton, New York, 2003).

299 'The responses to 11 September' Editorial by Mitchell Cohen in *Dissent*, Vol. 49, No. 1, Winter 2002.

300 'Certainly,' the *Washington Post* reported 'An Eminence with No Shades of Grey' by Michael Powell, *Washington Post*, 5 May 2002.

301 'There is no limit to the follies' 'Notes on Nationalism' by George Orwell, from *The Collected Essays, Journalism and Letters: Volume Three* (Penguin Books, London, 1970).

301 'A rhetorical tactic is at play' Editorial by Mitchell Cohen in *Dissent*, Vol. 49, No. 1, Winter 2002.

303 'May we now agree to cancel this crime' 'Stranger in a Strange Land' by Christopher Hitchens, *Atlantic Monthly*, December 2001.

304 'The leaders of the western nations' See 'It's a War Against Islam!' by Abu Musab, *Kcom Journal*, 30 September 2001.

305 'In the late nineteenth century' *Terror and Liberalism* by Paul Berman (W. W. Norton, New York, 2003).

308 'Aristotle crept back into Europe' *The Ethical Crises of Civilisation: Moral Meltdown or Advance?* by Leslie Lipson (Sage, Newbury and London, 1993).

309 'these fundamentalist thinkers expound' *The Challenge of Fundamentalism: Political Islam and the New World Disorder* by Bassam Tibi (University of California Press, Berkeley, 1998).

309 'neither . . . inordinately difficult nor illegitimate' *Modern Islamic Political Thought* by Hamid Enayat (Texas University Press, Austin, 1982).

310 'truth is great and will prevail' See *A Documentary History of Religion in America, Volume I: To the Civil War* by Edwin S. Gaustad (William B. Eerdmans Publishing Company, Grand Rapids, 1982).

311 'The Virginia act for religious freedom has been received' Letter from Thomas Jefferson to James Madison, 16 December 1786, quoted in *Paine and Jefferson on Liberty* edited by Lloyd S. Kramer (Continuum, New York, 1988).

Index

P.S.

Ideas,
interviews
& features ...

Interview with Francis Wheen

by Simon Jones, editor of
Third Way *magazine*

Would it be reasonable to describe you as a fundamentalist of the Enlightenment?
Not a fundamentalist. But I'm an admirer of what you might call 'Enlightenment values' (though they go way beyond the Enlightenment). Things like scientific empiricism, the separation of church and state, the waning of absolutism and tyranny, yes, I cling to those.

And did you yourself reach that position through the application of reason – rather than through indoctrination as a child, for example?
Certainly through thinking, yes. I had a lot of time for thinking when I was a child. I was packed off to boarding school at the age of about seven, and so in school holidays for the next ten years or so I was not exactly on my own, because I had an older and a younger brother, but all my friends were at school and I would spend long periods just sitting in my bedroom, brooding on things and reading a lot and observing. So it gave me plenty of chance to think.

It was quite a religious household. I wouldn't be surprised, frankly, if I'm the first Wheen to be an atheist. And so, of course, there was a lot of church-going and all the rest of it, and gradually, through my childhood, I found myself rejecting more and more of it, until finally all I was left with was the Litany and the hymns. I know the Book of Common

Prayer and Hymns Ancient and Modern and the King James Bible practically backwards, and I'm very fond of them all.

In the book, you quote Peter Gay: 'The Newtonian heavens proclaimed God's glory.' Did it not occur to you that these heroes of the Enlightenment never saw faith and reason as being opposed?
No, they didn't. Newton was into all sorts of things – astrology, alchemy – it's perfectly true; and it continues to be true to this day, of all sorts of people. It never ceases to surprise me: people I know who appear to be intelligent, sophisticated people you then discover have some fantastically eccentric peccadillo – they can't get out of bed in the morning, for instance, without reading what Jonathan Cainer says in his horoscope. So, faith and reason in that sense can often coexist in the same person.

Immanuel Kant believed the Enlightenment would free people from what he called their 'self-incurred immaturity'. That was a long time ago, of course.
Yes. He rather thought it would all be done by the year 1800. A tiny bit optimistic, I think.

It's easy to fault the Enlightenment on the grounds that it never delivered the Utopia it promised...
It's easy to say that, but I think its ▶

Interview *(continued)*

◀ achievements are not negligible. Of course
it's a slow process, but I do think that actually
over the 200 years since the Enlightenment
you can see the gradual acceptance, in
certain countries, of secularism, of liberal
democracy and so forth. And also scientific
progress (though of course we're not allowed
to use that word these days, because there's
a tremendous anti-science backlash).
That, too, you could say is a legacy of the
Enlightenment.

But over the last twenty or twenty-five
years there has been a retreat from that.
It seems to me that there is now a fierce
hostility to the Enlightenment, with a very
odd assortment of pre-modernists and
post-modernists ganging up on modernity.
And the pre-modernists are not just the
Taliban and al-Qaeda but also primitivists,
neo-Luddites, the deep-green Earth-Firsters
who are so technophobic they think the
invention of the plough was a bad thing
and we should all go and live in tiny, remote
communities – which is my idea of a
nightmare, because actually small
communities can be extremely oppressive.
One of the joys of the communications
revolution of the last 200 years – the
invention of the railways, the telephone – is
that you can more easily escape from the
tyranny of a small community and find
kindred spirits. It's very liberating.

**To go back to self-incurred immaturity: you
were not too impressed by the communal
grief that followed Princess Diana's death …**
I did find the mass ululating slightly creepy.

Such eruptions can turn into a form of tyranny – and also I think they are a form of narcissism. I'm not a cold ultra-rationalist to the total exclusion of emotion. I've nothing against people (to use a vogue phrase) having 'emotional intelligence', as long as it is allied with 'intelligent intelligence'. What I am less enamoured of is people diving into emotionalism and abandoning anything else at all.

Is it harder to be taken seriously as a political commentator when you're known as a humorist?
There was a review of my biography of Karl Marx in the *London Review of Books* which complained that it had jokes in it and therefore was frivolous. Personally, I think there are often occasions that are so serious that only humour can do justice to them. Sometimes the language of the absurd is the only style that does justice to an absurd world, or an absurd institution or train of events. Once I discovered that Marx was a fan of *Tristram Shandy*, that wonderful shaggy dog story of a novel, it seemed to me to explain an awful lot of strange and whimsical passages in *Das Kapital*. He knew what he was doing: he was using a topsy-turvy style because it was the only thing that could do justice to the topsy-turvy world he was describing.

Could the Church do with a sense of humour?
Yes, in a word. Some bits of it do have a sense of humour, though a lot of the humour is ▶

Interview *(continued)*

◄ unintended in my view. I am very fond of the Church of England as an institution, in spite of everything, because it seems to me to represent religion restrained by long experience which has come to a kind of accommodation with society and does not wish to boss us about and dominate all our lives. I'm passionately in favour of freedom of religion just so long as we have freedom *from* religion as well and I don't have the Pope telling me that the sun revolves round the earth and that I've got to say the same or else it's the rack for me, matey. ■

Mumbo-Jumbo Never Sleeps

by Francis Wheen

IT WAS SOMETHING I could have predicted confidently without any assistance from crystal balls, tea-leaves or horoscopes: that when the hardback edition of this book appeared, the forces of mumbo-jumbo would unwittingly act as my publicists by providing new instances every day of my argument that rational thought is in retreat.

So it proved. The schools superintendent for the American state of Georgia proposed that the word 'evolution' should be removed from all biology textbooks, explaining that it 'evokes the monkeys-to-man sort of thing' and might therefore distress pupils who believe that the earth began a few thousand years ago with Adam and Eve. Dr Percy Seymour published *The Scientific Proof of Astrology*, which claimed to demonstrate that our characters and destinies depend on where Mars, Saturn, Jupiter and Venus happened to be on the night of our birth. The Queen chose Dr Timothy Evans, who specializes in acupuncture and aromatherapy, to replace Sir Nigel Southward as the official royal doctor. Kabbalah was hailed by the tabloids as 'the trendiest faith around', endorsed by stars such as Madonna, Demi Moore and Britney Spears – all of whom apparently believe that they can absorb 'negative energy' by swinging a chicken above their heads, and that wearing red string knotted around their wrists will help ward off 'the evil eye'.

Having written a book which included ▶

‘ Madonna, Demi Moore and Britney Spears – all apparently believe that they can absorb "negative energy" by swinging a chicken above their heads ’

7

Mumbo-Jumbo Never Sleeps (continued)

◄ something to offend pretty well everybody, I also expected the publicity campaign to be assisted by a loud chorus of hostile reviews. This prophecy was less successful. Most reviewers were remarkably generous – notably Suzanne Moore in the *New Statesman*, who paid me several handsome compliments even though I take a swipe at her in my chapter on Princess Diana. More surprising still was a full-page eulogy in the *Daily Mail*, a newspaper described in my book as the chief British purveyor of mumbo-jumbo.

No such surprises from Professor John Gray, the Screaming Lord Sutch of academe. His review for the *Independent* complained that the book was a 'rambling and bilious tirade ... against Margaret Thatcher and the Ayatollah Khomeini, the Reverend Jerry Fallwell and Professor Noam Chomsky, Milton Friedman and the New Age guru Deepak Chopra ... As he flays out furiously against virtually every aspect of the current intellectual scene, one is irresistibly reminded of Victor Meldrew's plaintive cry in *One Foot in the Grave*: "I don't believe it!"' It's a treat to be accused of splenetic grumpiness by a man whose own jeremiads make Victor Meldrew sound like Milly-Molly-Mandy. Oddly, however, he omitted to mention that another target of 'Wheen's spleen' is none other than Professor John Gray, whose bizarre intellectual odyssey is chronicled in Chapter 8.

Since the book's publication I have spoken at dozens of bookshops and literary festivals, and one question is asked again and

❛ Having written a book which included something to offend pretty well everybody, I also expected the publicity campaign to be assisted by a loud chorus of hostile reviews. ❜

again: 'What about Iraq?' If you want a guide to the 57 varieties of human folly and idiocy, you certainly need look no further than the recent history of Iraq – or, more precisely, Western attitudes to Iraq. Before the war there were many predictions (gloomy or gleeful, according to who was making them) that the US-led forces would spend months bogged down on the outskirts of Baghdad, unable to break the defences of Saddam's 'elite Republican Guard'. It would, according to several pundits, be 'another Stalingrad'. In the event, as anyone surveying the scale of the invasion force could have guessed, the coalition forces reached the capital with little difficulty.

But then a far greater idiocy gradually became apparent. In all the extensive pre-war planning by the finest minds in the Pentagon, the State Department and the White House, no one had paused to think about what could or should be done once the military campaign achieved its objective. I was reminded of Michael Foot's jibe against the Tory minister Sir Keith Joseph, who presided over the destruction of British manufacturing industry in the 1980s. Foot likened Joseph to a magician who borrows an expensive watch from a member of the audience, smashes it with a hammer – and then, after much anguished brow-furrowing, confesses that he has forgotten the rest of the trick.

The catalogue of American blunders or outright crimes (including the torture and sexual humiliation of detainees) is well known, and too long to repeat here. But ▶

❛Most reviewers were remarkably generous – notably Suzanne Moore, who paid me several handsome compliments even though I take a swipe at her❜

Mumbo-Jumbo Never Sleeps *(continued)*

◄ what of the supposedly virtuous opponents of Messrs Bush and Blair? In Chapter 4 of my book I note that Alan Sokal's famous hoaxing of the post-modernists was prompted by his indignation, as a socialist, that the self-proclaimed Left was now championing obscurantism. This bizarre alliance between progressives and reactionaries has since reappeared in Britain's Stop the War Coalition, which is jointly led by the Socialist Workers Party and the Muslim Association of Britain (MAB) – a British affiliate of the ultra-Islamist Muslim Brotherhood of Egypt. The MAB's political aim is the establishment of a theocratic state in which apostasy from Islam is 'punishable by death'.

Thus a party supposedly committed to democracy, secularism and feminism embraced a movement that is violently hostile to all these values – purely because they happen to share a hatred of American policy. As the American socialist Paul Berman wrote recently, many people are blinded by the understandable revulsion they feel towards the US president who waged the war: 'They peer at Iraq and see [only] the smirking face of George W. Bush.' Following this logic, veteran left-wingers such as Tariq Ali and John Pilger became cheerleaders for the so-called Iraqi 'resistance' – even when this resistance was perpetrated by latter-day Nazis from Saddam's Ba'ath Party or Islamist goons from al-Qaeda, and even though its targets included UN workers, Kurdish democrats, Iraqi socialists and indeed many devout

❝ It's a treat to be accused of splenetic grumpiness by a man whose own jeremiads make Victor Meldrew sound like Milly-Molly-Mandy. ❞

Muslims, massacred in their mosques.

The Left used to believe that liberty, democracy and human rights were the birthright of everyone. Not any more, apparently. To quote Paul Berman again: 'Today, people say, out of a spirit of egalitarian tolerance: Social democracy for Swedes! Tyranny for Arabs! And this is supposed to be a left-wing attitude?' Seldom has a hefty dose of rational thinking been more necessary; seldom has it been harder to find. ■

If you want a guide to the 57 varieties of human folly and idiocy, you certainly need look no further than the recent history of Iraq

Have You Read?

Other works by Francis Wheen

Karl Marx

Francis Wheen's biography of Marx is an
international best-seller, translated into
more than twenty languages – prompting
the *Independent* to ask: 'Why is Karl Marx
even more popular than Harry Potter?'

'I'll read anything by Francis Wheen, even a
biography of Karl Marx, and my trust was
not misplaced: the simple elegance of the
writing, and Wheen's ability to winkle
humour out of the most unpromising
subject, results in a book which is far more
pleasurable than anyone had the right to
expect.' Nick Hornby, *Guardian*

....

The Soul of Indiscretion

Tom Driberg was one of the most flamboyant
British politicians of modern times, whose
friends included Evelyn Waugh, Mick Jagger,
W.H. Auden and the Kray twins. Francis
Wheen's classic biography describes a career
that shattered almost every convention of
polite society.

'Wheen chronicles this . . . rake's progress
with Hogarthian zest, exposing in the process
a whole hidden layer of English life.' Piers
Brendon, *Mail on Sunday*.

....

Who Was Dr Charlotte Bach?

The gloriously bizarre tale of a conman
extraordinaire, whose life of deception
culminated in his most outrageous

performance of all – as a female philosopher who claimed to have made
the greatest intellectual breakthrough since Charles Darwin.

'A mad, creepy tale told with Francis Wheen's characteristic dry and brilliant wit.' Roger Lewis, *Daily Express*

Hoo-Hahs and Passing Frenzies
This sparkling collection of essays and articles by Francis Wheen won the George Orwell prize in 2003.

'This is a writer who can dispatch an argument with the flick of a wrist, who can get humour to do in one well-timed movement what others labour over fifty pages to achieve. This is someone who seeks not just to entertain you, or even persuade you, but urgently to enlighten you by the means of his learning as well as his conviction.' David Hare ■

Francis Wheen's Guide to the Web

http://www.litrix.com/madraven/madne001.htm

Charles Mackay's *Extraordinary Popular Delusions and the Madness of Crowds* (1841), which I cite several times in this book, is essential reading for anyone interested in the history of mumbo-jumbo. The text is now available online via this link.

http://www.opendemocracy.net/
This ambitious online magazine, founded by my friend Anthony Barnett, has quickly established itself as one of the most intelligent, free-thinking forums for geopolitical debate.

http://www.csicop.org/si/
The website of the Committee for Scientific Investigation of Claims of the Paranormal includes many excellent debunking articles from its publication *The Skeptical Inquirer*, 'the magazine for science and reason'.

http://whyfiles.news.wisc.edu/
The Why Files, run by the National Institute for Science Education in the US, explores the science (and maths) behind recent news stories, from cellular biology to political opinion polling.

http://www.quackwatch.org/index.html
A comprehensive guide to health fraud and quackery which exposes the pseudo-science behind so-called 'alternative remedies'.

http://www.physics.nyu.edu/faculty/sokal/
A website run by Professor Alan Sokal which includes a comprehensive archive of papers relating to his famous hoaxing of the post-modernists at *Social Text*.

http://www.au.org/site/PageServer
The price of both secular and religious liberty is eternal vigilance, and since 1947 the pressure group Americans United for the Separation of Church and State has acted as an unsleeping watchdog. This is its homepage.

http://users.rcn.com/peterk.enteract/
Otherwise known as 'the unofficial Christopher Hitchens website'. Hitchens is an old friend of mine whose pugnacious, wide-ranging journalism both enlightens and provokes. This site enables one to keep up with his prolific output from publications on both sides of the Atlantic.

http://normblog.typepad.com/normblog/
A blog run by Professor Norman Geras, whose bracingly iconoclastic observations on modern political follies are interspersed with his thoughts on cricket, movies and the songs of Bob Dylan.

http://www.snopes.com/info/whatsnew.asp
This frequently updated register of urban legends should be the first port of call whenever you notice new stories or rumours which seem too good to be true. More often than not, they are indeed too good to be true. ▶

Francis Wheen's Guide *(continued)*

◄ http://www.creationism.org/
I recommend this loopy creationist website on the 'know your enemy' principle. These people truly believe, inter alia, that dinosaurs roamed the earth only a few thousand years ago.

http://www.richardthompson-music.com/default.asp
This has no particular connection with mumbo-jumbo or rationalism: it is simply the website of Britain's most brilliant and enduring singer-songwriter. Those who haven't yet discovered him should hasten to do so. ■